MARKETING MEASUREMENT AND ANALYTICS

To Lindsey, my partner in agility.

CONTENTS

PREFACE

A BRIEF HISTORY OF MARKETING MEASUREMENT

The evolution of marketing measurement has been both reflective and constitutive of broader changes in technology, media, and consumer behavior over the past century. Understanding this history helps in appreciating the sophisticated techniques used in today's digital marketing landscape.

The Early 20th Century

Marketing measurement in the early 1900s was rudimentary, primarily focused on increasing sales volumes and leveraging the burgeoning print advertising industry, as television and even radio communications were still several years away. As mass production took hold, businesses began to see the value in advertising their products to wider audiences.

The concept of measuring marketing effectiveness at this time was largely limited to noting an increase in sales following advertising campaigns. A key figure during this era was Daniel Starch, who developed the Starch score in the 1920s. This method assessed the effectiveness of magazine and newspaper ads by measuring readers' recognition and recall of printed advertising material[1].

The Mid-20th Century

It was only a matter of time before technologies originally developed for other purposes, such as warfare communication, were utilized to reach consumers. Radio was the first to do so, and brought with it the modernization of both entertainment as well as marketing and advertising.

By the mid-20th century, the proliferation of radio and television introduced new advertising opportunities and challenges, leading to more sophisticated measurement techniques. A.C. Nielsen Company, which was established in 1923, began using analytical methods to track product sales and media consumption, laying the groundwork for the Nielsen ratings. These ratings became crucial for measuring the reach and popularity of television and radio programs, and by extension, the effectiveness of advertisements broadcast during these programs (Napoli, 2003)[2].

The Late 20th Century

The late 20th century saw a major shift with the advent of digital technologies. Cable television fragmented the media landscape, necessitating more granular measurement techniques to understand the diverse and evolving viewing habits of consumers.

The introduction of the Internet in the 1990s revolutionized marketing, as online advertising grew exponentially with the expansion of investments into Web-based businesses and technologies, as well as the growing ubiquity of Web sites created for existing businesses. Web analytics tools began to emerge, allowing marketers to track Web site traffic, click rates, conversion rates, and other online behaviors in real time[3]. This included the expansion of email as a marketing and communications platform, and the growing field of Search Engine Optimization (SEO) as companies such as Google rose to prominence.

The Early 21st Century

The early 2000s introduced more advanced digital analytics and Customer Relationship Management (CRM) systems, enabling businesses to conduct detailed data analyses to tailor their marketing strategies to individual consumer preferences. The increasing adoption of mobile devices and the growth of social media platforms such as Facebook and YouTube further diversified the channels through which companies could engage with customers. The concept of multi-touch attribution models began to take shape, focusing on understanding the influence of each touchpoint in the consumer journey toward a conversion[4].

The Era of Big Data

With more sources of information to pull from (such as the explosion of the smartphone market with the introduction of the iPhone in 2007), businesses began to collect greater amounts of data. Thus, the explosion of "big data" analytics in the late 2000s changed the scale and scope of marketing measurement. The integration of big data tools with marketing strategies allowed businesses to process vast amounts of information to make data-driven decisions. This laid the groundwork for technologies such as machine learning and Artificial Intelligence (AI), which have been harnessed to predict consumer behavior, optimize ad placements, and personalize marketing messages at scale[5].

MEASUREMENT TODAY

Today, marketing measurement must contend with the complexities of a multi-platform, multi-device world where privacy concerns and data protection regulations, such as GDPR, are increasingly paramount. Marketers are now exploring privacy-friendly methods of measurement and attribution that do not rely on third-party cookies, while also striving to maintain measurement accuracy and actionable insights.

Marketing measurement and analytics have become increasingly important in today's business landscape, where every dollar of expense must be justified, and every customer is inundated with a multitude of choices. With the rise of digital marketing and the abundance of data available, it is more important than ever to be able to measure and analyze marketing efforts effectively. This book provides a comprehensive guide to marketing measurement and analytics and is designed to help marketers make data-driven decisions that will improve their overall performance.

Data and measurement are critical aspects of any marketing strategy, and how this is approached can make the difference between category leaders and those left behind. The performance of each individual channel in a brand's portfolio is important as each one contributes to the whole. This means that brands with the best insights about their customers, their products and services, and their business will pull ahead. Marketing leaders know this, too, with Chief Marketing Officers (CMOs) spending around 6.5% of their marketing budgets on analytics[6].

This book is designed to give marketers of all skill levels the knowledge and understanding to meaningfully measure the performance of their work while supporting the needs of the business and incorporating omnichannel customer behaviors into their view of marketing success. The pages that follow cover the fundamentals of establishing and prioritizing the right marketing Key Performance Indicators (KPIs) that align with business KPIs, and then working with internal teams to ensure they can be measured properly. The book concludes with a review of how to analyze and interpret the results of the measurements to ensure both marketing and overall business alignment and growth.

WHO THIS BOOK IS FOR

This book is for marketing leaders, aspiring leaders, and other marketing professionals who want to better understand how to be more effective at measurement or to guide their teams in the best ways. It is written from more of a senior marketer viewpoint, though the content, framework, and ideas within can be beneficial for marketers of all experience levels.

There is also no specific marketing *channel* that is favored over others. The examples used tend to include more digital channels than offline ones, though the concepts used within can be applied to any marketing channel, digital or non-digital. The concepts and ideas work well for anything, which is the intention.

Keep in mind that statistics is covered a few times in this book, though readers are not expected to have a thorough understanding of statistical concepts. Much the opposite, as the fundamentals of statistics, where they can best be applied to marketing, are addressed in the chapters that follow, but even a marketer without interest in these concepts can still get a lot out of this book.

WHAT WE WILL COVER

I'm excited to share my knowledge, my experience measuring and improving marketing efforts, and all the insights I've gained from talking with some of the world's leaders on this topic on my podcast, *The Agile Brand with Greg Kihlström*. This book is divided into five main sections:

- **Part 1: Aligning Measurement to Business Goals** The first section will give an overview of KPIs and metrics and how they tie into one another, how they're different, and how to pick the right ones for your efforts and your organization.
- **Part 2: A Marketing Measurement Framework** Next, a measurement framework will be introduced that you can adapt to your organization and marketing efforts that ties organizational goals to individual marketing tactics.

- **Part 3: Data Collection** Then, we will talk about the actual measurement of marketing and how to ensure it works effectively for you and your teams.
- **Part 4: Measurement and Testing** In the next section, we will discuss how to effectively interpret and analyze your marketing measurement and make the most of the information you have.
- **Part 5: Refining and Improving Your Results** In the last section, we will discuss improving your measurement, analysis, and, ultimately, your marketing results. This will include AI-based methods such as using predictive analytics and generative AI, in addition to analysis techniques that you and your team can adopt.

A balance has been struck between giving an overview of marketing measurement best practices while considering that every organization, industry, and situation might be a little different.

OUR RECURRING CASE STUDY: PB SHOES

FIGURE 0.1. A selection of shoes from our fictional case study brand, PB Shoes (image courtesy of Greg Kihlström, generated by ChatGPT and DALL-E, with editing in Adobe Photoshop).

Throughout the book, we're going to take a look at a hypothetical company, PB Shoes, that makes athletic shoes specifically for pickleball, but wants to expand its product offerings, as there appears to be an opportunity for growth there in the market.

This recurring case study will help to frame many of the ideas and concepts we'll be exploring and illustrate how to use them in your own marketing work.

ADDITIONAL RESOURCES

You can find some related resources, as mentioned within the chapters that follow, on the *Agile Brand Guide* Web site at *https://www.agilebrandguide.com.*

You can also find me on LinkedIn, so contact me if you have any questions or would like to be pointed in the direction of further information, *https://www.linkedin.com/in/gregkihlstrom.*

ENDNOTES

1. Jones, J.P. (1995). "Single-Source Research Begins to Fulfill Its Promise." *Journal of Advertising Research.*
2. Napoli, P.M. (2003). "Audience Economics: Media Institutions and the Audience Marketplace." *Columbia University Press.*
3. Kaushik, A. (2010). "Web Analytics 2.0: The Art of Online Accountability & Science of Customer Centricity." *Sybex.*
4. Li, H., & Kannan, P.K. (2014). "Attributing Conversions in a Multichannel Online Marketing Environment: An Empirical Model and a Field Experiment." *Journal of Marketing Research.*
5. Davenport, T.H. (2014). "Big Data at Work: Dispelling the Myths, Uncovering the Opportunities." *Harvard Business Review Press.*
6. Villanova Business School. "How Marketers Use Data and Analytics to Reach Customers." Retrieved July 2023 from *https://taxandbusinessonline.villanova.edu/blog/how-marketers-use-data-analytics-to-reach-customers/*

G. Kihlstrom
December 2024

ACKNOWLEDGMENTS

First, I want to thank JR Sherman, CEO of RainFocus for contributions to this book. Also, as with any book I've written, countless people had a hand in the thoughts and ideas contained within. I will endeavor to thank many of them, but a full list would take up its own book, so instead, I will cheat and make this a blanket list. Yes, it's a bit of a cop-out, but I am hoping the people who have been so helpful to me on this topic see themselves in this list:

- All the amazing clients and customers I've had the opportunity to work with related to this topic
- All the amazing consultants and team members I've worked alongside
- All the amazing thought leaders I have talked with on my podcast, at a conference, or in a virtual or in-person meeting
- All the amazing people who have commented on and given me feedback on my articles, books, keynote speeches, and other content I've put out into the marketing and CX world

Thanks also to my wife Lindsey, who always supports me, no matter how many books I write during a year (this year, it will be more than a few). She is forever an inspiration, and I'm thankful to have such a great partner in all things.

Finally, thanks to everyone reading this book, anyone who has listened to my podcast, read an article and supported me in any way over the last several years. I hope that the thoughts and ideas shared by myself and others have been helpful in your work.

Let's get started on our marketing measurement journey together!

ABOUT THE AUTHOR

Greg Kihlström is a best-selling author, speaker, and entrepreneur, and serves as an advisor and consultant to top companies on marketing technology, marketing operations, customer experience, and digital transformation initiatives. He has worked with some of the world's top brands, including Adidas, Coca-Cola, FedEx, HP, Marriott, Nationwide Insurance, Victoria's Secret, and Toyota.

He is a multiple-time co-founder and C-level leader, leading his digital experience agency to be acquired by the largest independent marketing agency in the DC region in 2017. He successfully exited an HR technology platform provider he co-founded in 2020, and led a SaaS startup to be acquired by a leading edge computing company in 2021. He currently advises and sits on the board of a marketing technology startup.

In addition to his experience as an entrepreneur and leader, he earned his MBA, is currently a doctoral candidate for a DBA in Business Intelligence, and teaches several courses and workshops as a member of the School of Marketing Faculty at the Association of National Advertisers. He has served on the Virginia Tech Pamplin College of Business Marketing Mentorship Advisory Board and the University of Richmond's CX Advisory Board, and was the founding Chair of the American Advertising Federation's National Innovation Committee. Greg is Lean Six Sigma Black Belt certified, is an Agile Certified Coach (ICP-ACC), and holds a certification in Business Agility (ICP-BAF).

Greg has had multiple best-selling books, including his 10-part *Agile Brand Guides* series on marketing technology platforms and practices. His recent book, the best-selling *House of the Customer (2023)*, discusses the 1:1 personalized customer experience of the future, and how brands can organize the people, processes, and platforms that enable it. His award-winning podcast, *The Agile Brand with Greg Kihlström,* now in its sixth year with over 500 episodes and 2 million downloads, discusses brand strategy, marketing, and customer experience with some of the world's leading experts and leaders.

Greg is a contributing writer to MarTech, CustomerThink, and CMSWire, and has been featured in publications such as Ad Age, Financial Times, and The Washington Post. Greg has been named a two-time Top 10 Marketing and Customer Experience Thought Leader by Thinkers360, was named one of ICMI's Top 25 CX Thought Leaders two years in a row, and has been named a DC Inno 50 on Fire as a DC trendsetter in Marketing. He's also participated as a speaker at global industry events and has guest lectured at prominent universities and colleges.

Greg lives in Alexandria, Virginia, with his wife, Lindsey.

PART 1: ALIGNING MEASUREMENT TO BUSINESS GOALS

When it comes to marketing measurement and analytics, it is essential to have a clear understanding of how your marketing efforts contribute to your organization's overall goals. This is why aligning business Key Performance Indicators (KPIs) with marketing KPIs is important. By aligning these KPIs, you can ensure that your marketing efforts are directly contributing to the success of your organization.

If your organization faces challenges in this area, you're not alone, though, as 38% of businesses say that data analytics is among their top five biggest issues. Yet, when done well, 21% say it's the single most effective way to obtain a competitive edge[1].

There are many reasons to align your marketing measurement to business goals, of course; we'll discuss a few of these in the chapters that follow in this section.

PRIORITIZATION OF RESOURCES

When your business and marketing KPIs are aligned, you can better prioritize your resources and budget to support the areas that have the greatest impact on your organization's goals. This can help you maximize your return on investment and ensure you are making the most of your marketing budget.

For instance, a digital marketer for an e-commerce brand might analyze past campaign data and discover that social media ads on a specific platform generate the highest conversion rate. Because of this insight, they could shift a greater portion of the budget into this channel, perhaps focusing on retargeting ads that have proven to be especially effective, while scaling back or optimizing less productive pay-per-click campaigns on search engines.

Prioritizing resources enables marketers to operate more strategically, investing in areas with proven success. It's about making informed decisions to allocate marketing budgets effectively, thereby improving the cost-efficiency and overall impact of marketing initiatives.

EFFICIENT DECISION-MAKING

Aligning business and marketing KPIs can also help to streamline your decision-making process. By clearly understanding how your marketing efforts contribute to your organization's overall success, you can make more informed decisions about where to allocate resources and how to optimize your marketing campaigns.

A digital marketer who monitors real-time analytics for a high-traffic online retail website might notice a sudden spike in traffic from a viral social media post. The marketer quickly allocates additional resources to increase server capacity, ensuring website performance remains smooth. Simultaneously, they adjust the advertising spend to capitalize on this newfound attention, thus making the most of the unexpected surge in potential customers.

Efficient decision-making lies in agility and the ability to use real-time data to guide actions. By being prepared to make and implement decisions swiftly, a marketing department can adapt to the dynamic nature of the digital landscape, ensuring opportunities are seized and potential issues are promptly addressed.

ACHIEVING A BETTER UNDERSTANDING OF CUSTOMER BEHAVIOR

Finally, aligning business and marketing KPIs can help you better understand how your customers interact with your brand. By tracking key metrics such as customer lifetime value and customer acquisition cost, you can gain insights into which marketing channels and campaigns are most effective at driving customer engagement and loyalty.

A marketer might use website analytics to observe that customers often visit an FAQ page before completing a purchase. Recognizing this behavior, the marketer develops a strategy to enhance the visibility and content of the FAQ page, along with implementing a chatbot that proactively assists users on this page. As a result, the company sees an increase in conversion rates, attributable to the improved support and clarity provided to customers at a critical point in their journey.

Deep insights into customer behavior empower marketers to craft strategies that resonate with their audience. It's about leveraging data to uncover the nuances of how customers interact with the brand, enabling the creation of tailored experiences that effectively guide them along the path to purchase.

Overall, aligning business and marketing KPIs is critical in any measurement approach. By doing so, you can ensure that your marketing efforts are directly contributing to the success of your organization and make more informed decisions about allocating resources and optimizing your marketing campaigns.

This alignment, combined with a marketing measurement framework such as the one introduced in Part 2 of the book, is essential for any business that wants to measure the success of its marketing efforts. By aligning your metrics and KPIs with your business goals and objectives, you can gain a broader view of your marketing efforts and understand how different channels contribute to your overall success.

WHAT WE ARE GOING TO DISCUSS IN PART 1

First, though, we're going to start by looking at definitions of some of the key terms and concepts we'll be using throughout this book, and how they fit together to form a complete line from organizational objectives to measurements of marketing campaign and initiative performance.

This part of the book includes the following:

- Exploring the terminology of the types of data used in marketing measurement, as well as how metrics and KPIs are used
- The hierarchy of goals and KPIs and how business goals relate to marketing goals
- How to choose the right marketing metrics to be successful in your work
- The unique characteristics of single-channel and multi-channel marketing measurement
- A brief introduction to using statistics for marketing measurement

This part of the book will form the foundation for our deeper exploration in subsequent chapters, including the introduction of a marketing measurement framework.

ENDNOTE

1 Villanova Business School. "How Marketers Use Data and Analytics to Reach Customers." Retrieved July 2023 from: *https://taxandbusinessonline.villanova.edu/blog/how-marketers-use-data-analytics-to-reach-customers/*

CHAPTER 1

Exploring the Terminology

While the focus of this book is on marketing measurement, as well as analyzing and interpreting those results, it is important to start off by ensuring that you have a solid understanding of the terminology that will be used.

Two terms you'll hear often in this book are key performance indicator, or KPI, and metric, and both of these are made from the building blocks of data (Figure 1.1).

Key terms

Key Performance Indicator (KPI)

Metric(s)

Data

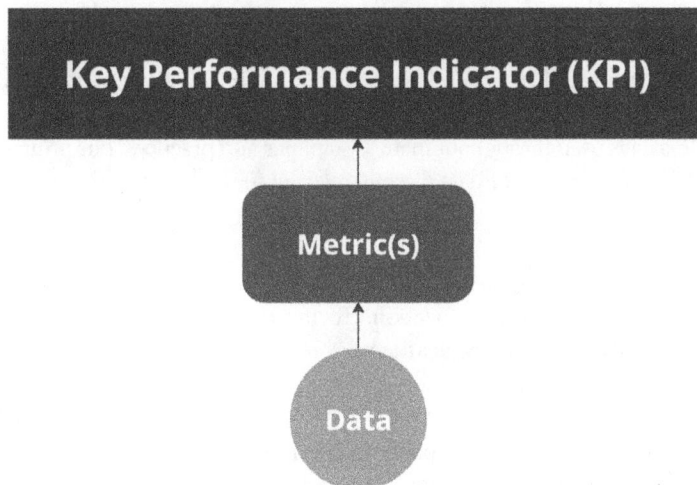

FIGURE 1.1. Key terms used in marketing measurement.

Although these terms are often used interchangeably (and wrongfully so), KPIs and metrics are not the same thing. This chapter will examine the difference between the two and why it matters.

DATA

This is our fundamental building block of information when discussing marketing measurement. Data is information that encompasses the quantitative characteristics of a variable or group of variables. It is typically documented as facts, figures, or details that can be processed or examined to acquire knowledge or make decisions.

Often, data is quantified, collected, and analyzed to facilitate decision-making and problem-solving across various fields, including science, business, and technology. In its simplest form, data can be numbers, words, measurements, observations, or even just descriptions of things.

Historical Origins of the Word "Data"

The word "data" is derived from the Latin word "datum," which translates to "something given." This reflects its origin from the Latin verb "dare," meaning "to give"[1]. Historically, in English, the term dates back to the 17th century, when it was singularly used as "datum." Initially, it referred to a premise or assumption that was used to base an argument or reasoning in philosophical or logical discussions[2].

Throughout the 20th century, the usage of the term "data" evolved significantly, perhaps in line with its growing usage across disciplines within the world of business and academics. With the rise of scientific research and quantitative methods, "data" began to be used in its plural form, symbolizing the collection of facts or measurements from which conclusions could be drawn[3]. This shift in usage paralleled advancements in areas such as statistics, computing, and information science, where data became a central element of analysis and decision-making.

In contemporary usage, "data" encompasses a wide range of information types and is crucial to data science—a field that focuses on analyzing and interpreting complex datasets. The nature of data can vary widely, being either structured or unstructured, and can reside in physical or digital form[4]. The analysis of data drives innovation, operational improvements, and strategic decisions across various industries and, as we will discuss in this book, it drives the work of marketers and their goal to reach customers, sell products, and increase sales.

Thus, while data is used throughout many disciplines and practices, our primary focus within this book is going to be on the types of data directly relevant to marketers and those in related fields.

The Types of Data

In the realm of marketing, data is the fuel that powers strategic decision-making, audience understanding, and campaign optimization. To harness this power, marketers must grasp the different types of data and their applications.

Qualitative Data

Qualitative data is descriptive and conceptual. It is data that can be observed but not measured. Think of it as the color palette that paints a detailed picture of customer opinions, sentiments, and experiences. For a marketer, qualitative data could include customer feedback collected through interviews, focus groups, or open-ended survey responses. This data offers insights into why customers behave a certain way, what they value in a product, or how they perceive a brand.

Example: A marketer might analyze customer reviews of their product to identify common themes or sentiments, which could inform product development or marketing messaging.

Quantitative Data

Quantitative data, in contrast, is numerical and can be counted or measured. It offers a statistical backbone that provides objective metrics to track and evaluate performance. For instance, it can measure how many visitors a Web site gets, the conversion rate of a campaign, or the average sales value per customer.

Example: A marketer could look at the number of shoes sold after a promotional email campaign (quantitative data) to determine the campaign's effectiveness.

Categorical Data

Categorical data represents characteristics that can be placed into categories but have no inherent numerical value. In marketing, categorical data is often used to segment customers into groups based on shared features or behaviors, such as by gender, age group, or buyer persona. This data is pivotal for targeting and personalizing marketing efforts.

Example: A marketing team for a sports brand might use categorical data to segment their market into "recreational" and "professional" athletes, tailoring marketing efforts to suit the interests and needs of each group.

Continuous Data

Continuous data refers to variables that can take on any value within a range. This data is measured along a continuum and can be broken down into finer scales, which is invaluable for tracking and analyzing variations over time. In marketing, continuous data might include the amount of time spent on a Web page or the number of shoes sold in a month.

Example: A brand could monitor the average daily duration that visitors spend on their product pages (continuous data) to gauge customer interest and engagement.

Understanding these types of data helps marketers draw a more nuanced picture of their audience and measure the impact of their marketing activities. By effectively capturing and analyzing both the narratives behind behaviors (qualitative) and the numbers that quantify those behaviors (quantitative), marketers can refine their strategies to better resonate with their target audience. Categorizing customers allows for more focused targeting, while continuous measures help track and optimize performance over time. Each data type serves as a critical piece in the complex puzzle of a modern marketing strategy.

Limitations of Relying on Data on Its Own

The constraints of data on its own are many. Thus, the information that the data itself represents lacks significance without interpretation based on context, relevance, and other factors.

For instance, knowing that we got 50,000 clicks on a social media ad last quarter does not tell us a lot. For instance:

- Is this more than we were anticipating?
- Did those clicks result in any purchase behavior?
- Is 50,000 clicks better or worse than the previous quarter?

Fundamentally, it is difficult to know whether 50,000 clicks is a good or bad thing, simply by knowing that number. Thus, data on its own only forms the foundations for the metrics and measurements we will be discussing in more detail.

METRICS

A metric is a quantifiable measure consisting of one or more data points used to assess the performance of a specific aspect of a marketing campaign, initiative, or business. While a metric may be a single data point, it generally includes several data points that, when used together, form a measure of an element's performance.

Additionally, even single data points that comprise a metric are often filtered or qualified; for example, a metric for Web site traffic would be filtered by date, source, page visited, or other criteria, rather than just being considered as a raw number, which might include search bots and internal employee traffic.

Examples of Metrics

Examples of metrics are social media engagement, filtered Web site traffic, email open rates, and Clickthrough Rates (CTRs) for ads, emails, or registration pages.

Limitations of Metrics on Their Own

Metrics give you a general idea of your campaign's performance, but they don't necessarily tell you how well you're meeting your goals. That's where KPIs come in.

Earlier, when we talked about data, the example of clicks on an ad was used. A metric could, by contrast, be considered the CTR, or, of the available impressions of an ad, how many people clicked on it.

So, for instance, knowing that the CTR on a social media advertisement for the last quarter was 3.1% does not have a significant inherent meaning unless you know that:

- The average social media advertising CTR worldwide from the 4th quarter of 2023 was only .98%[5], meaning that your CTR is three times the worldwide average.
- Your company's CTR in the previous quarter was 3.2%, meaning that, even though your CTR is well above the worldwide average, it actually declined from the previous quarter.

Thus, metrics give us more detail and context than individual data points alone, but still need both analysis and interpretation—the subject of several chapters of this book—as well as KPIs to make them more valuable.

KPIs

Key performance indicators—KPIs—are a specific metric, or quite often a calculation that consists of a set of metrics to measure the performance of important activities within a business. Because they determine whether a business or a team within it is achieving its goals, they are tied to a business objective or goal. KPIs help organizations track progress toward objectives, identify areas for optimization, and evaluate the effectiveness of marketing campaigns. In this chapter, we will discuss the importance of KPIs in achieving marketing success.

KPIs are used because they indicate how well you achieve your goals and are critical in helping you make informed decisions. Examples of KPIs include conversion rates, customer retention rates, cost per lead, and revenue growth. KPIs are quantifiable targets that help you monitor progress toward the overall objective of your marketing campaign or business.

Why KPIs Are Important

As a marketing leader, your primary goal is to drive business growth and improve Return on Investment (ROI), among many other things. How, though, can you measure your progress and identify areas for improvement? The answer lies in the use of KPIs.

KPIs allow you to set achievable goals aligned with your business objectives. By focusing on the performance of specific sets of metrics, and turning those into a larger view that you use as a KPI, you can determine what success looks like and track your progress toward that goal.

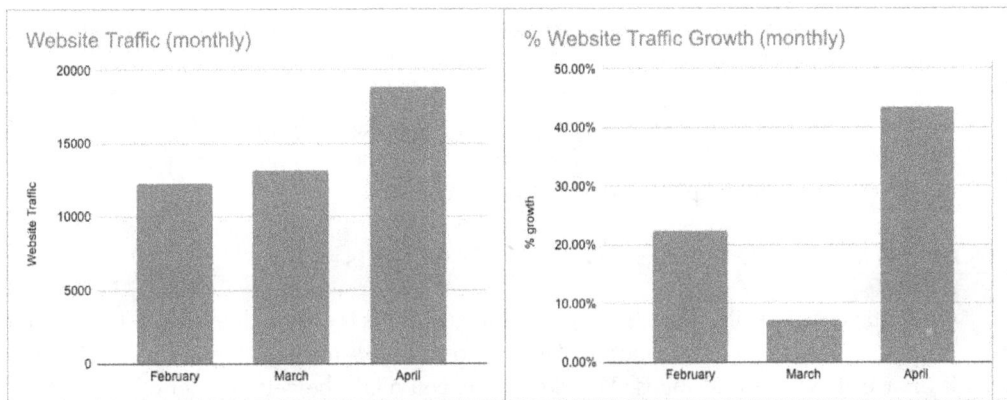

FIGURE 1.2. A comparison of KPI approaches.

For example, look at Figure 1.2. If your goal is to increase Web site traffic, you can set a KPI to measure the number of monthly Web site visitors, as shown on the chart on the left, which illustrates that monthly Web site traffic has increased month over month from February through April. Taken on its own, a Web site marketer could claim success.

A potentially more valuable KPI, however, would be the *growth* of monthly Web site visitors over time. This allows you to track your progress and determine whether the marketing initiatives you have implemented are driving the desired outcomes. Going back to Figure 1.2, you can see that the percentage of Web site traffic growth month over month severely dipped in March, from over 20% in February to lower than 10% in March. This decrease in the growth rate means that although overall numbers were slightly increasing (as shown in the chart on the left), the effectiveness of the efforts—or some yet-to-be-identified phenomenon—hindered the effectiveness of the Web site marketing efforts.

In this way, it is important that marketers choose the best possible KPIs that will enable them to have a clear view of the success of their efforts.

Benefits of KPIs

This section will detail some of the benefits of KPIs.

KPIs Increase Transparency and Accountability

Choosing KPIs that align with shared business objectives and communicating these goals with teams both within and outside of your immediate department or teams enables visibility on the measures of success and, in some cases, debate on the definition of success.

Well-chosen KPIs provide transparency throughout the organization, allowing everyone to see the progress toward the overall objectives. This helps to promote accountability and ensures that everyone is working toward the same goals. It also allows your marketing team to balance their activities more effectively and ensure they stay on track with KPIs.

Case Study: PB Shoes Need to Set KPIs

Let's say, for example, that we work for a hypothetical company, PB Shoes, that makes athletic shoes and wants to expand sales and market share of its shoes made specifically for pickleball because there appears to be an opportunity for growth in that sector of the market.

This is a case where KPIs can be incredibly helpful. After all, how does the company know that it is making progress toward its expansion of market share in the area of pickleball shoes?

Given this goal, their business KPIs should include market share expansion and an overall sales increase in the pickleball shoes sector. They may have other KPIs, but using both will help them tell that they are not only growing their own revenue from pickleball shoes but also outpacing the expansion of the pickleball shoe market in general.

KNOWING WHEN TO FOCUS ON METRICS OR KPIs

Understanding the difference between metrics and KPIs is essential because they have different purposes. Focusing solely on metrics can give you a false sense of accomplishment. For instance, if the metric you're tracking is Web site traffic, you might be getting a lot of traffic, but if that traffic is not translating into leads or sales, then it's not really helping you achieve your goals. If, however, you also track the KPI of conversion rates, you can see whether that traffic is translating to leads or sales and can make informed decisions on improving that KPI.

Moreover, if you're selecting the wrong metrics for your KPIs, you might be tracking progress that's not really relevant to your goals. For instance, if your objective is to increase revenue, you might be tempted to track the metric of Web site traffic. Web site traffic might, however, not have a direct correlation to revenue. Instead, you should track revenue growth as your KPI to measure progress more effectively.

CONCLUSION

Data, metrics, and KPIs are the building blocks for the marketing measurement that will be explored in the chapters that follow. While metrics and KPIs are similar in that they are both measurements used to track the success of a campaign or a business, they are also different. Metrics can give you valuable information about the performance of your campaign, but KPIs help you monitor progress toward specific business objectives.

Understanding the difference between the two is important to make informed decisions, achieve goals, and stay on track as a marketer.

By focusing on the right KPIs, you can measure success more accurately through individual metrics used together to tell the full story, adjust campaigns to improve performance, and meet your business objectives. By using relevant KPIs, you can set achievable goals, increase transparency and accountability, measure the effectiveness of campaigns, identify areas for optimization, and stay agile. Strategically aligned KPIs allow you to evaluate the ROI of marketing initiatives, adapt to changing market conditions, and make data-driven decisions to optimize overall business performance. As a marketing leader, strong KPIs tightly aligned with strategic business goals should be at the top of your priority list to improve your marketing ROI.

What is the difference, then, between business and marketing KPIs? If they are both KPIs, how do we know when each applies? The next chapter is going to answer this important question.

ENDNOTES

1 Harper, D. (2021). Online Etymology Dictionary. Entry "Data." Retrieved from *https://www.etymonline.com/word/data*

2 Harper, D. (n.d.). Datum. Online Etymology Dictionary. Retrieved October 6, 2024, from *https://www.etymonline.com/word/datum*

3 Oxford English Dictionary. (2022). Entry "Data." Retrieved from *https://www.oed.com/view/Entry/47444*

4 National Institute of Standards and Technology. (2019). NIST Big Data Interoperability Framework: Volume 1, Definitions. Retrieved from *https://nvlpubs.nist.gov/nistpubs/SpecialPublications/NIST.SP.1500-1r2.pdf*

5 Statista. "Social media advertising clickthrough rate (CTR) worldwide from 4th quarter 2022 to 4th quarter 2023." Retrieved May 26, 2024 from *https://www.statista.com/statistics/872099/social-media-advertising-ctr/*

CHAPTER 2

THE HIERARCHY OF GOALS AND MEASUREMENTS

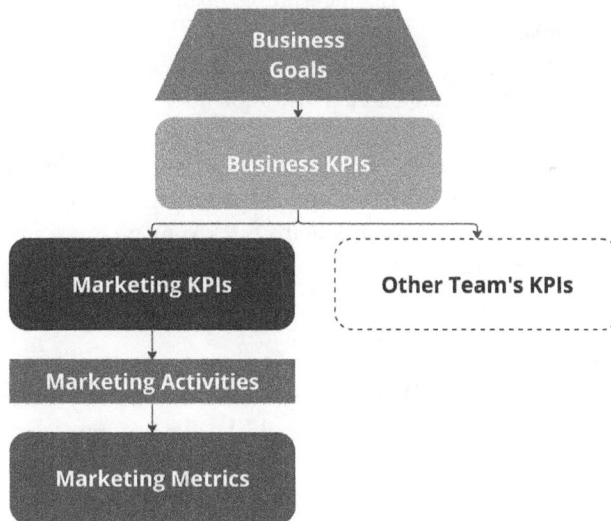

Let's begin with an overview of the hierarchy of goals and measurements (Figure 2.1) and how we will talk about these terms throughout this book. This will be reviewed in greater detail in the chapters that follow, but it will help to start with some context.

Hierarchy of Goals and Measurements

FIGURE 2.1. Hierarchy of goals and measurements.

The following sections provide a brief outline of each element of the hierarchy.

BUSINESS GOALS

Business goals are the specific, measurable objectives that a company aims to achieve to fulfill its broader mission and strategic vision. These goals are generally long-term and serve as guiding benchmarks for the overall progress of the organization.

Why They Are Important

Business goals are crucial because they provide a clear framework for strategic planning and decision-making across all levels of an organization. They help align the efforts of various departments and ensure that all activities contribute toward the overarching aims of the company. Effective business goals promote organizational focus, drive motivation, and foster a cohesive direction that is necessary for sustainable growth and success.

How to Know Whether They Are Well Defined

Well-defined business goals are SMART: Specific, Measurable, Achievable, Relevant, and Time-bound. This means they clearly outline what is to be achieved, allow for tracking progress through specific indicators, are attainable, align with broader business objectives, and have a defined timeline for achievement. A well-defined goal enables effective planning and precise performance assessment.

If you are not familiar with SMART goals, here is a brief overview of the terms that make up each part of the acronym, straight from The Agile Brand Guide's Martechipedia[1]:

- *Specific*: Make sure that your goals are precise and detailed. Instead of vague goals such as "Increase sales," make them specific, such as "Increase sales by 25% in three months."
- *Measurable*: Set a quantifiable target for your campaign goals. For example, "Increase Web site traffic by 30% in one month" is a measurable goal. It helps you to monitor the performance of your campaign.
- *Achievable*: Quantifying specific targets is important, but you must ensure your goals are achievable. Unrealistic goals can lead to frustration among your team members, which can kill their motivation.
- *Relevant*: Ensure your goals align with the overall strategy of your business. Your short-term objectives must contribute to your company's long-term ambitions.
- *Time-bound*: Setting a specific timeline helps track your progress and encourages you to work faster to meet deadlines. For example, "Increase social media engagement by 40% in six months" is time-bound.

Common Misconceptions

One common misunderstanding about business goals is that they are static and, once set, remain unchanged. Business goals, however, should be flexible and adaptable to changes in the business environment. Another misconception is that all business goals directly relate to financial gains, while in reality, they can also focus on customer satisfaction, market expansion, innovation, and other non-financial aspects that contribute to long-term business viability.

Examples of Business Goals

- *Increase market share*: An enterprise might aim to increase its market share in a specific region by 5% over the next year through strategic partnerships and enhanced marketing efforts.
- *Improve operational efficiency*: A business goal could be to reduce operational costs by 10% within two years by implementing new technologies and optimizing existing processes.

- *Enhance customer satisfaction*: Enterprises may set a goal to improve customer satisfaction scores by 15% through improved customer service training and a revamped feedback system.
- *Sustainability initiatives*: A company might aim to reduce their carbon footprint by 20% over the next five years through the adoption of cleaner technologies and more sustainable practices.
- *Employee engagement and retention*: A goal may be to increase employee retention rates by improving engagement through career development programs and enhanced work-life balance options.

Each of these examples demonstrates how enterprise organizations define specific targets that not only aim for immediate benefits but also align with long-term strategic plans that sustain business growth and adaptation in a competitive landscape.

BUSINESS KEY PERFORMANCE INDICATORS

Business Key Performance Indicators (KPIs) are quantifiable metrics used by organizations to evaluate their success in reaching targeted business goals. These indicators help measure the effectiveness of business strategies and activities in terms of performance and achievement.

Why They Are Important

Business KPIs are important because they provide an objective basis for measuring and tracking the efficiency and effectiveness of business operations. They enable organizations to make informed decisions, prioritize resources, and direct efforts where they are most effective. KPIs also facilitate clear communication about performance across different levels of an organization, fostering accountability and alignment with strategic objectives.

How to Know Whether They Are Well Defined

Well-defined business KPIs are directly linked to strategic business goals and tailored to reflect critical success factors. They should be clear and measurable and provide actionable insights. A well-defined business KPI will have a baseline measurement with set targets that reflect expected improvements or maintenance of performance, making it possible to track progress over time.

You can use the following checklist as a guide to determine whether a business KPIS is well defined:

- *Strategic alignment*: Does the KPI directly link to strategic business goals? Ensure each KPI is clearly connected to broader organizational objectives.
- *Specificity*: Is the KPI explicitly defined? Check that the KPI clearly specifies what is being measured.
- *Measurability*: Can the KPI be quantitatively measured? Verify that there is a method in place for accurately assessing the KPI.
- *Actionable insights*: Does the KPI provide insights that can lead to actionable steps? Ensure that the KPI helps in making informed decisions.

- *Baseline and targets*: Is there a baseline measurement established for the KPI? Confirm that there are specific targets set, reflecting expected improvements or necessary maintenance of performance.
- *Progress tracking*: Can progress be tracked over time? Make sure the KPI allows for periodic assessment to measure advancement toward targets.
- *Cross-disciplinary relevance*: Does the KPI reflect higher-level, cross-disciplinary performance and not just focus on one specific area, such as marketing? Ensure it provides a holistic view of business success.
- *Distinctiveness from marketing KPIs*: Ensure that the business KPIs are not a repeat of the marketing KPIs but complement them by providing a broader view of organizational success.
- *Regular review and adjustment*: Is there a process in place for regularly reviewing and updating the KPI based on evolving business needs and external conditions?
- *Integration with other KPIs*: Check how well the KPI integrates with other performance indicators across the organization to ensure a cohesive performance management system.

This checklist will help ensure that each business KPI is well defined and effective in contributing to the strategic success and overall health of the organization.

Common Misconceptions

A common misunderstanding about KPIs is that more is always better. In fact, focusing on too many KPIs can dilute an organization's strategic efforts and obscure key performance insights that would help with either continuous improvement or avoiding potential issues that inhibit growth. Another misconception is that KPIs are solely about financial metrics, such as revenue and profit margins; they can, however, also include customer satisfaction, employee engagement, operational efficiency, and other non-financial aspects critical to long-term success.

Examples of Business KPIs

- *Revenue growth rate*: Measures the rate at which revenue is growing from one period to another, indicating overall business growth and market acceptance.
- *Net profit margin*: A key financial metric that shows how much of each dollar earned translates into profits, reflecting the efficiency of cost management.
- *Customer retention rate*: Indicates the percentage of customers who remain with the company over a specific period, highlighting customer satisfaction and service quality.
- *Employee turnover rate*: Measures the rate at which employees leave the company, which can indicate the health of organizational culture and employee satisfaction.
- *Operational efficiency ratios*: These might include inventory turnover ratios or production efficiency ratios, which help measure how effectively resources are being utilized to maintain and increase business operations.

These examples show how business KPIs, both financial and non-financial, are crucial for monitoring the effectiveness of strategies implemented by enterprise organizations in pursuit of their broader goals.

MARKETING KPIs

Marketing KPIs are specific, quantifiable metrics used to measure the effectiveness and success of marketing initiatives against predefined targets. These measurements help marketing teams assess how well their activities are contributing to the business objectives.

Why They Are Important

Marketing KPIs are vital to companies, and the marketing teams within them, because they allow marketers to evaluate the performance of their campaigns and strategies in real time, providing data-driven insights into what's working and what isn't. These metrics help optimize the marketing spend, improve campaign strategies, and justify further marketing investment to stakeholders, who can often be wary of spending more without being able to see tangible results. Marketing KPIs align marketing efforts with the overall business strategy, ensuring that marketing contributes directly to achieving business goals.

How to Know Whether They Are Well Defined

Well-defined marketing KPIs are aligned with broader marketing objectives and, ultimately, with business goals. They should be Specific, Measurable, Attainable, Relevant, and Time-bound (SMART), a concept that has been touched on briefly and will be explored further in this book. A well-defined marketing KPI clearly states what is measured, how it is measured, and the timeframe over which it is measured. It also includes a benchmark or target that defines success or the need for adjustment.

You can use the following checklist to determine whether your marketing KPIs are well defined:

- *Alignment with marketing objectives*: Is the KPI directly aligned with the broader marketing objectives?
- *Connection to business goals*: Does the KPI support overarching business goals?
- *Specificity*: Does the KPI clearly state what is being measured? Is the definition precise and unambiguous?
- *Measurability*: Is there a clear method outlined for how the KPI is to be measured? Are the tools and data sources needed to measure the KPI specified?
- *Attainability*: Is the KPI realistically achievable given the current resources and market conditions?
- *Relevance*: Is the KPI directly relevant to the performance of the marketing department and its impact on the business?
- *Time-bound*: Does the KPI have a specified timeframe over which it is to be measured? Is this timeframe appropriate for the marketing goals it supports?
- *Benchmark or target*: Does the KPI include a specific benchmark or target that defines what success looks like?
- *Adjustability*: Is there a provision for adjusting the KPI based on performance data and market feedback?
- *SMART criteria*: Overall, does the KPI meet all the criteria of being specific, measurable, attainable, relevant, and time-bound?

Reviewing against this checklist ensures that each KPI is a strategic tool that drives and measures marketing success effectively. This will help you ensure your KPIs are robust, actionable, and aligned with broader business objectives.

Common Misconceptions

A common misunderstanding about marketing KPIs is that they are universally applicable, meaning that an "out-of-the-box" marketing dashboard can be used. Effective marketing KPIs are highly specific to the organization's market, strategy, audience, and objectives. Another misunderstanding is equating vanity metrics (such as page views or number of followers) with true KPIs, which should directly tie back to business impact, such as lead generation, sales conversions, or customer engagement.

Examples of Marketing KPIs

- *Conversion rate*: Measures the percentage of users who take a desired action, which helps in understanding the effectiveness of marketing campaigns in driving targeted actions.
- *Customer Acquisition Cost (CAC)*: The cost associated with acquiring a new customer, which is crucial for evaluating the efficiency of marketing investments.
- *Return on Advertising Spend (ROAS)*: A calculation of the profit generated by advertising spend compared to the cost of those activities, providing a direct financial impact of advertising efforts.
- *Lead generation*: The total number of new leads generated, indicating the effectiveness of marketing campaigns at filling the sales pipeline.
- *Engagement rate*: Used particularly in digital marketing, this measures interactions with content across digital platforms, reflecting customer interest and content relevance.

These KPIs help marketing teams in enterprise organizations to track performance, make informed decisions, and steer their activities in alignment with business objectives, ensuring that marketing efforts are not only creative but also quantifiable and strategically sound.

MARKETING ACTIVITIES

Marketing activities include the often large range of actions, initiatives, and campaigns performed by a marketing team and their agency partners and vendors to promote products or services, engage with customers, and ultimately drive the company's marketing objectives forward. These activities can span many channels and formats, including digital and traditional marketing.

In terms of our measurement hierarchy, these marketing activities are driven by the business goals and KPIs and determined by the marketing KPIs that need to be achieved.

Why They Are Important

Marketing activities are critical as they directly influence customer perceptions, generate leads, and drive sales. They are the tangible executions that deliver the brand message to the target audience, build customer relationships, and enhance Customer Lifetime Value (CLV). Effective marketing activities not only help in achieving specific marketing KPIs but also contribute to broader business goals by increasing market share, customer base, and revenue.

How to Know Whether They Are Well Defined

Well-defined marketing activities are clearly aligned with strategic marketing goals, as well as the business KPIs they support, and are designed to meet specific KPIs with target numbers assigned to them. They have clear objectives, target specific audience segments, and utilize appropriate channels and tactics to reach these audiences effectively. Additionally, they include metrics for measuring success and are adaptable based on performance data and market feedback.

Thus, you can use the following checklist to help determine whether a marketing activity is well defined and aligned with the other items in the hierarchy:

- *Alignment with strategic goals*: Does the marketing activity align with the broader strategic marketing goals of the organization?
- *Support for business KPIs*: Is the marketing activity designed to support specific business KPIs? Are these KPIs clearly identified?
- *Specific KPIs with targets*: Does the marketing activity have specific KPIs with target numbers assigned to measure success?
- *Clear objectives*: Are the objectives of the marketing activity clearly defined and understood by all stakeholders?
- *Target audience identification*: Does the marketing activity specify which audience segments it targets?
- *Appropriate channels and tactics*: Are the channels and tactics chosen for the marketing activity appropriate and effective for reaching the targeted audience?
- *Metrics for measuring success*: Are there clear metrics in place to measure the success of the marketing activity?
- *Adaptability*: Is the marketing activity designed to be adaptable based on performance data and market feedback?
- *Data-driven adjustments*: Are there processes in place to make adjustments to the marketing activity based on data and feedback?
- *Review and optimization*: Is there a regular review process to assess the effectiveness of the marketing activity and make necessary optimizations?

This checklist ensures that each marketing activity is aligned with the overall strategy as well as measurable, targeted, and adaptable, thereby maximizing the potential for success.

Common Misconceptions

While achieving measurable outcomes is always the goal, a common misunderstanding about marketing activities is that they should always lead directly to sales. While driving sales is a primary goal, marketing activities also focus on building brand awareness, enhancing customer engagement, and nurturing relationships, which are equally important for long-term success.

Another misunderstanding is that successful marketing requires huge budgets; creativity and strategic targeting, however, can often yield better results than sheer financial spend.

Examples of Marketing Activities

- *Social media campaigns*: Engaging with customers on platforms such as Facebook, Instagram, and Twitter to build brand awareness and foster community engagement.

- *Content marketing*: Creating and distributing valuable, relevant, and consistent content to attract and retain a clearly defined audience and, ultimately, to drive profitable customer action.
- *Email marketing*: Sending targeted and personalized messages to segmented customer lists to inform customers about new products, offers, and content.
- *Search Engine Optimization (SEO) and SEM*: Enhancing online visibility through and paying for advertisements on search engines to drive Web site traffic.
- *Trade shows and events*: Participating in industry events to network with potential clients, showcase new products or services, and strengthen brand presence.

These examples illustrate how varied and dynamic marketing activities are within large organizations, each tailored to different stages of the customer journey and designed to contribute collectively to achieving both marketing and business objectives.

MARKETING METRICS

Marketing metrics are quantitative tools used to track the performance and effectiveness of marketing activities. They measure specific aspects of marketing campaigns to evaluate progress toward achieving marketing goals and objectives.

Why They Are Important

Marketing metrics are crucial for understanding the impact of marketing efforts on the company's bottom line. They help marketers quantify success, make data-driven decisions, and justify marketing spend by demonstrating ROI. Metrics provide feedback that can be used to optimize ongoing campaigns, guide future marketing strategies, and ensure that marketing objectives are aligned with business goals.

How to Know Whether They Are Well Defined

Well-defined marketing metrics are specific, measurable, and directly linked to marketing objectives. They should be easy to track, relevant to the goals they are supposed to help achieve, and clearly defined so that there is no ambiguity about what is being measured. Effective metrics should also provide actionable insights that can be used to improve marketing performance.

You can use the following checklist to help determine whether your marketing metrics are well defined:

- *Specificity*: Does the metric clearly specify what aspect of marketing performance it is measuring? Ensure that the metric is focused and well defined to avoid ambiguity.
- *Measurability*: Can the metric be quantified? Verify that the metric can be measured with available tools and data to ensure accuracy and reliability.
- *Direct link to objectives*: Is the metric directly linked to specific marketing objectives? Check that each metric corresponds to particular goals to ensure alignment with overall marketing strategies.
- *Ease of tracking*: Can the metric be easily tracked with current systems and technologies? Confirm that the tools and processes are in place to regularly monitor this metric.

- *Relevance*: Is the metric relevant to the goals it is supposed to achieve? Ensure that the metric contributes to understanding and evaluating the effectiveness of marketing activities.
- *Clarity*: Is the definition of the metric clear and straightforward? Check for any potential confusion or misinterpretation in what the metric measures.
- *Actionability*: Does the metric provide actionable insights? Ensure that the data obtained from this metric can be used to make informed decisions to improve marketing performance.
- *Consistency*: Can the metric be consistently measured over time and across different platforms? This consistency is crucial for comparing performance over time.
- *Integration*: Does the metric integrate well with other metrics to provide a comprehensive view of marketing performance? Check how this metric fits into the broader set of marketing metrics.
- *Feedback mechanism*: Is there a mechanism in place to review and refine the metric based on its effectiveness and feedback from stakeholders? Regular reviews can help adapt metrics to changing marketing landscapes and objectives.

This checklist will help ensure that marketing metrics are practical, actionable, and effectively aligned with the strategic goals of the marketing department, thus enhancing the overall performance and success of marketing initiatives.

Common Misconceptions

A common misunderstanding about marketing metrics is that they can universally apply to all campaigns and objectives. In reality, the appropriateness of a metric can vary greatly depending on the specific marketing strategy and the channel being used. Another misunderstanding is equating high numbers directly with success; for example, high traffic to a Web site doesn't necessarily translate to high conversion rates. Marketers must look deeper to find metrics that truly correlate with business success.

Examples of Common Marketing Metrics

- *Clickthrough Rate (CTR)*: Measures the percentage of people who clicked on a link within an advertisement or content piece, indicating the effectiveness of the creative or the offer.
- *Cost per Acquisition (CPA)*: Tracks the average cost spent to acquire one customer, which is critical for budgeting and marketing ROI calculations.
- *Conversion rate*: The percentage of visitors who complete a desired action, such as filling out a form or making a purchase, which helps gauge the success of conversion-driven initiatives.
- *Social media engagement*: Measures interactions (likes, shares, and comments) on social media platforms to assess how engaging content is with the target audience.
- *CLV*: Calculates the total revenue a business can reasonably expect from a single customer account throughout their relationship with the company, helping to refine the marketing strategy and resource allocation.

These metrics, when tracked regularly and analyzed accurately, provide enterprise organizations with critical insights into their marketing effectiveness, guiding strategic decisions and operational improvements.

CONCLUSION

In this chapter, we have looked at the structured hierarchy of marketing measurement, starting from broader and strategic business goals down through measurable business KPIs, marketing KPIs, the specific marketing activities that support all of these, and, finally, the most granular level of marketing metrics. Each layer of this marketing measurement framework is essential for constructing a robust marketing strategy that aligns closely with the overarching business objectives. By understanding and implementing this hierarchy, organizations can ensure that every marketing effort is both purposeful and measurable, maximizing the impact of their marketing investments.

As we have seen, business goals set the strategic compass for the organization, while business KPIs track the company's progress toward these goals. Marketing KPIs, derived from business KPIs, focus specifically on the contributions of marketing efforts to the overall business strategy. Marketing activities are the tactics used to reach these KPIs, and marketing metrics provide the data needed to assess the effectiveness of each activity.

As we move to the next chapter, we will delve deeper into the distinctions between business KPIs and marketing KPIs. Understanding these differences is crucial for ensuring that marketing strategies not only support but also enhance the broader business objectives. We will explore how to tailor marketing KPIs to reflect and support business KPIs effectively, ensuring that marketing efforts are not only aligned with but actively driving toward the company's strategic goals. This knowledge will empower marketers to better demonstrate the strategic value of their work and optimize the contributions of marketing within the business landscape.

ENDNOTES

1 The Agile Brand Guide's Martechipedia. "SMART GOALS." Retrieved July 2023 from *https:// agilebrandguide.com/wiki/measurements/smart-goals/*

CHAPTER 3

DISTINGUISHING BETWEEN BUSINESS AND MARKETING KPIS

Today's businesses must stay competitive to remain relevant. Part of this competitiveness involves setting goals that help achieve strategic objectives, as we explored in the last chapter. These objectives are backed by the specific Key Performance Indicators (KPIs) that we discussed in the previous chapters. As we saw, there are two types of KPIs that businesses must be aware of. These are business KPIs and marketing KPIs. This chapter aims to provide a clear understanding of the difference between the two, how they're used, and how to develop them.

One of the key differences between marketing KPIs and business KPIs is the level of influence they have on the overall strategy of their organizations. Marketing KPIs are used to measure a specific aspect of the marketing strategy; they don't drive the organization's overall strategic direction. On the other hand, business KPIs align with the broader strategic direction of the business and help guide decision-making to achieve business objectives.

When developing marketing and business KPIs, clear objectives and actionable metrics must be set. Marketing KPIs should align with business KPIs to ensure marketing efforts drive long-term business growth. With aligned KPIs, organizations can focus on approaches that impact both the quantity and quality of leads, create more conversion opportunities, and drive overall growth. As such, business KPIs inform marketing KPIs to help them create strategies to help achieve overall business objectives.

CASE STUDY: PB SHOES' MARKETING KPIs

Let's go back to PB Shoes. When we left them, they had aligned around some business KPIs, including market share expansion and an overall sales increase in the pickleball shoes sector.

Now, the marketing team at PB Shoes needs to create marketing KPIs that align with the business goal of growing their pickleball shoes business, and the related business KPIs.

For instance, their marketing KPIs may include an increase in e-commerce sales for pickleball shoes, or they may even get more specific and focus on increasing sales of pickleball shoes to existing customers—or maybe they do both!

In this case, the marketing team at PB Shoes chose to have both as marketing KPIs. After all, a team can have multiple marketing KPIs as long as they are relevant and are tied to a business goal and KPI.

PLAYING TO THEIR STRENGTHS

Marketing KPIs and business KPIs are essential performance indicators supporting business growth, but it is important to distinguish between the two. Marketing KPIs focus on measuring specific marketing strategies in play to achieve a business objective. Business KPIs focus on broader performance indicators, such as revenue growth, margins, and customer satisfaction. When developing KPIs, keep in mind that both marketing and business KPIs are essential to drive business growth; they must align and provide insights to help inform the decision-making process and maintain long-term business growth.

Chief Marketing Officers (CMOs) and marketing leaders should work together with other leaders and stakeholders within the business to align the marketing and business KPIs, ensuring that the marketing strategies implemented drive the overall business strategy.

ALIGNING MARKETING KPIs AND BUSINESS KPIs

Although, as we just saw, marketing KPIs can be distinct from business KPIs, that doesn't mean it should stay like that within your organization. Ideally, you align your marketing KPIs with the business KPIs, which will ultimately benefit your marketing teams, customers, and the business itself. Marketing KPIs should align with business KPIs to ensure marketing efforts drive long-term business growth, assuming that stronger marketing drives revenue, new customer acquisition, and customer loyalty and lifetime value.

By aligning marketing and business KPIs more closely, you can track the impact of marketing initiatives on the business's overall success, optimize marketing efforts to support business objectives, and enhance the credibility of marketing as a strategic function. This will support greater investments in resources, infrastructure, and more. Let's explore these benefits in more detail.

TRACKING THE IMPACT OF MARKETING INITIATIVES ON OVERALL BUSINESS SUCCESS

By aligning marketing KPIs with business KPIs, marketing leaders can track the impact of marketing initiatives on overall business success. This alignment allows marketing teams to quantify the impact of their work on business objectives such as revenue, customer acquisition, and customer retention. By tracking these metrics, marketing teams can demonstrate how their efforts contribute to overall business growth and success.

This is critical to not only the success of the marketing team but also the overall growth and sustainability of the brand. This impact should also involve tying direct lines between marketing efforts and longer-term customer relationships. This is why I stress the concept of a Customer Lifetime Value (CLV) model so much with the customers I work with. Using CLV as a business KPI and having marketing metrics and KPIs roll up to that can positively influence how business is done and ensure that marketing teams are front and center in the discussion.

ENHANCING THE CREDIBILITY OF MARKETING AS A STRATEGIC FUNCTION

By aligning marketing KPIs with business KPIs, marketing leaders can enhance the credibility of marketing as a strategic function. This alignment ensures that marketing is viewed as a critical business function that contributes to overall business success rather than just a support function. By demonstrating the impact of marketing on business success and using metrics relevant to the business, marketing can become a more valued and strategic function within the organization.

This is especially helpful when the marketing function needs to ask for further investment in areas such as:

- Expanding teams and the number of members within marketing teams
- Expanding or modernizing marketing technology infrastructure
- Making further investments in customer data integrations
- Performing transformations to gain greater efficiency to support time- and resource-intensive activities, such as expanded personalization

Of course, the preceding are just a few areas where further investment might be needed.

MAKING DATA-DRIVEN DECISIONS

Aligning marketing KPIs with business KPIs is essential for ensuring that marketing efforts contribute directly to overarching business objectives. This alignment allows leaders to make decisions based on comprehensive data that reflects both marketing effectiveness and its impact on the business as a whole. It bridges the gap between marketing activities and broader business goals, such as revenue growth, market expansion, and customer satisfaction.

For instance, if a business objective is to increase market share, relevant marketing KPIs could include lead generation rates, conversion rates, and customer acquisition costs. By focusing on these KPIs, marketing efforts can be directly correlated with their contribution to gaining market share, allowing for adjustments in strategy that are informed by actual performance against business targets.

Case Study: PB Shoes' Alignment of Business and Marketing KPIs

At PB Shoes, aligning marketing and business KPIs has transformed their strategic planning and resource allocation processes. One of PB Shoes' objectives is to expand into new geographic markets. The business KPIs might include increased overall revenue and market penetration rates. Corresponding marketing KPIs would focus on regional brand awareness and the effectiveness of localized marketing campaigns.

By tracking both sets of KPIs, PB Shoes can evaluate how well their marketing strategies in new regions are contributing to the desired increase in market penetration and revenue. For example, if a campaign in a new market is successful in driving high engagement but fails to convert engagement into sales, the marketing team can investigate and adjust their tactics, such as by optimizing call-to-action messages or improving post-engagement follow-ups.

This unified approach enables PB Shoes to ensure that all departments are not only aware of but also working toward the same goals. It facilitates better communication and coordination across teams, as everyone uses a common language of metrics. Additionally, it helps in justifying marketing expenditures by directly linking them with their impact on business outcomes, thereby enhancing accountability and transparency.

In this example of using a common set of metrics, PB Shoes can more effectively communicate successes and areas needing improvement to stakeholders, from team members to external investors. It also aids in strategic adjustments, as real-time data feedback allows the company to pivot quickly in response to market dynamics, ensuring that both marketing and business objectives are met.

Aligning marketing KPIs with business KPIs is not just about tracking numbers but about integrating marketing efforts into the fabric of business strategy. This alignment is crucial for making informed, data-driven decisions that propel the company toward its long-term goals. It ensures that every marketing initiative undertaken is justifiable in terms of business value, fostering a culture of accountability and strategic focus across the organization.

BUILDING A CULTURE OF ACCOUNTABILITY

Aligning marketing KPIs with broader business KPIs is a strategic approach that can significantly enhance accountability within an organization. For CMOs and other marketing leaders, this alignment is crucial not only for justifying marketing spend but also for ensuring that the marketing department's efforts are in harmony with the company's overall objectives. This strategic alignment helps bridge any gaps between marketing initiatives and business outcomes, fostering a culture where every team member understands how their actions contribute to the company's success.

Case Study: PB Shoes' Culture of Accountability

At PB Shoes, the marketing team aligns their KPIs, such as lead generation and customer engagement rates, with the company's business KPIs, such as revenue growth and market share expansion. This alignment allows marketing leaders to clearly demonstrate how marketing efforts directly influence the overall business performance. For instance, if the goal is to expand into new geographic markets, marketing KPIs would focus on increasing brand awareness and customer acquisition in those specific areas, directly supporting the business KPI of market expansion.

This approach ensures that everyone in the organization, from the top executives to the frontline employees, is focused on delivering measurable results that drive the company forward. It creates a shared understanding across departments, reducing silos and enhancing cross-functional collaboration. By using a common set of metrics, it becomes easier for all employees to see the direct impact of their work on the organization's goals, which in turn can boost morale and increase motivation.

When everyone is evaluated based on the same set of clear, quantifiable objectives, it also establishes a fair and transparent basis for accountability. This is crucial for maintaining high performance and continuously improving the quality of work across all levels of the organization. In the context of PB Shoes, for example, the marketing department can be held accountable not just for the number of marketing leads generated but for how well these leads convert into actual sales, directly reflecting their contribution to the business's primary goal of revenue growth.

Aligning marketing KPIs with business KPIs is not just about measuring success; it's about creating a culture where accountability is part of the daily operations. For companies such as PB Shoes, this means ensuring that each department and team member is not only aware of how their efforts align with broader business goals but also committed to achieving them. This unified approach not only drives company-wide success but also fosters an environment where continuous improvement is a shared responsibility.

MAP MARKETING KPIs TO STAKEHOLDERS

As we've explored so far in this book, your challenge as a marketer is to identify the right KPIs that not only measure marketing performance but also support your company's wider business objectives, and "speak the language" of others within the business. When this happens, it is easier to demonstrate your success, make the case for additional investments, and ensure alignment of expectations between marketing and other areas of the business.

Let's explore the process of confirming that your marketing metrics resonate with your stakeholders across the organization.

Think Outside Marketing: What Is Best for the Business at Large?

To select the right marketing KPIs, you need to understand your company's overarching goals and how marketing fits into them. Also, in a large, siloed organization, it can sometimes be hard to think outside a single marketing channel, let alone the entire marketing organization.

Ask yourself questions such as: What are we trying to achieve as a business? How can marketing contribute to these goals? What are the measurements that will best showcase our contribution to the organization at large? For example, if your company aims to increase revenue from new customer acquisition, you may focus on revenue growth metrics such as conversions, average order value, or CLV.

Identify Stakeholder Priorities

Marketing KPIs are not just about showing marketing's performance. They need to align with the goals and priorities of your stakeholders across the company, including your CEO, CFO, sales team, customer support staff, and others. Identify who your stakeholders are and what they care about. What metrics will best showcase the value that marketing brings to their area?

For example, your CFO may be interested in metrics that show a strong Return on Investment (ROI), such as customer acquisition cost and ROI. At the same time, your sales team may care more about lead generation and conversion rates.

Consider Your Competitive Landscape

Your marketing KPIs should also help you benchmark your performance against your competition because others in the business are surely looking at that component and will want your organization's marketing component to keep pace, if not leading in the space. If possible, look at what metrics your competitors are tracking and consider which ones are relevant to your business.

For example, your industry may have benchmarks for Web site traffic, social media engagement, or market share. Use your competitors' metrics as a starting point to identify gaps in your performance and improvement opportunities.

Choose a Meaningful Measurement Cadence

Additionally, the frequency and timeframes you measure matter and should be picked strategically. There are a few ways to look at this, including comparing the current period to the previous one, such as comparing this month's metrics to last month's. This is generally referred to as Month over Month (MoM), and the same can be done quarterly (Quarter over Quarter—QoQ) or annually (Year over Year—YoY).

Pay attention to seasonality as well, which means that there may be patterns throughout the year that make a comparison of one month or quarter to the previous one a less-than-equal comparison. For instance, if PB Shoes sells more pickleball shoes at the beginning of the summer than any other time of the year, they should compare May of this year to May of last year, not the month of May to April.

Keep It Straightforward

Finally, while tracking as many KPIs as possible is tempting to avoid missing an important component, too much data can be overwhelming and counterproductive. Choose a manageable set of metrics that provide a holistic view of your marketing performance and can be easily tracked and reported. Consider creating a dashboard that consolidates your key metrics and provides real-time visibility into your performance.

CONCLUSION

Aligning marketing KPIs with business KPIs brings many benefits to marketing leaders. By doing so, you can track the impact of marketing initiatives on overall business success, optimize marketing efforts to support business objectives, enhance the credibility of marketing as a strategic function, make data-driven decisions, and build a culture of accountability.

By aligning your marketing KPIs with business KPIs, you can ensure that marketing is contributing to the business's overall success and that marketing is viewed as a critical and valued function within the organization.

You should now have a good understanding of KPIs and how to use them. In the next chapter, we are going to explore the criteria of how to choose the right marketing metrics

CHAPTER 4

CHOOSING THE RIGHT MARKETING METRICS

Having explored why alignment between marketing and business KPIs is so important, let's discuss how to determine which marketing metrics we should focus on to evaluate the success of marketing and strategic business goals.

How do you know if your marketing efforts truly align with your business KPIs and marketing KPIs? The answer lies in selecting the right marketing metrics to evaluate success. With so many metrics to choose from, however, it can be overwhelming to pick which ones to prioritize.

CHECKLIST BEFORE STARTING

Let's explore how to determine which marketing metrics to use when evaluating success and aligning with the business strategy.

Understand Your Business and Marketing Goals and KPIs

The first step in selecting the right marketing metrics is to understand your business goals, which translate into business KPIs and marketing KPIs, as we've previously discussed. If you have inherited a set of business or marketing KPIs that were not created using best practices, strongly consider making Specific, Measurable, Achievable, Relevant, and Time-bound (SMART) goals that can help you and your team think more strategically about the goals and metrics you set.

For example, the following questions should be answerable before you begin choosing marketing metrics:

- What are you trying to achieve for the business with your marketing efforts? (For example, are you looking to increase brand awareness, drive Web site traffic, or boost sales?)
- What timeframe do these results need to be achieved within?
- Are there benchmarks that you need to reach and/or exceed?

Of course, specifics will vary greatly from company to company and marketing team to marketing team. Once you clearly understand your goals, you can select the metrics that will demonstrate progress toward achieving them.

Consider Your Audience(s)

Another factor to consider when selecting marketing metrics is your target audience. Who are you trying to reach with your marketing efforts, and what types of marketing are most relevant to each type of audience? For instance, do you segment by:

- Age or other demographics: by generation (Gen Z, Millennial, Gen X, or Boomer), household income, or geographic location
- Stage in the customer journey: prospective, current, or lapsed
- Interest (outdoor activities, foodies, etc.)
- Preferred platform (email, SMS, etc.)

Understanding your audience will help you select the most relevant metrics. For example, if you're targeting a younger demographic, social media engagement metrics on a popular platform such as TikTok or SMS engagement could be more useful in evaluating success than evaluating email opens, which are not as widely used with those age groups.

Alternatively, if you are targeting only lapsed customers, you can likely rely on your CRM data since you already have information about them (versus prospective customers who may not have provided you with their information yet).

Additionally, you likely have multiple audiences, so what impact does that have on your measurements? Do you need to rely on different metrics for each audience, or is there a core set of measurements you can use across all of them?

Understand the Available Data

While your organization may have access to vast amounts of information, it should not be a foregone conclusion that any piece of data you desire is immediately available. Therefore, it is important to understand the data that is available to you, how easy it is to obtain on a regular basis, and more. Here are some examples of the questions you should ask:

Is this data…

- Readily available without making a request to an internal (or external) team?
- Presented in an existing dashboard, or only via an API?
- Refreshed at a regular frequency, or is a manual data request process required?
- Available for all customers or only a subset or audience segment?
- Compiled from multiple sources or coming from a single source?
- Available from x months or more, or only from the past few weeks at most?

Of course, there may be other considerations as well, depending on your exact needs.

Evaluate Your Marketing Activities

Look at the activities that you will be performing to achieve your marketing KPIs. You may be running multi-channel campaigns, posting content on social media, creating a Web site landing page, and more. Looking at these activities, consider the metrics that will show you and your team whether or not your efforts are successful. For instance, looking at the following table (Figure 4.1), you can see the variations of metrics that can be chosen, based on just a few of the potential marketing channels that can be used:

Channel	Potential Metrics
Website	Page views, returning visitors, form fills, referrals from source
Social media	Engagement, followers, clickthroughs
Email	Open rates, Clickthrough Rates (CTRs), sign-ups, unsubscribes
Digital advertising	Impressions, CTRs, Return on Ad Spend (ROAS)

FIGURE 4.1. Marketing metric examples by channel

CHOOSING YOUR METRICS

After reviewing the checklist, you are now ready to begin choosing the marketing metrics that will be the most useful. As with marketing KPIs, it is generally not a case of more being better, but of finding the right balance between having enough information to give marketing teams information that helps them perform better while not overwhelming anyone with information overload.

Let's look through the criteria for choosing the best marketing metrics now.

Map Marketing Metrics to Your Marketing KPIs

While it might seem like it goes without saying, you might be surprised at how often marketing metrics are chosen in a vacuum, only for teams to later find that they have a hard time justifying their marketing efforts when comparing to business KPIs, or sometimes even their own marketing KPIs!

Thus, before getting too far down the path of defining marketing metrics, it is important to make sure that the marketing metrics you have chosen can help you demonstrate your success toward business and marketing goals, as defined in those KPIs.

This also helps to reduce waste in the process. While it might seem great to report on everything that could be relevant, remember that there is some type of cost associated with any metric you create, whether it is the time to update reports, explaining results to stakeholders, and so on.

With your marketing KPIs in place and strategically aligned with the business goals and KPIs, as well as your marketing activities defined, you can now enumerate the marketing metrics for all of your activities that will indicate whether you are on track to achieve your marketing goals, which are defined by your marketing KPIs.

Choose Metrics That Tell a Story

Marketing metrics don't just need to be data points on a report. They need to paint a picture of your marketing performance that is easy to understand and compelling for your stakeholders. Choose metrics that tell a story and showcase the impact of marketing on your business goals.

For example, rather than simply presenting Web traffic numbers, you may showcase how your content marketing efforts increased Web site traffic by 20% month over month, leading to a 10% increase in lead generation.

This shows that rather than a series of disconnected charts on a dashboard, the marketing measurements you've chosen to track are all working together to tell the story of generating leads from Web site visitors, and the points in between—and, ideally, those points' contributions to the lead.

Identify Where AI Can Provide Value

There can sometimes be areas where marketing metrics are valuable but difficult to gather or analyze on a timely basis. In other cases, the sheer quantity of information can be difficult to parse, or understanding trends over time can be valuable but impossible for a human to do on their own.

In these cases, and more, Artificial Intelligence (AI) tools can be helpful in the process. In other words, you and your team should identify when data would be valuable, but solely relying on humans to do the work may not be feasible.

Several areas where AI tools can be utilized will be explored later in this book, but suffice to say that there are plenty of areas where AI can provide a boost to marketing measurement and analytics teams where the processing of large sets of data, understanding of patterns, and other issues are present.

Continuously Improve

Once you have selected your marketing metrics, it's important to analyze your data regularly to track progress and make data-driven decisions. Analytics tools such as Google Analytics, Hootsuite, and HubSpot can help you collect and analyze data. By analyzing your data, you can identify trends and patterns and optimize and adjust your marketing strategy accordingly.

Also, remember that marketing metrics are not set in stone. They can change over time, depending on your business and industry. As your business grows and evolves, it's important to continuously evaluate and adjust your marketing metrics to stay aligned with your business goals. Regularly revisit your KPIs and adjust them as necessary based on what you're learning from your data.

Selecting the right marketing metrics is crucial for evaluating success and aligning your marketing strategy with your business objectives. By understanding your business goals, identifying your KPIs, considering your audience, analyzing your data, and continuously improving, you'll be well on your way to measuring the success of your marketing efforts and driving business growth.

CASE STUDY: DETERMINING MARKETING METRICS FOR A NEW SHOE LINE

Let's return to PB Shoes, the growing athletic footwear brand. They recently launched a new line of women's pickleball shoes. With the new product line rollout, PB Shoes needed to identify the right marketing metrics to measure the performance and success of their campaigns. Let's look at how the company approached the process of determining the most effective marketing metrics to evaluate their launch.

Defining the Business and Marketing Objectives

PB Shoes began the process by aligning their marketing activities with broader business goals. Their primary business objective for the new women's pickleball shoes was to increase market share in the women's athletic footwear sector while generating a 15% growth in revenue within the next 12 months. From a marketing perspective, the company aimed to enhance brand awareness, drive Web site traffic, and increase conversions through direct sales of the new shoe line.

Given the strategic importance of the launch, PB Shoes set specific marketing KPIs to track progress:

- Increase brand awareness in the women's pickleball community by 25%.
- Drive a 20% increase in Web site traffic specifically to the pickleball shoe pages.
- Achieve a 10% conversion rate from targeted digital advertising campaigns.

Understanding the Target Audience

PB Shoes segmented their audience carefully, focusing on women in the 35–55 age range who are active in recreational sports, particularly pickleball. This target audience was further divided into two sub-groups: avid pickleball players and those who are new to the sport but are looking for comfortable, performance-oriented footwear.

For each segment, different marketing tactics were employed. PB Shoes used social media campaigns to target the younger end of the spectrum, leveraging platforms such as Instagram and Facebook to engage their audience. For more seasoned players, they focused on email marketing campaigns and influencer partnerships within the pickleball community.

Choosing the Right Marketing Metrics

With their objectives and audience in mind, PB Shoes followed a strategic approach to selecting the most relevant marketing metrics. Drawing insights from the process outlined in Chapter 4 of the guide (202), PB Shoes ensured that each chosen metric was specific, measurable, attainable, relevant, and time-bound (that is, it followed the SMART principles).

The company selected the following key marketing metrics to track:

- *Brand awareness*: Social media impressions and reach on Instagram and Facebook, measuring the number of unique users exposed to the marketing campaigns
- *Engagement*: The number of comments, likes, and shares on social media content, particularly focused on pickleball-specific posts
- *Website traffic*: Tracking total page views, bounce rates, and the time spent on the product pages for the new shoe line using Google Analytics
- *CTRs*: Monitoring the CTR from email campaigns sent to existing customers, as well as display and search ads targeting pickleball players
- *Conversion rates*: Measuring how many users who visit the Web site complete a purchase, specifically for the women's pickleball shoes
- *ROAS*: Assessing the effectiveness of paid digital advertising campaigns by comparing revenue generated from these ads against the total ad spend
- *Customer Acquisition Cost (CAC)*: Calculating the cost of acquiring each new customer through paid campaigns, ensuring profitability.

Leveraging Available Data and Tools

PB Shoes utilized a combination of analytics tools to collect and analyze the data necessary to track these metrics. Google Analytics provided detailed insights into Web site traffic and conversions, while social media platforms, such as Instagram and Facebook, offered in-platform analytics to measure engagement and brand awareness. Additionally, email marketing platforms provided data on open rates, CTR, and conversion rates from email-driven traffic.

To monitor ROAS and CAC, PB Shoes integrated their digital ad platforms (such as Google Ads and Facebook Ads Manager) with their e-commerce analytics to directly link advertising efforts to product sales.

Results and Insights

Through regular data analysis and reporting, PB Shoes was able to track the performance of their women's pickleball shoe marketing campaign. They achieved a 30% increase in brand awareness, exceeding their original goal, largely driven by the success of influencer collaborations and targeted social media content. Their Web site traffic increased by 22%, slightly above their target, with high engagement on the product pages for the pickleball shoes.

In terms of conversions, PB Shoes achieved a 12% conversion rate from their digital advertising campaigns, surpassing their 10% goal. The company's ROAS remained strong, with a return of $4 for every $1 spent on digital advertising. PB Shoes, however, recognized that their CAC for new customers was higher than anticipated, prompting the team to refine their targeting and optimize the cost-efficiency of their ad campaigns.

Continuous Improvement

PB Shoes continues to analyze their marketing metrics regularly to refine their strategy. They've already begun implementing changes to reduce CAC by optimizing ad targeting and testing new creative content. Additionally, the company is exploring the use of AI-driven analytics to predict trends and improve personalization in their marketing efforts, ensuring that they remain competitive in the growing pickleball market.

Final Assessment

By clearly defining their business objectives and aligning them with relevant, well-defined marketing metrics, PB Shoes successfully measured the performance of their new women's pickleball shoe line. The company's data-driven approach allowed them to track their progress, optimize their campaigns, and exceed many of their initial goals. This case study highlights the importance of selecting SMART marketing metrics that are aligned with both strategic goals and the available data, providing actionable insights to improve future marketing performance.

CONCLUSION

Selecting the right marketing metrics is not a one-size-fits-all approach. It requires a deep understanding of your business goals, stakeholder priorities, competitive landscape, and storytelling abilities. As a marketer, your role is to filter through the noise, choose the metrics that matter most to your stakeholders, and showcase the value marketing brings to the business.

Use these tips to select the right metrics and gain stakeholder support across the organization. Remember, the right metrics can lead to better decision-making, increased credibility, and, ultimately, better business outcomes.

The next chapter will explore how to use these metrics effectively in both single-channel and multi-channel marketing measurement scenarios.

CHAPTER 5

SINGLE-CHANNEL VS MULTI-CHANNEL MEASUREMENT

N ow that we've explored KPIs and aligned them with marketing and business goals, let's look at measurement approaches. We're going to start by talking about single-channel versus multi-channel measurement approaches. While it might seem straightforward, understanding the difference between them is essential to improving your marketing strategies.

So, let's delve into the primary differences between single-channel and multi-channel marketing measurement. First, however, remember that it's not an either/or situation: both are important and necessary to doing marketing well. After all, it would be impossible to market on only a single channel and be effective, yet you need to understand how your marketing is performing in both dimensions: single-channel and multi-channel.

SINGLE-CHANNEL MARKETING MEASUREMENT

Single-channel marketing measurement is a method used to assess the effectiveness of marketing efforts by focusing on a single marketing channel. This approach measures conversions and tracks performance metrics generated by a particular strategy, such as email marketing, SEO, Pay-per-Click (PPC) advertising, or social media campaigns. By isolating one channel for analysis, marketers can gain specific insights into how well that particular channel is performing. While this method is straightforward, it may lack the depth and context necessary to fully understand the broader impact of a marketing campaign, especially if other channels are also in play. After all, most consumers do not relegate their activities to a single channel but rather engage in "channel-switching," or moving between devices (such as mobile to desktop) or channels (email to Web site) on a regular basis.

A major advantage of single-channel marketing measurement is its simplicity and focus. It allows marketers to drill down into one area, making it easier to attribute conversions and other metrics directly to a specific marketing effort. For example, if a company is running a social media ad campaign, using single-channel measurement helps identify the number of conversions or Web site visits directly stemming from that channel. This method provides a clear-cut view of the campaign's success without the noise and complexity of multi-channel data.

Single-channel marketing measurement is particularly useful in several situations. One of the main use cases is when a business is running a campaign focused solely on one channel with little overlap from others. For example, an email marketing campaign designed to increase conversions through targeted messaging would benefit from single-channel measurement. Another scenario would be when a company lacks the budget for a broader multi-channel campaign and needs to maximize effectiveness within one specific platform.

Another common use of single-channel measurement is when marketers are exploring a new channel. When venturing into untested waters—whether experimenting with a new PPC strategy or testing the potential of a social media platform—it's essential to measure the effectiveness of that channel on its own. By isolating the metrics, companies can gather important insights about whether the channel is worth incorporating into their broader marketing mix. In this context, single-channel measurement serves as a useful exploratory tool.

Additionally, single-channel measurement is valuable for validating new marketing strategies. When a marketing team launches a new initiative, they need to determine whether that strategy can generate meaningful results. By focusing exclusively on one channel, they can validate the success (or lack thereof) of the strategy and determine whether to scale it further or adjust their approach.

Single-channel marketing measurement has its limitations, however. While useful for channel-specific teams, it does not provide a holistic view of customer behavior across multiple touchpoints. In reality, customers often engage with a brand across different channels, moving from social media to search engines, emails, and direct Web site visits before converting. Single-channel measurement does not capture these interactions or reveal how different channels interact to influence a customer's journey.

Thus, single-channel marketing measurement can be a valuable tool in specific situations where marketers need to evaluate the effectiveness of individual marketing efforts. It is, however, limited in scope when it comes to understanding the broader customer journey, making it insufficient for teams that require a multi-channel perspective. For businesses looking to optimize their entire marketing ecosystem, combining single-channel insights with multi-channel data will offer a more comprehensive view of marketing performance.

When to Use Single-Channel Measurement

- *When focusing on a campaign specific to one channel*: If your marketing effort is dedicated to a single channel with minimal crossover from other channels, single-channel measurement provides targeted insights.
- *When budget constraints limit multi-channel campaigns*: If you're working with a limited budget and need to ensure the effectiveness of one channel, measuring performance at the single-channel level is essential.
- *When testing a new marketing channel*: If you're exploring a new platform or strategy for potential future use, single-channel measurement helps assess its effectiveness in isolation.
- *When validating a new marketing strategy on a single channel*: If you're launching a new approach within a specific channel, using single-channel measurement allows you to evaluate its success before scaling or expanding.

When Not to Use Single-Channel Measurement

- *When running a multi-channel campaign*: If your marketing efforts span multiple platforms and channels, single-channel measurement won't provide the necessary insights to understand how different channels interact and contribute to conversions.

- *When focusing on customer journey analysis*: Single-channel measurement fails to capture the full customer journey, especially when customers engage with multiple touchpoints across various channels before making a purchase.
- *When optimizing for long-term marketing strategies*: If your goal is to assess and optimize the overall performance of your marketing strategy, relying on one channel's metrics alone may lead to skewed results and an incomplete understanding of your marketing's effectiveness.
- *When marketing channels are heavily integrated*: In campaigns where marketing channels are closely interconnected (e.g., social media driving traffic to a PPC landing page), single-channel measurement won't capture the cross-channel influence and attribution that are crucial for accurate analysis.

While single-channel marketing measurement is useful in analyzing performance for teams responsible for those individual channels, it is not ideal for understanding your customers' behavior across multiple marketing channels.

MULTI-CHANNEL MARKETING MEASUREMENT

Multi-channel marketing measurement involves evaluating the performance and effectiveness of multiple marketing channels simultaneously. Unlike single-channel measurement, this approach provides a comprehensive view of how different channels contribute to a marketing campaign's success, and by analyzing all the touchpoints that customers interact with, marketers can gain insights into the connections between channels and understand how each one plays a role in driving conversions, engagement, and overall sales. This method is particularly useful for businesses running integrated marketing campaigns that span various platforms, such as social media, email, SEO, and PPC.

One of the biggest advantages of multi-channel marketing measurement is that it provides a more holistic view of the customer journey. In today's digital landscape, customers typically interact with a brand multiple times before making a purchase decision. They may encounter a product through a social media ad, then research it via search engines, and finally convert through an email offer. By measuring performance across these various channels, marketers can map out the path customers take, revealing the sequence and influence of different touchpoints along the way.

Furthermore, multi-channel measurement enables marketers to see how channels work together rather than in isolation. For instance, a business may find that while social media ads drive awareness and traffic, it's email marketing that eventually converts visitors into customers. With this understanding, marketers can allocate resources more effectively, ensuring that high-performing channels receive the necessary investment while optimizing channels that play a supportive or complementary role in the customer journey.

Another significant benefit of multi-channel marketing measurement is the ability to optimize budget allocation. Since marketers can see how different channels contribute to overall conversions and sales, they can make data-driven decisions about where to allocate their budgets. Channels that deliver a strong Return on Investment (ROI) may receive more funding, while underperforming channels can be re-evaluated or adjusted to better meet campaign goals. This strategic budget allocation allows businesses to maximize the impact of their marketing dollars.

Measuring across multiple channels, however, also comes with challenges. One of the most notable difficulties is attribution—understanding which channel or touchpoint deserves credit for the conversion. Multi-channel attribution models, such as first-click, last-click, or multi-touch attribution, help marketers navigate this complexity by assigning value to the different touchpoints in a customer's journey. Implementing the right attribution model is crucial to obtaining accurate insights and optimizing marketing strategies.

Additionally, multi-channel measurement requires robust tools and technology to capture and analyze data across platforms. Marketers often rely on advanced analytics platforms that integrate data from multiple sources, such as Google Analytics, CRM systems, and social media platforms, to gain a comprehensive view. These tools help in consolidating data and providing actionable insights that drive better decision-making. Without the proper tools, it can be challenging to track and measure performance effectively.

Therefore, multi-channel marketing measurement is an essential method for businesses that engage customers across various platforms and want to optimize their overall marketing performance. By providing insights into how different channels interact and contribute to the customer journey, this approach enables marketers to make informed decisions about their campaigns, budget allocation, and channel optimization. While it requires more sophisticated tools and methodologies compared to single-channel measurement, the benefits of gaining a holistic view of the marketing ecosystem far outweigh the challenges.

When to Use Multi-Channel Measurement

- *When tracking multiple channels in a single campaign or overall marketing strategy*: Use multi-channel measurement when your campaign spans several platforms, as it provides a comprehensive view of how each channel contributes to your goals.
- *When comparing performance across different channels*: If you need to evaluate and compare the effectiveness of each marketing channel, multi-channel measurement allows for direct comparisons and performance analysis.
- *When analyzing the customer journey across various touchpoints*: Multi-channel measurement is essential when you want to understand how customers interact with your brand across different channels before converting.
- *When optimizing performance across all channels*: To ensure your entire marketing ecosystem is working efficiently, use multi-channel measurement to identify opportunities for optimization across platforms.

That said, focusing on the big picture doesn't allow meaningful improvements on single channels that can make big contributions to the whole, which is why single-channel marketing measurement is still a critical function.

When Not to Use Multi-Channel Measurement

- *When running a campaign focused solely on one channel*: If your campaign is limited to a single marketing channel, multi-channel measurement may add unnecessary complexity without providing valuable insights.
- *When budget or resources are limited for advanced analytics*: Multi-channel measurement often requires more sophisticated tools and data collection methods, so if resources are limited, it may be more practical to focus on single-channel measurement.

- *When you're testing the effectiveness of a new channel in isolation*: If the goal is to evaluate a new channel's performance on its own, multi-channel measurement could dilute the results, making it harder to assess the new channel's impact.
- *When the campaign or strategy has no overlap between channels*: If different channels are used independently without influencing one another, multi-channel measurement might not provide additional benefits, as each channel can be assessed separately.

More often than not, however, this is not an either/or choice, but rather marketers will utilize single- or multi-channel measurement at different points in their work.

DIFFERENCES BETWEEN SINGLE-CHANNEL AND MULTI-CHANNEL MEASUREMENT

While both single-channel and multi-channel marketing measurement tools focus on measuring metrics, they have several significant differences.

Firstly, single-channel measurement tools only allow marketers to analyze a single channel's performance. In comparison, multi-channel measurement tools help businesses understand the impact of all their marketing channels on their overall performance. Secondly, single-channel measurement tools are relatively easy to implement, while multi-channel measurement tools require more in-depth knowledge and a more complex setup process. Finally, multi-channel measurement provides a more comprehensive picture of customers' interactions across various marketing channels, while single-channel measurement may result in an incomplete or inaccurate view of consumers' behaviors.

CONSIDERATIONS FOR ONLINE VERSUS OFFLINE MEASUREMENT

Some considerations should be taken into account when your organization has both digital and offline channels. One of the biggest implications for marketers trying to measure online versus offline marketing channels is the need to use different metrics and methods to evaluate their effectiveness.

Online marketing channels, such as social media and search engines, can be measured using metrics such as Web site traffic, engagement, and conversion rates. Offline marketing channels, such as print ads and billboards, are more difficult to measure and may require the use of surveys, focus groups, or other research methods to gather data. Additionally, online marketing channels often have more detailed and real-time data available, which can be used to optimize campaigns and make data-driven decisions. On the other hand, offline marketing channels may have less data available and may require more creative and intuitive approaches to measurement. Overall, marketers need to be aware of these differences and use appropriate methods to measure the effectiveness of their online and offline marketing efforts.

CONCLUSION

Measuring the performance of your marketing channels is an essential aspect of evaluating the effectiveness of your campaigns. Whether to use a single-channel or multi-channel measurement approach depends on your team's goals and objectives and the story you need to tell.

Understanding which approach to employ gives you a clear blueprint for making intelligent decisions to optimize your ROI.

Ultimately, however, your marketing measurement needs to account for consumers' cross-channel behaviors. This means that single-channel measurement can play a key role, but you need a way to tie multiple channels together.

While many marketers are able to rely on reporting that exists within platforms and applications they frequently use, a basic knowledge of statistics can often help uncover deeper insights. The next chapter will provide a brief overview of how marketers can utilize statistics in their measurement work.

CHAPTER 6

A BRIEF OVERVIEW OF STATISTICS FOR MARKETERS

As data now plays a stronger role in all types of marketing, an understanding of statistics can serve as the basis for better data-driven decision-making. By applying statistical analysis, marketers go beyond guesswork and intuition, basing their strategies on empirical evidence and measurable outcomes.

This chapter is designed to introduce you to the increasingly important role statistics plays in deciphering market trends, understanding consumer behavior, and optimizing marketing campaigns. While this is far from an exhaustive guide to statistics and statistical modeling, we will cover some of the fundamental approaches and principles that marketers can rely on to ground their strategies and tactics in a solid understanding of data. Thus, we'll focus on commonly used concepts and ideas that empower marketers to craft compelling narratives grounded in data, predict future market movements with greater confidence, and make informed decisions that align closely with customer needs and business goals.

CHOOSING THE RIGHT TYPES OF DATA TO ANALYZE

Using your understanding of the types of data outlined in Chapter 1, the first step in using statistics is understanding the type of information you have (e.g., qualitative or quantitative), as well as how it relates to what you are trying to statistically evaluate, which might include categorical or continuous data. It is also important to understand what type of evaluation you would like to perform. To do this, let's look at two approaches: measures of central tendency and measures of variability.

Measures of Central Tendency

Measures of central tendency are tools in statistics used to summarize and describe a set of data by identifying the "center" or most typical value. They provide a single value that represents the entire dataset, making it easier for marketers to understand and interpret their data.

Using these measures helps you to establish a baseline for marketing performance, compares your efforts to industry benchmarks, and proves useful in other types of comparisons.

Mean

The mean, often referred to as the average, is one of the most commonly used measures of central tendency. It is calculated by adding all the values in a dataset and dividing the result by the number of data points. The result represents the average value of the dataset. You have likely used this many times in your marketing measurement, as well as in other areas of life, to get a general idea of some quantity that occurs on a recurring basis.

For instance, understanding the average number of page views that the home page of your Web site gets on a monthly basis can help you to understand when there is a sharp increase or steep decline, and do further exploration to determine the causes.

Thus, if the last 5 months of home page traffic looked like this:

- Month 1: 100,000
- Month 2: 100,000
- Month 3: 100,000
- Month 4: 100,000
- Month 5: 5,000,000

The mean would be 1,040,000, as that is the sum of all the traffic from months 1 through 5 (5,500,000) divided by the number of months (5). You can easily see which month the company decided to run a Super Bowl ad that drove an inordinate amount of traffic to the home page using these numbers. Thus, using the mean has benefits when working with sets of data that are largely similar, but can have some challenges when working with data that is irregular.

When to Use

For example, if PB Shoes wants to calculate the average amount spent by customers during a promotional period, the mean would provide a straightforward insight into customer spending behavior. This average could be used to benchmark against other promotional periods or forecast revenues for similar future initiatives.

Median

The median is another measure of central tendency that represents the middle value in a dataset when the data points are arranged in increasing or decreasing order. If there is an even number of data points, the median is calculated by taking the average of the two middle values.

While on the surface, this sounds similar to the mean, or average, there are some key differences, and the median is particularly useful when you have outlier data that might skew an average. For instance, as we saw in the previous section, if you ran a Super Bowl ad that drove a disproportionate amount of traffic to your home page one month, it might distort your monthly average traffic.

Thus, if the last 5 months of home page traffic looked like this:

- Month 1: 100,000
- Month 2: 100,000
- Month 3: 100,000
- Month 4: 100,000
- Month 5: 5,000,000

The median would be 100,000, as that is the value that falls in the *middle* of the set of data when the numbers are ordered in terms of value from lowest to highest.

A median, then, would not skew based on a single month of a high amount of traffic and could potentially account for seasonality or other one-time factors that might create sharp increases or steep declines.

When to Use

For instance, if PB Shoes has a wide range of shoe prices and a few high-end products are significantly more expensive than the rest, the median would give a better understanding of the central price point at which most sales occur, guiding pricing strategies more reliably than the mean.

Mode

The mode is the value that occurs most frequently in a dataset. It can be used for both numerical and categorical data and is useful for identifying the most common response or category in a given dataset.

Thus, if the last 5 months of home page traffic looked like this:

- Month 1: 100,000
- Month 2: 100,000
- Month 3: 100,000
- Month 4: 100,000
- Month 5: 5,000,000

The mode would be 100,000, as that is the value that occurs most often in the dataset—four times, to be specific.

When to Use

For example, PB Shoes might analyze customer shoe size selections and find that size 8 is the mode. This information could inform inventory decisions, ensuring the company stocks more of this size to meet the highest demand and avoid potential stockouts.

Summary

Each of these measures of central tendency—mean, median, and mode—serves a distinct purpose in marketing measurement. Selecting the right one depends on the data distribution and the specific insights a marketer is looking to glean from the analysis. Together, they offer a comprehensive view of customer behaviors and preferences, which is crucial for informed decision-making in marketing strategies.

Measures of Variability

While marketers often focus on central tendency measures such as the mean, median, and mode to summarize data, understanding variability, or how much data points differ from each other, is equally important. Measures of variability that we will take a look at here are range, variance, and standard deviation. These measures offer deeper insights into the spread of your data, helping you grasp the full story behind your marketing metrics.

Range

The range is the simplest measure of variability, calculated by subtracting the lowest value in your dataset from the highest value. In marketing data analysis, the range can quickly give you a sense of how wide the spread of your data is—from the least to the most engaged Web site visitors, the lowest to the highest campaign conversions, or the smallest to the largest transaction amounts. Though simplistic, the range provides an initial overview of the variability within your data, indicating the potential opportunities and risks in your marketing strategies.

The range is the simplest measure of variability, calculated as the difference between the maximum and minimum values in a dataset. It provides a quick sense of the spread of data points, which can be particularly useful in marketing when assessing the diversity or dispersion in consumer behaviors or sales performance across different regions or products.

For example, if PB Shoes wants to analyze the spread in daily sales figures during a promotional week across various store locations, the range will show the gap between the highest and lowest sales days, giving a sense of potential volatility or stability in sales performance. This can help in identifying outliers and understanding the overall consistency of sales across different stores.

Variance

Variance goes a step further by quantifying the average of the squared differences from the mean. In practical terms, it tells you how much your data points, such as individual sales figures or clickthrough rates, deviate from the average performance. For marketers, analyzing variance is crucial for understanding the consistency of campaign results across different channels or periods. A high variance might indicate fluctuating performance, signaling the need for strategy adjustments, while a low variance suggests stability.

Visualizing Variance

Let's say we have data from a marketing campaign that indicates the number of sales of pickleball shoes over the last 10 months. The data looks like this:

- Month 1: 5
- Month 2: 15
- Month 3: 25
- Month 4: 35
- Month 5: 45
- Month 6: 55
- Month 7: 65
- Month 8: 75
- Month 9: 85
- Month 10: 95

We can see a few things with this data. First, by adding all the monthly sales numbers together and dividing by the total number (10), we can calculate the mean. All the numbers added together equal 500, thus 500 divided by 10 equals 50. This means that our mean, or average, is 50.

Calculating Variance

In Figure 6.1, we can see a visualization of variance in our 10 months of data using bar charts.

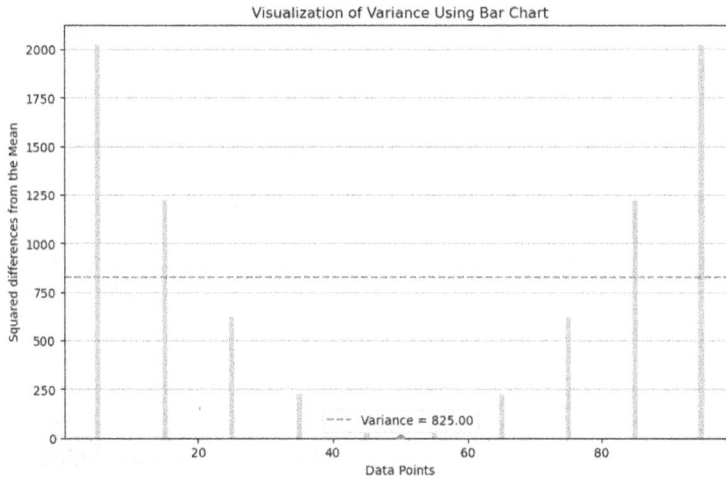

FIGURE 6.1. Visualizing variance.

You can see how our mean, 50, is in the center of the chart, with the numbers both lower and higher and their differences from the mean squared on either side. The variance is calculated as 825. To calculate variance, do the following:

1. Find the mean (or average) of your dataset. In the example in Figure 6.1, it is 50.
2. Subtract the mean from each data point and square the result. For instance, in month 10, according to our dataset, we had 95 pickleball shoe sales. 95 minus our mean of 50 equals 45. Then, we square 45 (multiply 45 by itself) and get 2,025.
3. Then, we do the same for each of the other months' data, and calculate the mean, or average, of these squared differences.

Variance measures the average degree to which each point differs from the mean. In marketing, variance is useful for quantifying the spread of data around the mean, which can indicate the consistency of customer behavior or campaign results.

For instance, if PB Shoes launches a new advertising campaign and measures the variance in Web site traffic or purchase frequency before and after the campaign, a lower variance in the post-campaign period could indicate that the campaign has led to more consistent customer engagement. Variance provides deeper insight into the distribution patterns of data, helping marketers understand not only the average effect of their strategies but also the reliability and predictability of those effects.

Standard Deviation

While variance provides valuable insights, its squared units can be hard to interpret in a practical context. This is where standard deviation comes in, offering a more digestible measure of variability. Standard deviation, the square root of variance, measures the average distance between each data point and the mean in their original units, making it easier to understand and communicate.

In the marketing domain, standard deviation helps assess the reliability and risk of different campaigns or strategies. For example, a small standard deviation in weekly sales figures suggests consistent performance, while a large one might warn of unpredictable outcomes, guiding budget allocation and strategic planning decisions.

Why Standard Deviation Matters

Understanding standard deviation is vital for:

- Segmenting your market effectively, identifying stable versus volatile segments.
- Evaluating the risk of new campaigns by comparing their expected outcomes' variability.
- Benchmarking and improving the consistency of customer experiences across touchpoints.

Standard deviation is the square root of the variance, providing a measure of variability that is in the same unit as the data. This measure is critical in marketing when comparing the dispersion of data across different datasets with potentially different means.

For example, if PB Shoes is comparing the spending habits of two different customer segments, the standard deviation allows them to assess which segment shows more variability in spending. This can be crucial for tailoring marketing strategies either to target the more predictable segment or to address the variability in the less predictable one. Standard deviation helps marketers gauge the risk and potential reward in targeting specific segments based on the consistency of their behaviors.

Applying Measures of Variability in Marketing

Incorporating these measures of variability into your data analysis can transform how you view and manage your marketing efforts. By going beyond averages and looking at the spread and consistency of your data, you gain a more nuanced understanding of your marketing activities' effectiveness and efficiency.

Whether assessing campaign performance, customer engagement levels, or sales trends, measures of variability equip you with the insights to make data-driven decisions that enhance the impact of your marketing strategies, mitigate risks, and capitalize on opportunities for growth and optimization.

Together, these measures of variability offer valuable insights that help marketers make informed decisions. The range provides a quick snapshot of data spread, variance shows the consistency around the mean, and standard deviation brings the variability measurement back to the original units of data for easier interpretation. By using these statistics, marketers can better understand their data's behavior, leading to more effective and targeted marketing strategies.

Remember, the goal of utilizing statistics in marketing isn't just about collecting data; it's about extracting meaningful insights that drive actionable strategies. By mastering measures of variability, marketers can ensure that they're not just seeing the average picture but understanding the full landscape of their data's story.

INFERENTIAL STATISTICS

When you have a complete set of information about an audience, you don't need to *infer* anything, because you can simply pull the data fields you need and get an exact view of the group in question. Often, however, marketers need to draw conclusions about a population based on a sample of data from a larger group that they don't have full access to information about.

In marketing, populations might refer to the total number of potential customers for a product in a given market, while a sample might represent a survey response from a subset of that market. Inferential statistics bridges the gap between these groups, providing insights and supporting decision-making without the need for feedback from every potential customer.

The real power of inferential statistics lies in its ability to predict and infer trends from sample data. For instance, after analyzing the purchasing behavior of a sample of 1,000 customers, marketers can use inferential statistics to predict the purchasing behavior of all potential customers in the market.

Populations vs Samples

It is important to understand the distinction between a population and a sample, so let's explore:

- *Population*: This is the total group of individuals relevant to a particular marketing research question. It could represent all potential consumers of a product within a geographic area.
- *Sample*: A sample is a subset of the population, selected for the actual study. It should be representative of the population to ensure the results are applicable to the broader group.

By focusing on samples, marketers can conduct research more feasibly and cost-effectively, as studying an entire population is often impractical.

Hypothesis Testing

Hypothesis testing is a statistical method used to decide between two competing hypotheses about a population, based on sample data. In marketing, this can be employed to test ideas and predict outcomes:

- *Formulate hypotheses*: Typically, this involves stating a null hypothesis (H0), which represents no effect or no difference, and an alternative hypothesis (H1), which suggests a potential effect or difference.
- *Choose the right test*: Depending on the data type and distribution, marketers must select an appropriate statistical test.
- *Decision-making*: Based on the p-value obtained from the statistical test, marketers can reject the null hypothesis in favor of the alternative if the evidence is strong enough.

For example, a marketer might test whether a new ad campaign leads to a statistically significant increase in product sales compared to sales before the campaign.

We will explore this concept in more detail in Chapter 18, including how to construct a good hypothesis as well as some things to avoid. So don't worry if you still have some questions about best practices in hypothesis testing.

Confidence Intervals

Of course, regardless of how much rigor a marketer uses in their methods, there is always some degree of uncertainty that inferring outcomes from a sample of a larger population will yield 100% accuracy. Therefore, marketers need a way to express their certainty that the outcomes of a statistical analysis are accurate, which introduces the need for confidence intervals.

Confidence intervals provide a range of values within which the true population parameter is expected to fall, expressed at a certain confidence level. While degrees of certainty can vary, a 95% confidence level is regarded as trustworthy. This statistical measure helps marketers assess the certainty of their sample estimates.

For instance, if a survey of 200 customers shows that 60% are satisfied with a product, with a confidence interval of ±4%, the marketer can be 95% confident that between 56% (60% minus 4%) and 64% (60% plus 4%) of the total population is satisfied with the product.

CORRELATION AND CAUSATION

While some marketers simply enjoy analyzing data for its own sake, the reason that measurement, analysis, and the statistics that support them are necessary is so that marketers can make better decisions about what to do next. To do that, marketers need to be able to draw conclusions from their analysis, which often includes establishing that factor a causes factor b.

For instance, if factor a is an advertisement placed on a social network and factor b is an increase in sales referred by that same social network from people who saw that same advertisement, a relationship has been established between the two.

At its core, correlation indicates a relationship or association between two variables wherein changes in one variable are mirrored by changes in another. For instance, as in the example earlier, there may be a positive correlation between social media advertising spend and increased sales. Correlation, however, does not imply that one variable causes the other to change.

Causation, on the other hand, denotes a cause-and-effect relationship, suggesting that changes in one variable directly result in changes in another. Establishing causation implies that any variation in the outcome variable is directly due to the manipulation of the predictor variable.

The Importance of Understanding the Difference

The distinction between correlation and causation is critical for marketers as misinterpreting the relationship between variables can lead to faulty conclusions and ineffective strategies. For instance, a marketer might observe a correlation between the number of blog posts published and an increase in Web site traffic. Without further investigation, one might hastily conclude that publishing more blog posts will always increase traffic, overlooking other factors such as content quality, relevance, and distribution channels that could affect outcomes.

Establishing Causality

To determine causality, marketers must rely on well-structured experimental designs. Experiments typically involve the manipulation of one variable (independent variable) to observe the effect on another variable (dependent variable), while controlling for external factors that might influence the outcome. Randomized Controlled Trials (RCTs) are considered the gold standard in experimental design as they randomly assign subjects to treatment or control groups, mitigating the risk of bias and confounding variables.

A/B Testing as a Marketing Tool

A practical example of experimental design in marketing is A/B testing, where two versions of a Web page, advertisement, or email campaign (A and B) are tested against each other to determine which one performs better on a specified metric. A/B testing allows marketers to make data-driven decisions about changes to their marketing strategies with a higher degree of confidence in causality.

We will talk about creating tests in more depth in Chapter 15, so don't worry if you would like more details about this.

Common Mistakes in Proving Correlation and Causation

One of the most common mistakes in marketing research is assuming causation based on correlation. This fallacy can lead to misguided strategies that may not yield the desired results. Additionally, overlooking lurking variables—factors that affect both variables of interest—can also skew interpretation of the data. For example, a marketer might conclude that higher email open rates lead to increased sales without considering the impact of holiday seasons, during which both open rates and purchase intent might naturally increase.

Another frequent oversight is neglecting to consider reverse causation, where it is assumed that variable A affects variable B, whereas in reality, B could be influencing A. Establishing a temporal relationship, where the cause precedes the effect, is crucial in determining the correct direction of causality.

Understanding the nuances between correlation and causation and the importance of experimental design is foundational to making informed marketing decisions. By testing hypotheses and acknowledging the limitations of their data, marketers can avoid common pitfalls and contribute to the development of effective, evidence-based marketing strategies.

This can be where critical thinking with marketing measurement can be as important as capturing the right data in the first place.

PROBABILITY

Another common question that marketers need to answer is how likely an event is to occur. This is where probability factors into the discussion of statistics in marketing. Probability is a fundamental concept in statistics that allows marketers to assess and quantify uncertainty in relation to an event.

Imagine that a marketing manager at PB Shoes wants to evaluate the likelihood of customers purchasing a new line of pickleball shoes after receiving a promotional email. In this context, probability is the measure of the likelihood that a customer who received the email will make a purchase. Based on historical data, if 100 customers received similar emails in the past and 20 of them made a purchase, the probability of any given customer making a purchase after receiving the email is 20%. This can be expressed as 0.20 or 20%, where the probability is calculated by dividing the number of favorable outcomes (customers making a purchase) by the total number of events (total emails sent).

Probability Distributions

Many times, marketers need to predict the likelihood of several possible outcomes, which is referred to as a *probability distribution*. This is a mathematical function that provides the probabilities of occurrence of different possible outcomes for an experiment.

Continuing from the preceding example, let's assume the marketing manager at PB Shoes decides to analyze the responses to the promotional emails over several months to predict future responses. They track the number of purchases made each month after sending out 1,000 emails. Over 9 months, the number of purchases might be:

- Month 1: 180
- Month 2: 200
- Month 3: 230
- Month 4: 220
- Month 5: 230
- Month 6: 180
- Month 7: 210
- Month 8: 230
- Month 9: 190

A probability distribution, such as the one shown in Figure 6.2, would map each of these outcomes to its relative probability, showing how likely each possible number of purchases is.

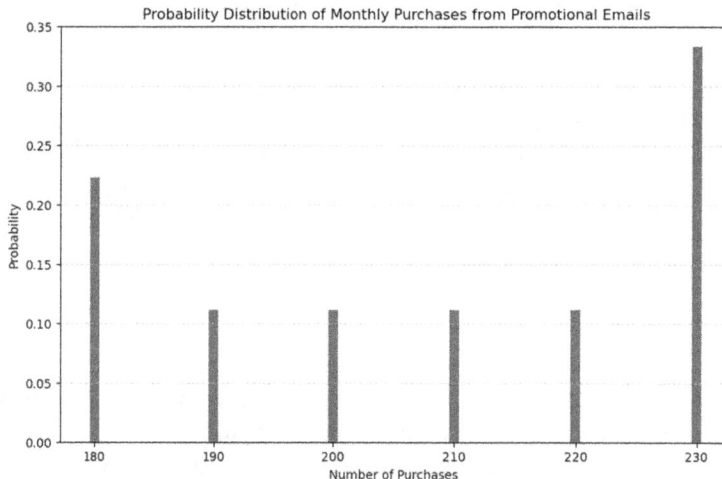

FIGURE 6.2. Probability distribution map.

This distribution could be visually represented as a graph, where the X axis represents the number of purchases (200, 220, 180, etc.) and the Y axis represents the frequency or probability of these purchase counts occurring. Such a distribution helps the marketer understand the variability and expected range of responses to the campaign. For instance, it might show that the probability of getting at least 200 purchases is high but getting more than 230 is very unlikely.

Based on this, we can see how probability gives a simple metric of likelihood based on historical data, whereas a probability distribution provides a fuller picture by showing all possible outcomes and their likelihoods. Marketers can use this approach for planning campaigns, as it helps predict customer behavior and allocate resources efficiently.

Types of Probability Distribution

There are several types of probability distribution, each serving distinct purposes in analyzing and predicting market dynamics. Two of the most important distributions are binomial and normal.

Binomial Distribution

The binomial distribution is particularly useful in marketing for modeling events that have two possible outcomes, such as conversion or no conversion, click or no click, and purchase or no purchase. It helps in calculating the probability of achieving a specific number of successes (e.g., sales) in a fixed number of trials (e.g., leads), given the success probability in each trial.

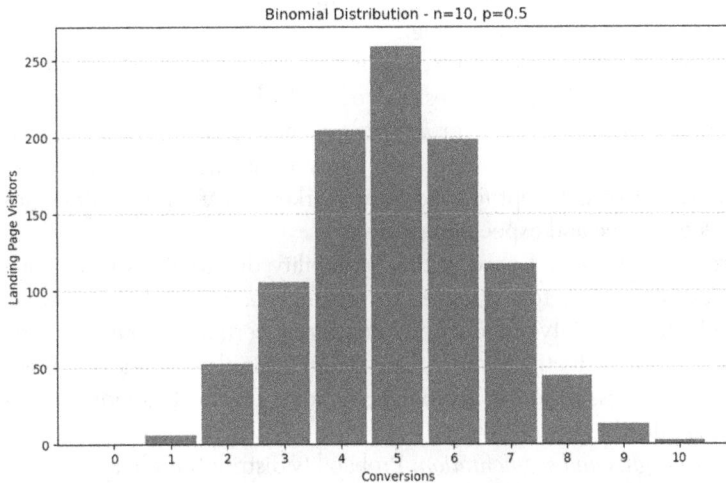

FIGURE 6.3. An example of binomial distribution.

For instance, as shown in Figure 6.3, knowing the conversion rate from a landing page, marketers can use the binomial distribution to estimate the probability of obtaining a certain number of conversions from a set number of visitors. This aids in evaluating the effectiveness of marketing campaigns and optimizing strategies accordingly.

Normal Distribution

Often referred to as a bell curve, the normal distribution is crucial in marketing for handling data that clusters around a mean. It is applicable in numerous scenarios, ranging from customer satisfaction scores to the average time spent on a Web site.

The normal distribution assists marketers in understanding variability and standard deviation, enabling them to make predictions about consumer behavior, sales trends, and other marketing-related phenomena. For example, analyzing customer purchase amounts during a specific period can reveal patterns that aid in inventory management and promotional planning.

Role of Probability in Making Decisions

Probability plays a pivotal role in marketing decisions at multiple levels. From forecasting sales and customer behavior to evaluating the success of marketing campaigns and understanding market trends, the application of probability helps marketers mitigate risks and allocate resources more effectively.

By quantifying the chances of various outcomes, marketers can better predict the future performance of their strategies, products, and services, leading to more calculated and informed decisions that align with business objectives and market needs.

Here are a few examples of how probability and probability distributions can benefit marketers:

- *Forecasting and predictability*: Probability distributions allow marketers to forecast customer behaviors and market trends. By understanding the distribution of possible outcomes, such as the range of potential sales figures or customer responses to a campaign, marketers can predict the most likely outcomes and plan accordingly. This ability to forecast based on a distribution of outcomes rather than a single average value enables more robust, data-driven decision-making.
- *Risk assessment*: With probability distributions, marketers can quantify the risk associated with different marketing strategies. For example, by analyzing the probability distribution of potential returns on an advertising campaign, marketers can assess the likelihood of various levels of success or failure. This helps in making informed decisions about budget allocations and strategy optimizations, as marketers can choose strategies that align with their risk tolerance and expected returns.
- *Resource optimization*: Knowing the probability distributions of customer purchases or responses helps marketers optimize resource allocation. For example, if the distribution shows a high probability of increased sales during certain periods, marketing resources can be focused more effectively during these times. Similarly, understanding the distribution of responses across different customer segments can lead to more targeted and efficient marketing efforts.
- *Customer insights and segmentation*: Probability distributions help in understanding the behaviors and preferences of different customer segments. By analyzing how likely different segments are to respond to marketing initiatives, marketers can tailor their approaches to meet the specific needs and preferences of each segment. This segmentation can lead to more personalized marketing, which typically yields better customer engagement and loyalty.
- *Scenario analysis*: Marketers often use probability distributions to perform scenario analysis. By considering a range of possible outcomes and their probabilities, they can prepare for various scenarios, including less likely but potentially impactful events. This preparation ensures that marketing strategies are resilient and adaptable, even in uncertain or volatile market conditions.

Common Challenges with Probability and Marketing

While probability offers valuable insights, marketers face several challenges in its application:

- *Data quality and availability*: Reliable predictions require high-quality, ample data. Incomplete or inaccurate data can lead to incorrect probability estimations and misguided decisions.

- *Overreliance on historical data*: Past data may not always be indicative of future events, especially in rapidly changing markets.
- *Interpreting results*: Misinterpretation of probability distributions and statistical significance can mislead marketing strategies.
- *Complexity in application*: Some probability models may be complex and beyond the grasp of marketing practitioners without a statistical background.

Probability and its distributions are indispensable tools in the marketer's arsenal, offering a systematic approach to navigating uncertainty. By leveraging these concepts, marketers can enhance their decision-making processes, forecast outcomes with greater accuracy, and, ultimately, drive better business results.

It is, however, critical to acknowledge and address the challenges that come with applying probability in marketing. Ensuring data integrity, staying adaptable to market changes, accurately interpreting statistical findings, and continually improving statistical literacy can empower marketers to harness the full potential of probability in crafting successful marketing strategies.

CONCLUSION

Of course, we have only scratched the surface when it comes to statistics and marketing, but we have provided a foundation for the remaining chapters in the book, and you are encouraged to continue your exploration of statistics by reading more from resources specifically focused on that area.

As we continue, you can carry the knowledge from this chapter that being intentional in the way that data is collected, measured, and analyzed, as well as how conclusions are drawn from it, is of utmost importance to your work as a marketer.

Another important aspect of marketing that benefits from measurement is the implementation of AI and AI models. The next chapter will explore some methods to set measurement goals to understand and assess AI's contribution to marketing efforts.

CHAPTER 7

MEASUREMENT OF AI IMPLEMENTATION AND AI MODEL QUALITY

While Artificial Intelligence (AI) has existed for several decades, the recent focus on generative AI tools such as ChatGPT has brought it to the forefront of the marketing landscape, offering new capabilities for data analysis, customer engagement, and personalization at scale. As AI becomes more integrated into marketing strategies, it is critical to measure the effectiveness of AI implementations and the quality of the models powering these tools.

This chapter will explore the best practices of AI in marketing measurement and the necessity of ongoing evaluation to ensure these advanced tools contribute meaningfully to marketing objectives in the present and future.

UNDERSTANDING AI IN MARKETING

AI marketing tools generally fall under three categories:

- *Generative AI*: Tools that generate content in a variety of mediums (text, images, audio, video, software code, and more) based on prompts from users. These tools range from text generation applications to generative AI capabilities within existing tools such as Adobe Photoshop, HubSpot, and Salesforce.
- *Predictive analytics*: These tools leverage machine learning and data analytics to predict customer behavior, automate decisions, and provide actionable insights. They range from personalization engines that use behavioral data to show recommendations to a customer to sophisticated analytics platforms capable of processing vast quantities of data to inform marketing strategies.
- *Workflow automation*: These tools help marketing teams to be more efficient in creating and delivering marketing content, campaigns, and other initiatives. They range from automations within project management tools, such as Asana, Adobe Workfront, or Atlassian's Jira, to other automations and syncing using tools such as Zapier that connect multiple products and platforms to perform automatic updates.

The potential benefits of using AI within marketing are immense, leading to more efficient resource allocation, higher conversion rates, and a deeper understanding of customer needs and market trends.

That said, to achieve greater success, there need to be metrics to measure both the *outcomes* of the marketing work generated by AI as well as the AI models themselves and what those models are producing. Without the latter, for instance, it may be difficult to detect whether the AI engine that is powering the tool is increasing or decreasing in effectiveness over time.

KEY PERFORMANCE INDICATORS FOR AI

Establishing the appropriate Key Performance Indicators (KPIs) is a pivotal aspect of measuring the triumph of AI strategies within an organization. A thorough analysis conducted by MIT reveals that enterprises integrating AI-informed KPIs are markedly more proficient—at a rate of threefold—when it comes to adaptability and speed in response to market changes compared to those who have not adopted this approach. For marketing leaders seeking to leverage AI, the KPIs must encapsulate:

- *Operational efficiency*: This includes the measurement of time and financial efficiencies brought by AI systems. Consider metrics such as process cycle times, cost reductions, error rates, and the amount of manual labor hours saved thanks to AI automation.
- *Marketing effectiveness*: Evaluate how AI contributes to reaching and surpassing core marketing objectives. Enhancement of customer experiences, boosting customer loyalty, and achieving higher engagement rates are quintessential metrics. For instance, tracking increases in Customer Lifetime Value (CLTV), customer retention rates, and Net Promoter Scores (NPSs) can indicate customer satisfaction levels.
- *Customer engagement*: This evaluates how effective AI-generated content or experiences are at converting customers or solving customer issues.

For marketing executives, it's not only about setting these KPIs but also about finding the granularity within each to offer actionable insights. Establishing precise benchmarks helps you discover the true Return on Investment (ROI) of AI integrations and ensure they contribute substantively toward overarching business goals.

Beyond the Initial Bump

It is also likely that the adoption of an AI-based tool will greatly increase efficiency or enable suddenly personalizing content for audiences that had previously received similar messaging regardless of audience segment. Thus, an initial bump in results may occur from AI adoption. While this is welcome in any marketing team, it is important to ensure continual boosts to performance beyond this initial bump.

Metrics should be regularly reviewed and tailored to reflect the rapidly evolving market dynamics and technological advancements in AI. By continuously calibrating KPIs, marketing leaders can ensure they remain in lockstep with their strategic vision, thus empowering their organizations to harness AI with finesse and deliver quantifiable outcomes.

AI MODEL USAGE

While small businesses will likely rely on off-the-shelf AI tools and existing Large Language Models (LLMs) for generative AI that are present in tools such as OpenAI's ChatGPT and

DALL-E or Google's Gemini, enterprise organizations are more often looking for customized solutions.

This means that these enterprise organizations are training their own LLMs for generative AI, and their own machine learning models for predictive analytics. Even if they rely on a starting point in either case that is "off the shelf," so to speak, they will not want to share their data outside of the organization, and they may also only want to train their AI models on their own company information, to prevent misinformation or "hallucinations" from occurring.

That said, just as these enterprise organizations will be measuring the marketing outcomes of using these AI-based tools and platforms, there also needs to be a way to measure and evaluate the AI models themselves.

Evaluating AI Model Accuracy

Maintaining and monitoring the performance metrics of AI models from the inception stage all the way through their active use goes beyond just quality control—it's about fostering ongoing improvements and sparking innovative leaps forward. For marketing professionals, emphasizing model quality delivers critical insights into the model's real-world utility rather than limiting its evaluation to controlled training environments, simultaneously reducing the risk of unexpected errors, often referred to colloquially as "hallucinations."

It's key for marketing leaders to assess the strengths and weaknesses of these AI tools, taking into account the context in which they are deployed, the references they use for learning, and their sample selections. To this end, employing a breadth of varied datasets remains crucial, regardless of the technological framework in place.

Keeping a close eye on vital performance indicators both pre- and post-launch is akin to taking the pulse of your model, ensuring it fulfills its intended functions effectively. The feedback loop is essential: as user responses are gathered, they should be reincorporated into the model to promote improved outcomes over time. It's a positive feedback loop that encourages constant refinement of the model. Conversely, errors that aren't caught can become compounded, making early and frequent corrections a top priority.

To give you a handle on measuring AI model accuracy and performance, here are several metrics that we advocate for marketing experts to track:

- *Quality index*: This composite metric offers a macro view of overall model health by aggregating various performance indicators (examples are BLEU, ROUGE, or CIDEr metrics).
- *Error rate*: Track the proportion of the model's outputs that are off the mark or not applicable. Bringing in human reviewers to help calibrate this measure is highly advisable.
- *Latency*: Measure the response time from the moment the AI model receives a user query until the moment it delivers an answer. Factors affecting this include the model's processing speed, its design, and the robustness of the deployment environment.
- *Accuracy range*: Set and monitor the target precision thresholds the model should achieve. Engage a dedicated team, sometimes known as a "red team," to rigorously test and critique the AI's performance.
- *Safety score*: Evaluate the frequency with which the model encounters or generates content that could be deemed detrimental or sensitive for your brand.

For those in the marketing vanguard, these measurements are not just numbers—they are the breadcrumbs that lead to a deeper understanding of your customers and continuous AI model optimization.

ASSESSING AI's CONTRIBUTION TO ROI

AI tools play a role in driving strategic growth and gaining a competitive edge. The real worth of AI-driven strategies, however, often comes down to their impact on ROI. Understanding this impact requires a three-part approach:

- *Quantitative analysis*: To begin with, concrete numerical data forms the foundation for ROI assessment. Marketing professionals need to monitor KPIs both before and after integrating AI to gauge the lift that it can have on efforts. These metrics may include conversion rates, customer retention statistics, and marketing cost effectiveness. The pre-AI metrics act as a baseline for comparison, allowing for an evaluation of any changes in performance following the adoption of AI solutions.
- *Qualitative assessment*: Additionally, nuanced factors that encompass customer attitudes and sentiment play a key role in marketing success and thus shouldn't be ignored. These impacts of AI can sometimes be hard to quantify purely with numbers, impacting customer engagement and satisfaction (CSAT). Understanding how the market responds to AI-enhanced experiences through feedback or NPS surveys can provide insights into how these technological advancements are perceived, ultimately influencing customer loyalty and brand image.
- *Validation through A/B testing*: To further validate assessments, A/B testing proves to be a tool. By comparing the effectiveness of AI-enhanced marketing strategies, with methods within a structured trial-based framework, marketing experts can not only determine whether AI outperforms its counterparts but also gain insights into the reasons behind its success. Key factors such as customizing message models for customer behavior and chatbot efficiency in customer support can be analyzed separately to evaluate their impact on the overall ROI.
- *Efficiency metrics*: Additionally, marketers should take into account not only the effectiveness of the efforts but also the quantity of resources required to do the work. For instance, if the same marketing results were achieved (e.g., 10,000 conversions from an email), yet 50% fewer resources were expended because of AI-based automation and content generation, the overall ROI of the effort is still considerably greater.

Combining qualitative evaluations with controlled A/B testing, marketing professionals can more accurately assess how AI contributes to ROI. This deeper comprehension of how AI tools influence key aspects of marketing activities allows for informed strategic choices, efficient resource management, and, ultimately, more competitive results.

Monitoring AI for Continuous Improvement

Continuous monitoring systems are essential for maintaining the relevance and accuracy of AI models over time. By tracking performance against KPIs and paying close attention to shifts in customer behavior and market conditions, marketers can refine AI tools to adapt to new data. Regular updates and adjustments ensure that AI implementations continue to provide value and support marketing objectives effectively.

CASE STUDY: PB SHOES' AI JOURNEY

PB Shoes recognized that there was great potential in leveraging AI for their digital marketing efforts. Let's explore how they approached AI adoption, with a focus on measuring both outcomes and the process itself.

Personalized Product Recommendations

The journey began with PB Shoes implementing an AI system designed to analyze customer data, including past purchase history, browsing behavior, and preference surveys. Utilizing a sophisticated algorithm, the AI system curated a personalized selection of pickleball shoes for each visitor. The recommendations evolved in real time, responding to the customers' interactions to refine the selections further.

Measuring AI's Impact on Engagement and Conversions

The true test of AI's effectiveness lies in its tangible impact on business outcomes. PB Shoes meticulously tracked the changes in online engagement metrics, noting substantial increases in time spent on the site and interaction with product pages. More significantly, sales conversion rates saw a notable uplift. The correlation between the introduction of AI recommendations and these metrics was clear evidence of success.

Continuous Learning and Model Refinement

Embracing a philosophy of continuous improvement, PB Shoes established feedback loops wherein customer responses and evolving purchase patterns were fed back into the AI system. This input triggered ongoing model refinements, allowing the AI to become more attuned to the shifting tastes and preferences of the pickleball community.

Measuring the Effectiveness of Their AI Model

To ensure that the AI system retained its efficacy over time, PB Shoes adopted a set of longitudinal performance indicators. They monitored the quality index, tracking a suite of metrics indicating customer satisfaction and engagement. Error rates in product recommendation mismatches were analyzed and reduced over time, reflecting the AI's growing sophistication.

Creating Transparency to Evaluate Bias

Aware of the potential pitfalls of AI, PB Shoes committed to maintaining transparency in their AI models. They conducted regular audits to pinpoint any bias in the AI's decision-making process, particularly biases that could skew product recommendations. By identifying areas where bias might be introduced, PB Shoes could take corrective action, ensuring fairness and relevance in the AI's operations.

The adoption of AI-based methods marked a transformative period for PB Shoes. The technology enabled them to offer unparalleled personalization in their marketing efforts, leading to higher customer engagement and increased sales. Through vigilant measurement and a commitment to transparency, PB Shoes not only maximized the effectiveness of their marketing but also set a standard for responsible AI use in the industry. This case study serves as a testament to the power of AI in marketing when applied thoughtfully and measured rigorously.

CONCLUSION

AI in marketing measurement is not only about embracing new technology but also about understanding and critically evaluating its impact. By setting the right KPIs, rigorously assessing AI model accuracy and ROI, and monitoring AI systems continuously, marketers can harness the full potential of AI. With careful consideration of ethical implications and biases, the journey with AI can be as responsible as it is innovative.

Marketers should approach AI with a combination of scientific rigor and an eye toward innovation. This will help their organization achieve meaningful momentum in their marketing while ensuring their AI tools are performing with the best interests of the organization and its stakeholders in mind.

PART 1 RECAP QUIZ

Welcome to the end of the first section of this book. To help you see whether you have mastered the concepts we've covered so far, we're going to provide a short quiz on some of the key concepts. To check your answers, refer to Appendix B, which lists all of the answers for the quizzes in the book.

Let's look at three questions on the content in Part 1.

Question 1
Which of the following are true about Key Performance Indicators (KPIs)? Choose all that apply:
a) KPIs help you set achievable goals
b) KPIs increase transparency and accountability
c) KPIs help you measure the effectiveness of campaigns
d) KPIs improve the customer experience
e) All of the above

Question 2
Which of the following are part of gaining stakeholder support? Choose all that apply:
a) Think outside marketing: what is best for the business at large?
b) Make sure stakeholders understand the marketing jargon you use
c) Choose metrics that tell a story
d) Keep it straightforward
e) All of the above

Question 3
Which kind of data does this describe?
It is descriptive and conceptual. It is data that can be observed but not measured.
a) Quantitative data
b) Qualitative data
c) Categorical data
d) Continuous data

PART 2: A MARKETING MEASUREMENT FRAMEWORK

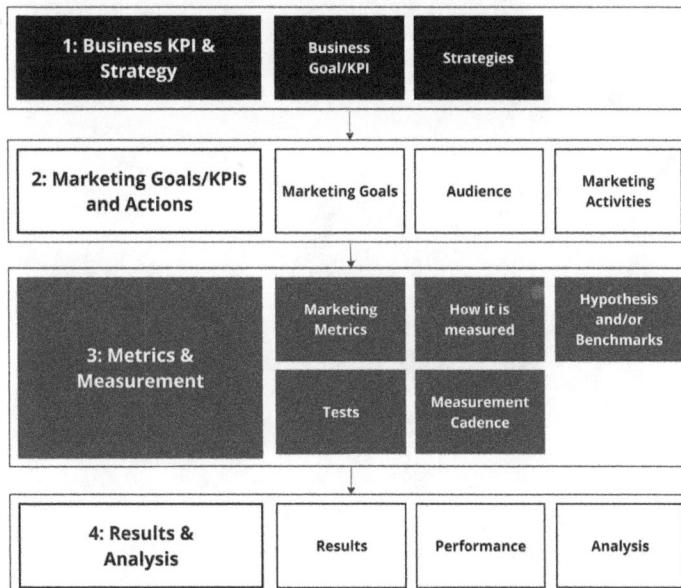

In this section of the guide, we will walk through a measurement framework (Figure P2.1) that you can use to measure the success of your marketing efforts, and that utilizes many of the ideas and concepts we have reviewed thus far, such as business and marketing KPIs and marketing metrics. There are also areas that we will explore in later chapters related to measurement and analysis.

The marketing measurement framework has been designed to be flexible enough to handle most marketing channels and campaigns, including complex, multi-channel marketing and advertising initiatives.

Marketing Measurement Framework

1: Business KPI & Strategy	Business Goal/KPI	Strategies	
2: Marketing Goals/KPIs and Actions	Marketing Goals	Audience	Marketing Activities
3: Metrics & Measurement	Marketing Metrics	How it is measured	Hypothesis and/or Benchmarks
	Tests	Measurement Cadence	
4: Results & Analysis	Results	Performance	Analysis

FIGURE P2.1. The marketing measurement framework.

While there are many frameworks available, there is value in consistency. Thus, it is important to use a consistent marketing measurement framework across your marketing teams because it allows you to compare the performance of different marketing channels and campaigns, identify areas for improvement, and make data-driven decisions. A consistent framework ensures that all teams are measuring and reporting on the same metrics, which makes it easier to analyze and interpret the data. This, in turn, helps improve your marketing efforts' overall effectiveness.

Additionally, a consistent framework helps to ensure that all teams are aligned on the goals and objectives of the marketing campaigns, which can improve collaboration and coordination across teams. By having a shared understanding of the important metrics, teams can work together more effectively to achieve their goals.

WHAT WE ARE GOING TO DISCUSS IN PART 2

In this next part of the book, we will discuss the following:

• The benefits of investing in a marketing measurement framework
• A high-level review of a marketing measurement framework
• A detailed review of the components of the framework
• Recommendations on incorporating AI-based tools into your marketing measurement

While you may find areas that need adjustment for the specifics of the way your business operates, or how your marketing is performed, there should be a solid foundation to build small improvements upon by using this framework.

CHAPTER 8

INVESTING IN A MARKETING MEASUREMENT FRAMEWORK

I
n this chapter, we will explore a Marketing Measurement Framework (MMF) you can use and adapt to your work. First, however, let's discuss why, exactly, an MMF is important.

As businesses become more analytics-driven and consumers continue to move online, marketers need a sound system or framework to guide their marketing activities. An MMF is a key tool that should be used by all businesses looking to keep their marketing efforts accountable, targeted, and efficient. A well-defined MMF is essential to track, analyze, and align marketing activities with business objectives.

ALIGNMENT OF METRICS AND KPIs TO THE STRATEGY AND GOALS OF THE BUSINESS

Investing in an MMF is essential because it creates a direct link between your marketing activities and your overarching business goals. Without this alignment, marketing efforts can become fragmented and misdirected, failing to support the broader objectives of the company. The framework acts as a guide to ensure that every campaign and marketing initiative is intentionally designed to contribute to these higher-level goals. This alignment makes it easier to justify marketing spend and to demonstrate the value marketing brings to the business in tangible terms. By linking metrics and KPIs directly to business objectives, marketing teams ensure that their activities are focused on what matters most to the company's growth and success.

The MMF is also a vital tool for defining and prioritizing goals. When setting up an MMF, marketers must carefully identify the metrics that are most relevant to the company's strategic priorities, whether it's growing brand awareness, increasing market share, or driving conversions. This process forces marketing teams to prioritize the outcomes that align with the company's overall direction, eliminating less impactful or irrelevant metrics. By defining Key Performance Indicators (KPIs) that mirror business objectives, the framework provides clarity on what success looks like. This structured approach ensures that all marketing efforts are purpose-driven, improving both focus and efficiency in achieving desired outcomes.

Moreover, the framework helps to measure progress consistently and transparently. With clearly defined KPIs and metrics aligned with the strategy, it becomes easier to track and evaluate the success of each marketing activity over time. This provides real-time insights into whether a campaign is on track to meet its objectives or whether adjustments need to be made. By measuring performance against the business goals, marketers can make data-driven decisions that directly impact their strategies. For example, if a campaign underperforms, the framework allows for quick identification of which specific KPIs are lagging and why, making it easier to implement course corrections that keep the business on track to meet its goals.

An MMF also plays a critical role in refining marketing tactics and improving Return on Investment (ROI). Once marketing metrics are aligned with business objectives, the data collected can help marketers fine-tune their tactics and optimize future campaigns. By continuously assessing which strategies are contributing most effectively to key business goals, marketing teams can abandon or recalibrate underperforming initiatives and double down on those that deliver strong results. The process of measurement and evaluation, guided by the framework, ensures that marketing spend is optimized and delivers maximum ROI. Over time, this alignment can lead to better decision-making, more efficient use of resources, and a more significant impact on the bottom line.

Finally, having an MMF in place enhances accountability across marketing teams and ensures a shared understanding of priorities. Since the framework ties marketing efforts to the company's strategic goals, it helps teams stay focused on what's most important. This alignment fosters a sense of shared responsibility across departments, ensuring that every marketing activity contributes to a common goal. Additionally, by clearly defining metrics and KPIs, the framework provides transparency to all stakeholders, from the C-suite to marketing teams. This visibility allows everyone to see how marketing activities are contributing to broader business success, reinforcing the importance of investing in well-defined, goal-oriented marketing strategies.

CONSISTENCY IN COLLECTING, MEASURING, TESTING, AND ANALYZING MARKETING EFFORTS

Consistency is a cornerstone of any successful MMF. By establishing a standard process for collecting, measuring, testing, and analyzing marketing efforts, businesses can achieve a more accurate and reliable understanding of their marketing performance. This consistency ensures that all data is gathered and evaluated in a uniform manner, reducing the chances of discrepancies or misinterpretations. A sound MMF defines clear procedures and tools for these processes, making it easier for marketers to compare results across campaigns, channels, and timeframes while providing the transparency needed to make informed, data-driven decisions.

A well-structured MMF provides a clear set of guidelines for data collection. It ensures that the same metrics are gathered across all marketing activities, whether it's a social media ad, an email marketing campaign, or a content marketing effort. Without these guidelines, marketers may inadvertently collect data inconsistently, leading to inaccurate comparisons and faulty conclusions. For example, one team might measure clickthrough rates in a social media campaign, while another team focuses on conversion rates in an email campaign. By having a unified approach to data collection, the MMF ensures that all relevant metrics are tracked in the same way, creating a complete and comparable picture of marketing performance.

The framework also outlines how to measure the performance of marketing efforts consistently. By defining the KPIs and metrics that are most relevant to the company's goals, the MMF ensures that marketing teams are not only collecting data but measuring it against clear, predefined benchmarks. This consistency is crucial for analyzing trends and identifying areas of improvement. When marketers measure campaign performance using standardized metrics, they can spot patterns that would otherwise be missed if each campaign was measured differently. This also makes it easier to assess whether specific tactics or strategies are working as expected, leading to more efficient optimization efforts.

Testing is another vital aspect of marketing that benefits from the consistency provided by a robust MMF. The framework should include protocols for A/B testing, multivariate testing, and other experimental methods used to optimize campaigns. Without standardized testing procedures, marketing teams may struggle to interpret test results correctly or apply insights consistently across channels. A sound MMF ensures that tests are designed and executed in a way that produces reliable, actionable data. It also encourages a culture of continuous testing, where marketers regularly evaluate their tactics and make data-backed adjustments to improve outcomes.

Once data has been collected, measured, and tested, the next step is analysis. Here, the consistency provided by an MMF becomes especially valuable. The framework ensures that marketing teams are using uniform methods to interpret data, reducing the risk of biased or inaccurate conclusions. It also fosters a data-driven culture, where decisions are made based on evidence rather than assumptions. By providing consistent analytics tools and methodologies, the MMF enables marketing teams to dig deeper into their data, uncover insights, and apply those insights to refine their strategies. Whether it's identifying the most effective channels, understanding customer behavior, or optimizing messaging, the analysis component of an MMF is essential for driving continuous improvement.

Finally, consistency in collecting, measuring, testing, and analyzing marketing efforts streamlines the entire marketing process, making it more efficient and accountable. Marketers are able to work within a structured system that eliminates guesswork and reduces the chances of errors or wasted resources. This consistency also facilitates better communication and collaboration among teams, as everyone is working from the same playbook. Whether coordinating cross-channel campaigns or presenting data to stakeholders, having a unified framework in place ensures that all efforts are aligned and easily understood, leading to better decision-making and improved marketing results over time.

FLEXIBILITY TO BE APPLIED TO MANY DIFFERENT MARKETING CHANNELS

One of the greatest strengths of a well-designed MMF is its flexibility to adapt across a wide variety of marketing channels. In today's complex marketing environment, businesses engage with audiences through multiple touchpoints, including social media, email, search engines, content marketing, and paid advertising. Each of these channels comes with its own set of metrics, tools, and measurement demands. A robust MMF must have the versatility to handle these differences while still providing a unified system for evaluating marketing performance. This flexibility ensures that regardless of the platform, marketers are working within the same framework, enabling consistent tracking and reporting across the board.

The adaptability of an MMF is key because each marketing channel serves a different role in the customer journey and requires its own set of metrics to measure effectiveness. For example, social media marketing may focus on engagement metrics such as likes, shares, and comments, while email marketing may prioritize open rates, clickthrough rates, and conversions. Paid advertising campaigns, on the other hand, may center around impressions, Cost per Click (CPC), and Return on Ad Spend (ROAS). Despite these variations, a flexible MMF can encompass all these metrics, creating a comprehensive picture of how each channel contributes to the broader marketing strategy. This ensures that the performance of different channels can be evaluated on an even playing field.

Flexibility in an MMF also makes it easier to compare performance across different marketing channels. By standardizing the way metrics are measured and reported, marketers can more easily analyze which channels are driving the most value. This cross-channel analysis is crucial for understanding which platforms are performing best, where to allocate more budget, and how to improve underperforming channels. For example, a business might find that social media is generating a large volume of traffic, but paid search is yielding higher conversions. With a flexible MMF, these insights can be easily surfaced, allowing for better-informed decision-making.

Moreover, this flexibility ensures that marketing efforts are not confined to silos. In organizations without a cohesive framework, marketing teams may focus on individual channels in isolation, leading to disconnected strategies and fragmented data. A well-integrated MMF breaks down these silos by aligning all marketing activities under one system of measurement. This integration encourages teams to collaborate, share insights, and work toward unified marketing goals, rather than optimizing one channel at the expense of others. By fostering a more holistic approach, a flexible MMF ensures that marketing efforts across different channels work together to drive overall business success.

Another advantage of having a flexible MMF is the ability to scale it as new marketing channels emerge. The digital landscape is constantly evolving, and new platforms, tools, and tactics are regularly introduced. Whether it's a new social media platform, an innovative form of content marketing, or emerging technologies such as voice search or augmented reality, a flexible framework can easily incorporate these new channels into the existing measurement system. This agility allows businesses to stay ahead of the curve and continue optimizing their marketing efforts as new opportunities arise. A rigid, channel-specific measurement approach would quickly become outdated, but a flexible MMF ensures that your marketing strategy remains adaptable and future-proof.

Finally, a flexible MMF maximizes the effectiveness of marketing efforts by enabling marketers to quickly identify what works and what doesn't across all channels. Since the framework is applied uniformly, it becomes easier to test new ideas, run experiments, and measure their impact on the overall strategy. If a particular campaign isn't performing as expected, marketers can use the framework to identify where the issue lies—whether it's within the messaging, targeting, or channel selection. On the flip side, high-performing channels or tactics can be quickly scaled up for greater impact. This constant process of testing, learning, and optimizing is critical for achieving sustained marketing success, and it's only possible when the MMF is flexible enough to adapt to the unique demands of each marketing channel.

INCREASED ORGANIZATIONAL ACCOUNTABILITY

One of the most significant benefits of an MMF is that it fosters increased organizational accountability. By establishing clear goals, metrics, and performance indicators, businesses can ensure that every marketing initiative is aligned with broader business objectives and stakeholders' expectations. Accountability is critical in today's data-driven marketing environment, where proving the value of marketing efforts is more important than ever. An MMF provides the structure needed to demonstrate how marketing activities directly contribute to business success, making it easier to justify investments, optimize resources, and identify areas for improvement.

A well-defined MMF helps create transparency across departments, particularly between marketing and sales. Both teams can access the same set of metrics and performance data, ensuring that everyone is on the same page regarding expectations and outcomes. For example, marketing teams can show sales teams exactly how their campaigns are driving leads or increasing brand awareness. Similarly, sales teams can provide feedback on the quality of leads being generated by marketing. This reciprocal flow of information fosters greater collaboration and trust, as both departments can see how their efforts align and contribute to the organization's overall success.

Stakeholders, including executives and investors, benefit from the increased accountability provided by an MMF. With a clear framework in place, it becomes easier to communicate the impact of marketing campaigns in tangible, quantifiable terms. Rather than relying on vague or subjective reports, marketers can present data-backed insights that directly link their efforts to ROI and other business metrics. This level of accountability builds confidence among stakeholders, as they can clearly see how marketing investments are paying off. Moreover, it allows marketers to make a stronger case for additional budget or resources, as the results of past efforts are clearly demonstrated and justified.

Another key aspect of accountability is the ability to identify areas for improvement. An MMF provides a structured approach to testing, measuring, and analyzing marketing performance, making it easier to pinpoint where campaigns may be falling short. Whether it's a specific channel underperforming or a message not resonating with the target audience, the framework allows marketers to quickly identify these issues and take corrective action. This process of continuous evaluation and optimization ensures that marketing teams are always working to improve their performance and contribute more effectively to the company's goals. The ability to assess what's working and what's not leads to better decision-making and resource allocation over time.

By linking metrics and KPIs to business objectives, an MMF also establishes clear standards for success. It outlines the goals that marketing activities should aim to achieve and provides benchmarks for measuring progress. These standards make it easier for businesses to hold themselves accountable, as they can objectively assess whether they are meeting their goals or falling short. If a campaign isn't delivering the expected results, the MMF provides the tools to analyze why that might be and adjust strategies accordingly. On the other hand, if goals are exceeded, the framework enables teams to replicate those successful strategies across other campaigns.

Finally, the MMF fosters a culture of accountability across the entire organization. By providing a clear, consistent, and data-driven approach to measuring marketing success, it ensures that everyone involved in marketing efforts, from junior marketers to C-level executives, understands their role in achieving business goals. This culture of accountability helps create a shared sense of responsibility for marketing performance, driving better outcomes for the entire company. Additionally, it encourages a proactive approach to problem-solving, as teams are empowered to use data to identify challenges and implement solutions before issues escalate. In short, an MMF not only holds the organization accountable for its marketing efforts but also provides the tools and processes needed to drive continuous improvement.

CONCLUSION

An MMF is essential in bringing accountability, clarity, flexibility, and visibility to your marketing efforts. Utilizing this framework across the entire business ensures that everyone is moving in the same direction toward common goals, improving the marketing ROI and success rate for all campaigns undertaken.

Without a sound MMF, businesses risk marketing in the dark, entangling themselves in complex, multi-channel operations without measurable results. With an MMF, however, businesses can confidently and efficiently position themselves for success.

Now that the rationale behind establishing a marketing measurement framework has been established, the next chapter will provide details on the components of the MMF and the value of each.

CHAPTER 9

COMPONENTS OF THE MARKETING MEASUREMENT FRAMEWORK

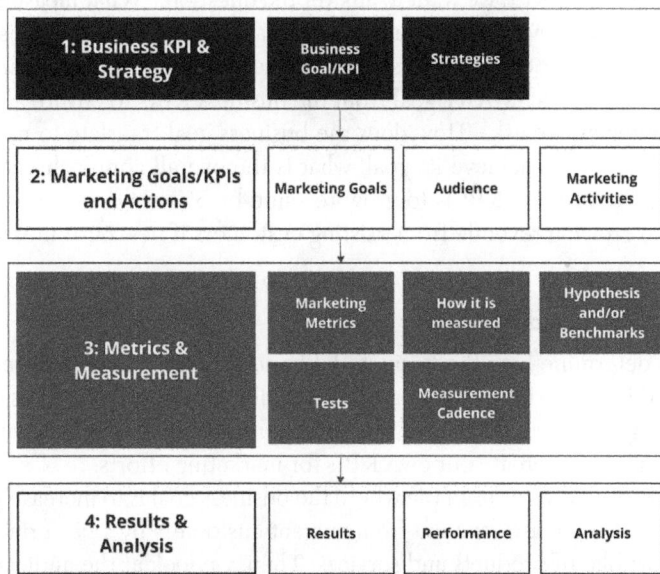

There are four primary components of the marketing measurement framework, and we will discuss each and their component parts. The four parts are:

- Step 1: Business KPI and strategy
- Step 2: Marketing goals and actions
- Step 3: Metrics and measurement
- Step 4: Results and analysis

Each of these components has multiple subcategories that go along with them, as you can see in the following figure (Figure 9.1).

Marketing Measurement Framework

1: Business KPI & Strategy	Business Goal/KPI	Strategies	
2: Marketing Goals/KPIs and Actions	Marketing Goals	Audience	Marketing Activities

3: Metrics & Measurement	Marketing Metrics	How it is measured	Hypothesis and/or Benchmarks
	Tests	Measurement Cadence	

4: Results & Analysis	Results	Performance	Analysis

FIGURE 9.1. The Marketing measurement framework.

After we review these in detail, we will look at the framework in practice by running through an example. Let's begin!

Step 1: Business KPI and Strategy

Step 1 is to define the business Key Performance Indicators (KPIs) and strategy. Since we've already discussed what a KPI is, we can talk more specifically about what a *business* KPI is, as opposed to a *marketing* KPI (which we will explore in the next step), to ensure our marketing measurement framework is effective.

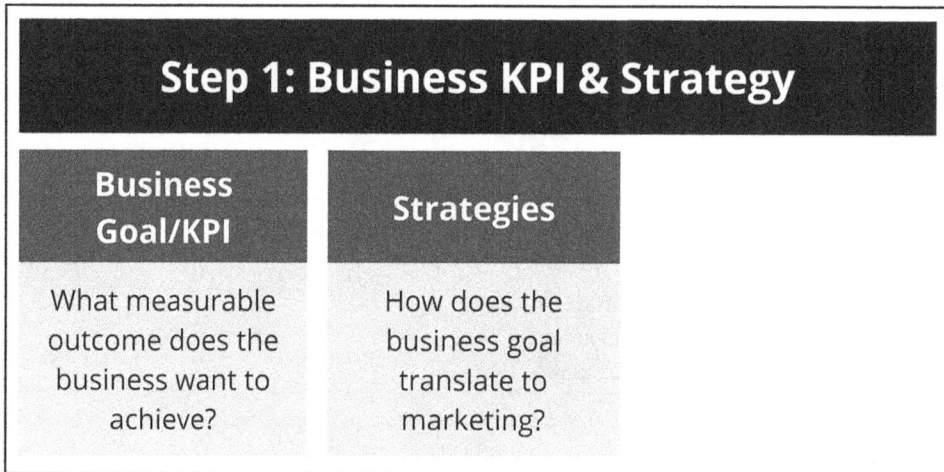

Step 1: Business KPI & Strategy

Business Goal/KPI	Strategies
What measurable outcome does the business want to achieve?	How does the business goal translate to marketing?

FIGURE 9.2. Step 1: Business KPI and strategy.

For the business goal/KPI, we want to answer the question, "What measurable outcome does the business want to achieve?" If the business goals are well constructed, this won't be an issue, as they will already be articulated and shared by executives and stakeholders. If not, however, remember how to create a SMART goal from the business KPIs to ensure alignment.

Next, for strategies, we ask, "How does the business goal translate to marketing?" In other words, for the business to achieve its goal, what is the overall approach marketing must take? For instance, if the business KPI is to grow revenue by 5% in Q1 of the year, marketing may need to focus on growing revenue from existing customers if new customer acquisition is a less viable option.

Step 2: Marketing Goals and Actions

Step 2 is to determine how the business KPI and strategy translate to marketing goals and actions. We do this by looking at three areas, each with a question to help us clarify.

For marketing goals, we ask, "What measurable marketing goal aligns with the strategy and business goal?" Then, we create our own KPIs for marketing efforts.

Going back to the previous example where the business goal is to increase revenue, a marketing KPI might be to increase revenue from current customers by 12%, primarily by expanding the business' portfolio of products and services. Then, we look at the audience or who is being

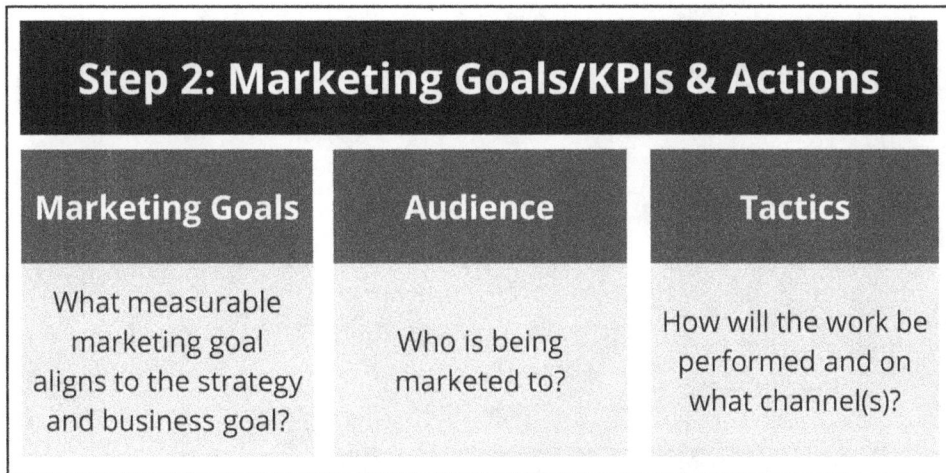

FIGURE 9.3. Step 2: Marketing goals and actions.

marketed to. Following this example, our audience would be current customers, though we will likely want to narrow that down to a group with the highest propensity to expand their usage of our products and services. Then, we look at tactics or how the work will be performed and on what channel(s).

For instance, if we have a great customer loyalty program that ties into our mobile app, we might consider utilizing a combination of push notifications through the app and emails to drive greater app usage.

Step 3: Metrics and Measurement

With all our goals established from both a business and marketing perspective, it is now time to measure the effectiveness of our work.

We start with marketing KPIs, which translate our marketing goals into metrics that quantify success. This is accompanied by determining how those marketing KPIs will be measured, including the methods to collect data on the channels or methods we use to run a campaign or initiative.

Then, we establish a hypothesis (as discussed earlier) about what we believe can be achieved, or we rely on pre-established benchmarks to determine whether we achieve success or not. Accompanying our hypothesis is the test(s) we perform to understand the elements that can enable further optimization and improvement of our marketing results.

Finally, we want to establish a measurement cadence that allows us to collect a statistically significant amount of data without requiring too much time to pass before we analyze our results to look for opportunities to optimize.

So, for instance, we might create a hypothesis for our example scenario that if we can increase the number of times a current customer logs in to our mobile app by 25%, we are likely to increase our sales by 12% over the course of a quarter.

Step 3: Metrics & Measurement		
Marketing Metrics	**How it is measured**	**Hypothesis and/or Benchmarks**
What is/are the metric(s) that can quantify success?	What methods are used to collect data about this type of marketing?	How do we know if it is successful?
Tests	**Measurement Cadence**	
What elements are being tested for further optimization?	At what frequency will it be most beneficial to measure?	

FIGURE 9.4. Step 3: Metrics and measurement.

Step 4: Results and Analysis

Once we have measurements from our marketing work, we then review the results and analyze them to determine the best next steps that will help bring us closer to achieving both our marketing and business goals.

Looking at the results of our efforts so far, we need to be able to determine what was achieved. If you cannot clearly articulate this and tell the story of how you started with business goals, then translate those to marketing goals and a strategy using measurable marketing KPIs on one or more channels. Then, your results will have the necessary level of detail.

Case Study: PB Shoes' Usage of a Marketing Measurement Framework

Let's go back to PB Shoes and their need to grow market share in the ever-expanding pickleball shoes sector. They could say something like the following:

By increasing the frequency of push notifications and other communications driving current customers to our mobile app, we were able to increase the frequency that a current customer logs in to the mobile app by 27% (our goal was 25%), resulting in an increase in revenue from additional sales of 13.5% (our goal was 12%). We did this by increasing the frequency and changing the messaging used to engage our customers.

In any type of marketing measurement, looking at the results from a single period is not enough to understand the context and whether or not the outcomes are objectively good or not.

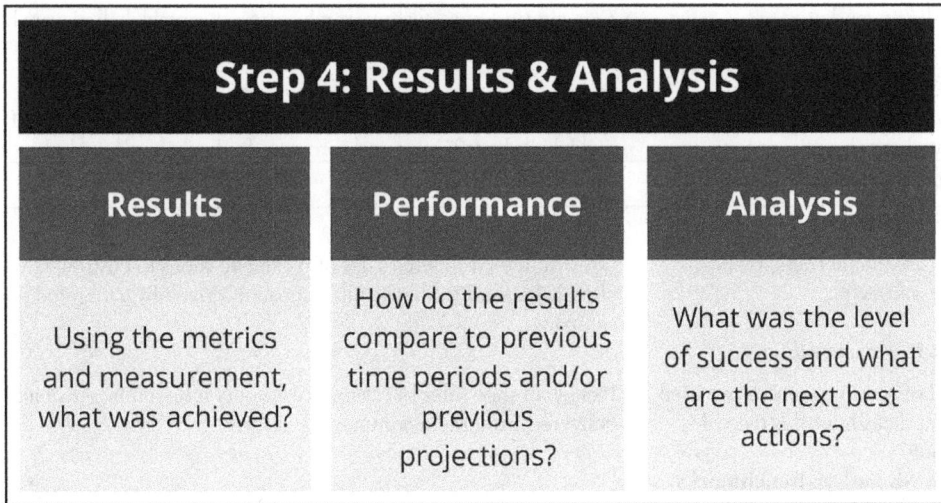

FIGURE 9.5. Step 4: Results and analysis.

Thus, we look at performance as the amount of increase (or decrease) achieved through marketing efforts relative to the prior periods, usually defined in our cadence (from the previous step of metrics and measurement).

Analysis

Finally, and perhaps most importantly, is the analysis. So, we achieved additional sales of 13.5%, which exceeded our goal of 12% for the quarter. What exactly does that mean? This requires asking a few questions:

Step 1: Business KPI and Strategy	
Business Goal	
Overall goal	Become the leading pickleball shoe manufacturer in the world by achieving 27% market share by Q1 of 2026
Business KPI	
What measurable outcome does the business want to achieve?	Increase revenue from sales of pickleball shoes by 20% within the calendar year and each subsequent year
Strategies	
How does the business goal translate to marketing?	Expand awareness of the company's pickleball shoe offerings to existing customers who already love the brand
Step 2: Marketing Goals/KPIs and Actions	
Marketing Goals/KPIs	
What measurable marketing goal aligns with the strategy and business goal?	Increase adoption of PB Shoes' pickleball shoes by existing PB Shoes customers by 35% Year over Year (YoY)
Audience	

FIGURE 9.1. The marketing measurement framework in action.

Who is being marketed to?	Existing PB Shoes customers who are active pickleball players but haven't tried PB Shoes' pickleball shoes

Marketing Activities

How will the work be performed, and on what channel(s)?	Awareness campaign that asks, "Did you know PB Shoes also offers pickleball shoes?" executed across multiple channels, including email

Step 3: Metrics and Measurement

Marketing Metrics

What is/are the metric(s) that can quantify success?	Growth in e-commerce sales of pickleball shoes to customers who already have a PB Shoes online account, driven by a targeted email campaign

How It Is Measured

What platforms or methods are used to collect data about this type of marketing?	Pickleball shoe sales to existing customers referred by email and delivered from the e-commerce platform

Hypothesis and/or Benchmarks

How do we know whether it is successful?	We know whether it is successful if this month's sales of pickleball shoes outpace both last month's sales (MoM) as well as the same time last year (YoY)

Tests

What elements are being tested for further optimization?	We will test several elements (one at a time), including the subject lines of the email, send times, the imagery used in the email, and the landing page that customers are sent to once they click the call to action

Measurement Cadence

At what frequency will it be most beneficial to measure?	This will be measured weekly for the duration of the campaign, compared both Week over Week (WoW) as well as to the same week during the previous year

Step 4: Results & Analysis

Results

Using the metrics and measurement, what was achieved?	12,250 existing customers who received an email that is part of the campaign bought a total of 14,375 pairs of pickleball shoes

Performance

How do the results compare to previous periods and/or previous projections?	In the second week of the campaign, there was a 6.25% increase in sales WoW, and overall, 12.5% more pickleball shoes were sold to existing customers than during the same period last year

Analysis

What do the results and performance mean to both the marketing efforts and the business? Is more testing required? Are the goals being met or projected to be met soon? Is a different approach required?	While we are happy with the increase in results, we feel that with further testing, we can continue to increase the results. There is not enough YoY growth, particularly because we didn't run a specific campaign for pickleball shoes last year.

FIGURE 9.6. (Continued) The marketing measurement framework in action.

- Why could we achieve it, and do we believe it to be repeatable?
- Could we improve upon these results, and how?
- Are there circumstances that were particularly favorable (or unfavorable) that impacted our results?
- What would we like to test about this moving forward?

We will explore analysis further in the next section as well, so stay tuned for more insights on how to make the most of this step.

THE FRAMEWORK IN ACTION: PB SHOES

Let's return to our example company, PB Shoes, and look at this framework filled out. In the following table (Figure 9.6), you can see that we've gone through each of the steps and filled them out for a single objective related to our planned expansion of pickleball shoe sales.

CONCLUSION

Keep in mind that your specific circumstances may require you to approach a few of these steps differently. Whether or not you are focused on a single marketing channel, there may be some additional considerations.

Regardless, the marketing framework is flexible enough to handle from the largest needs to a small campaign or single-channel measurement.

With the rapid rise of AI tools and methods being used in marketing, it is important to understand how artificial intelligence can augment your marketing measurement framework. The next chapter will explore how you can start to incorporate AI into your measurement.

CHAPTER 10

INCORPORATING AI-BASED TOOLS AND METHODS

The integration of AI into marketing measurement marks a significant shift toward data-driven decision-making. AI's capacity to analyze vast datasets allows for more nuanced insights into customer behavior, campaign effectiveness, and overall marketing performance. Just a few of the potential applications are the following, many of which we'll explore in further depth in later chapters:

- *Predictive analytics*: Powered by AI, predictive analytics uses historical data to forecast future outcomes. In marketing measurement, these predictions can help anticipate changes in consumer behavior, demand for products or services, and the potential impact of marketing strategies. This foresight enables businesses to adapt their marketing efforts proactively, optimizing resources for maximum impact.
- *Customer segmentation*: AI enhances customer segmentation by analyzing behavioral data, purchase history, and engagement patterns at an unprecedented scale. These granular insights aid in identifying distinct customer groups, enabling marketers to tailor campaigns that resonate on a more personal level. Custom-tailored campaigns not only improve customer experience but also elevate the efficiency of marketing spend by targeting prospects with the highest conversion potential.
- *Media Mix Modeling (MMM)*: This is a statistical analysis technique that quantifies the impact of various marketing tactics on sales. Incorporating AI into MMM enables real-time data processing and a more agile response to market changes. AI algorithms can sift through and analyze the effects of multiple variables, from digital campaigns to offline events, providing a holistic view of marketing effectiveness.
- *Sentiment analysis*: This utilizes AI to process and analyze customer opinions, reviews, and social media conversations. Understanding sentiment not only reveals customer preferences but also gauges brand perception. By measuring sentiment, businesses can nip potential issues in the bud, enhance customer experience, and adjust strategies to align better with customer expectations.

ALIGNING AI TOOLS WITH YOUR MARKETING MEASUREMENT FRAMEWORK

Integrating AI tools without a strategic framework can lead to disjointed insights and missed opportunities. A structured approach to aligning AI within a marketing measurement framework ensures that every tool serves a clear purpose, contributing to overarching business objectives.

Define Objectives

It all starts with clear marketing objectives, and this applies whether you are incorporating AI-based tools or not. That said, understanding what you aim to achieve—whether it's increasing brand awareness, boosting sales, or enhancing customer loyalty—will guide the selection and implementation of AI tools and prevent costly changes down the road.

Without defining clear objectives upfront, you run the risk of being led by choosing AI-based tools that have interesting or novel features, rather than selecting those that are directly aligned with helping you achieve your goals.

Select Relevant AI Tools

When it comes to enhancing your marketing efforts through technology, the selection of the right AI tools is paramount. These tools should not just be advanced in their capabilities but, more importantly, must align with your specific marketing measurement needs. This precision in selection ensures that you are not merely collecting data but are gathering insightful information that can drive strategic decisions.

For those looking to leverage predictive analytics, there's a wealth of options available. Google Analytics, known for its robust tracking capabilities, offers predictive features that can forecast future customer behaviors based on historical data. Such predictions can be instrumental in anticipating market trends, customer churn rates, and potential revenue opportunities. Some scenarios, however, might require even more tailored solutions. In these instances, custom models built with machine learning platforms step in. By feeding these models with your unique datasets, they can uncover patterns and insights that off-the-shelf solutions might miss, offering a competitive edge that is precisely catered to your business's needs.

On the other hand, when the focus shifts toward understanding your customer base more granularly, AI-powered Customer Relationship Management (CRM) software becomes invaluable. Such platforms go beyond the traditional storage of customer contact information, evolving into sophisticated systems that can analyze customer interactions, segment audiences based on behavior, and even gauge customer sentiment toward your brand or products. The actionable data derived from these platforms enables marketers to craft highly targeted campaigns that resonate on a personal level with each segment, thereby increasing engagement and loyalty.

Knowing When an AI Tool Is Not the Right Fit

While the allure of AI in marketing is undeniable, it is crucial to recognize when an AI tool may not be relevant to your needs. This discernment is essential to avoid unnecessary expenditures on technology that doesn't add value to your marketing efforts. An AI tool might not be relevant if:

- *It does not integrate well with your existing marketing stack*, leading to fragmented data and insights.

- *Its capabilities are too generic* and don't provide the depth of analysis required for your specific marketing objectives.
- *The learning curve and operational overhead outweigh the potential benefits*, making it a resource-intensive option without offering proportional advantages.

To ensure you're leveraging the most suitable AI tools, start with a clear understanding of your marketing objectives and required outcomes. Investigate how each tool integrates with your current systems and whether it requires additional resources for operation and maintenance. Furthermore, closely monitor the performance and relevance of deployed AI tools, remaining open to making changes as your marketing goals evolve or as more advanced solutions become available.

Thus, the strategic selection and constant evaluation of AI tools in marketing are not just about harnessing advanced technology. It's about making informed, data-driven decisions that propel your marketing strategies forward in the most efficient and effective way possible.

Integrate and Implement

To seamlessly integrate AI tools into existing marketing measurement frameworks, organizations must undertake a series of strategic and operational steps. This process is both nuanced and multifaceted, involving careful consideration of the team's capabilities, the quality of the data being utilized, and the methodologies employed to ensure the evolution and refinement of these practices over time. Furthermore, it is critical to prioritize and uphold data privacy and ethical standards throughout the implementation and operation of AI technologies in marketing.

1. *Planning and strategy development*: The integration process begins with a solid plan that aligns AI tools with the organization's marketing goals and objectives. Understanding the specific outcomes you wish to achieve with AI will guide the selection of appropriate tools and technologies. This stage should involve a comprehensive assessment of the existing marketing measurement framework to identify areas where AI can add value.

2. *Team training and preparation*: For AI integration to be successful, it's imperative that the team managing and executing marketing campaigns is well versed in the use of selected AI tools. This involves not only technical training but also a shift in mindset to fully leverage AI capabilities. Training programs should cover data analysis, interpretation of AI-generated insights, and the effective use of these insights in strategic decision-making.

3. *Ensuring data quality*: The efficacy of AI in marketing heavily depends on the quality of the data fed into the system. Organizations must establish strict data management practices to ensure that the data is accurate, comprehensive, and timely. This involves regular data audits, cleaning processes, and the establishment of data governance policies to maintain the integrity of the data over time.

4. *Setting up processes for continuous learning and adjustment*: AI integration is not a set-and-forget solution. Continuous learning and iterative adjustment are integral to harnessing the full potential of AI in marketing measurement. Organizations should establish feedback loops that allow for the constant refining of AI models based on real-world outcomes and shifting marketing dynamics. This iterative process will enable the continuous enhancement of marketing strategies and campaigns.

5. *Maintaining data privacy and ethical standards*: With the increased reliance on AI and data analytics, safeguarding customer data privacy and adhering to ethical standards is more important than ever. Organizations must implement robust data privacy measures and ensure compliance with relevant regulations. This includes securing customer consent for data use, anonymizing data where possible, and implementing transparent AI operations that can be audited for accountability.

By meticulously planning the integration, preparing the team, ensuring data quality, setting up processes for continuous learning, and upholding high ethical standards, organizations can unlock the full potential of AI in their existing marketing measurement frameworks. This not only enhances the effectiveness of marketing campaigns but also ensures that operations are sustainable, ethically responsible, and aligned with the long-term objectives of the organization.

Measure and Optimize

Continuous measurement and optimization are key to leveraging AI in marketing. It's imperative for marketers to not solely rely on AI tools for the measurement of traditional metrics but also to assess the impact and effectiveness of AI implementations within their campaigns. This dual-focused approach ensures a comprehensive understanding of both conventional marketing outcomes and the innovative enhancements brought about by AI.

For instance, AI-powered analytics platforms can go beyond tracking basic metrics such as Clickthrough Rates (CTRs) and engagement levels. They are capable of providing deeper insights into customer behavior patterns, predictive analysis on future trends, and even sentiment analysis from social media engagements and customer feedback. These AI-driven insights enable marketers to not only see what happened but also understand why it happened and how it can inform future strategies.

Practically, this could involve using AI tools to perform A/B testing on different versions of a campaign to determine which performs better in real time, adjusting strategies promptly based on data-driven insights. AI can also help in optimizing email marketing campaigns, where it analyzes the best times of day to send emails, predicts subject lines that will result in higher open rates, and segments users into highly targeted groups for personalized marketing efforts.

Furthermore, AI plays a crucial role in content optimization. It can recommend changes to Web site content, test different Calls to Action (CTAs), and personalize the site experience for individual users to increase the likelihood of conversion. For example, if an AI tool identifies that visitors to a sports apparel Web site are most engaged with running gear in the spring, the site can dynamically highlight running shoes and attire during those months.

Regularly reviewing these AI-driven insights is critical. It allows marketers to adjust their strategies in alignment not only with the nuanced shifts in business goals but also with the dynamic changes in market dynamics. This iterative process of measuring, analyzing, and adjusting ensures that marketing efforts are perpetually refined and optimized for the highest possible efficacy and Return on Investment (ROI).

In essence, the integration of AI in marketing goes beyond automating tasks; it's about harnessing the power of machine learning and data analytics to make smarter, more informed decisions. By actively measuring both traditional metrics and the effectiveness of AI implementations, and routinely adjusting strategies based on these insights, businesses can ensure their marketing endeavors are consistently aligned with overarching goals and responsive to the evolving landscape of consumer behavior and market trends.

CASE STUDY: PB SHOES

PB Shoes, specializing in athletic footwear for pickleball enthusiasts, realized that in order to stay ahead in the competitive market, they needed to leverage AI-based tools for their marketing measurement initiatives. The company began by clearly defining their goals, understanding that a sharp focus was crucial to select the most relevant AI technologies.

Goal Definition

Their primary goal was to enhance customer engagement through personalized marketing. This meant diving into customer data to understand buying patterns and preferences. The secondary goal was to optimize their ad spend to increase the ROI while maintaining a strong brand presence across various channels. Lastly, they aimed to improve customer retention by identifying key factors that influenced repeat purchases.

Tool Selection

With these goals in place, PB Shoes sought out AI-based tools that could deliver on these specific fronts. For the first goal, they implemented an AI-driven recommendation engine that could analyze individual customer data and predict preferences, enabling personalized product suggestions on their e-commerce platform. To address the second goal of optimizing ad spend, they adopted an AI tool designed for marketing mix modeling, which could assess the effectiveness of different marketing channels and reallocate budgets in real time for maximum impact. To support the third goal, they utilized a customer data platform with AI capabilities to segment customers based on predicted lifetime value, thus identifying and targeting high-value customers for retention campaigns.

Results

By aligning their tool selection with clear, defined goals, PB Shoes was able to not only select AI tools that were fit for purpose but also measure their success effectively. The recommendation engine led to a 25% increase in customer engagement, as reflected in longer session times and higher CTRs on personalized content. The marketing mix tool provided insights that resulted in a 15% increase in ROI from digital ad campaigns. The AI-enhanced customer segmentation contributed to a 10% improvement in retention rates within 6 months.

PB Shoes' experience exemplifies how clearly defined goals are essential in choosing the right AI-based tools for marketing measurement. By starting with specific objectives, the company could sift through the plethora of available AI technologies and pinpoint the ones that would truly drive their marketing strategy forward. This careful selection process, guided by strategic goals, enabled PB Shoes to harness the power of AI effectively, translating into measurable success in their marketing initiatives.

CONCLUSION

The integration of AI into marketing measurement represents a monumental leap forward in how businesses understand and engage with their markets. The true power of AI, however, lies not just in its technological capabilities but in its strategic alignment within a marketing measurement framework. By meticulously integrating AI tools that complement and enhance traditional measurement techniques, businesses can unlock deeper insights, drive more targeted strategies, and ultimately achieve a significant competitive advantage in the digital age.

Part 2 Recap Quiz

Welcome to the end of the second section. Check that you've mastered the ideas we've covered in this section by answering the three questions here. To check your answers, refer to Appendix B, which lists all of the answers for the quizzes in the book.

Let's look at three questions on the content in Part 2.

Question 1
True or false: Alignment of metrics and KPIs to the strategy and goals of the business is a key reason to invest in a marketing measurement framework.

Question 2
Which of the following are reasons an AI tool may not be a good fit for your marketing measurement framework? Choose all that apply:
a) It does not integrate well with your existing marketing stack, leading to fragmented data and insights
b) Its capabilities are too specific to your needs, and it doesn't provide generic functionality you may need at some point in the future
c) The learning curve and operational overhead outweigh the potential benefits, making it a resource-intensive option without offering proportional advantages
d) a and c
e) All of the above

Question 3
True or false: The fourth step in our Marketing Measurement Framework (MMF)—results and analysis—is where we set our business goals and KPIs.

PART 3: DATA COLLECTION

Effective measurement provides you with the insights you need to understand what is working and what is not and to allocate your marketing budget to maximize your Return on Investment (ROI). That measurement, however, requires that the right data is in place.

Without effective measurement, it is difficult to know whether your marketing efforts are having the desired impact, and you may be wasting resources on campaigns and channels that are not delivering results. Effective measurement also helps you demonstrate your marketing efforts' value to stakeholders, such as senior management or the board of directors.

WHY DATA COLLECTION MATTERS

Data collection is the bedrock of marketing measurement and analytics. It involves systematically gathering information about market conditions, customer behaviors, and the effectiveness of marketing strategies. This data is crucial because it forms the foundation upon which all analytical activities rest. Without accurate and comprehensive data, any conclusions or insights derived are likely to be flawed or misleading. For marketers, robust data collection ensures that decisions are made on a solid factual basis, enhancing both the effectiveness and efficiency of marketing strategies.

Enabling Precision in Targeting and Personalization

The more precise the data, the more targeted and personalized marketing efforts can be. Consumers expect marketing messages to be relevant and tailored to their preferences and behaviors. Detailed data collection allows marketers to understand their audience at a granular level—tracking everything from basic demographic information to complex interaction patterns across multiple channels. This deep understanding enables marketers to create highly personalized customer experiences, which can significantly improve engagement rates, customer satisfaction, and, ultimately, conversion rates.

Facilitating Strategic Decision-Making

Data collection also plays a pivotal role in strategic decision-making. With comprehensive data, marketers can identify trends, forecast future behaviors, and assess the competitive landscape. This information is invaluable for developing strategic initiatives that are proactive rather than reactive.

For example, by analyzing customer feedback and sales data, a company can identify emerging trends in customer preferences and adjust their product offerings accordingly before their competitors do, gaining a crucial market advantage.

Improving ROI and Accountability

Furthermore, effective data collection enhances the ROI and accountability in marketing campaigns. By meticulously tracking which strategies drive customer actions, marketers can allocate resources to the most effective tactics, thereby maximizing the ROI.

Accountability is also heightened as data provides a clear trail of evidence to evaluate the performance of each campaign. Marketing teams can justify their budget requests and demonstrate the tangible benefits of their work, fostering greater transparency and trust with stakeholders.

EXPLORING DATA COLLECTION

Now that we've explored how to align our marketing measurements to business goals in the preceding parts of the book, let's begin with this section of the book on ensuring data collection is in place.

Here is what we'll cover in this part:

- Determining what data is needed to measure your metrics
- What to think about when measuring on a single marketing channel, or across multiple channels
- Creating a sustainable approach to data collection
- AI-based methods to collect data and augment your existing data collection

Upon finishing this part of the book, you will have a better understanding of when different types of data can be the most beneficial and best practices for collecting them to support your marketing, measurement, and analysis efforts.

CHAPTER 11

DETERMINING WHAT DATA IS NEEDED

The analysis and optimization of marketing campaigns and initiatives are more successful when the corresponding data is collected. This requires planning before measurement ever begins.

Now that we've looked at how to measure our marketing channels and efforts effectively, we need to ensure that we are capturing the right data and other information to make our measurements accurate and meaningful. Let's look at a way to categorize our data types (Figure 11.1) to ensure we aren't missing any crucial information.

Types of Data

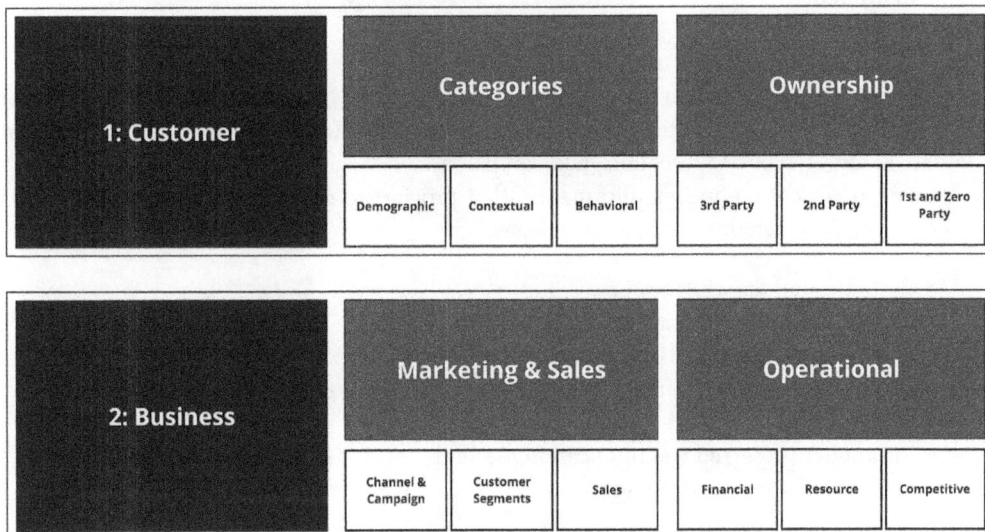

FIGURE 11.1. Types of data.

As you can see, we're going to look at two main categories of data: customer and business. Then, we'll break down each to better understand what is relevant and when they are needed to assist your marketing measurement.

THE TYPES OF DATA

We will need to collect several types of data to report on and analyze our marketing efforts effectively. Let's explore these types of marketing data.

Customer Data

First, we'll look at the categories of customer data, which help you identify individuals and their preferences and can assist you with personalizing their experience or understanding their individual buyer's journey. This is also where we get into the very important aspect of data ownership: who owns the information about your customers?

Categories

Demographic information consists of an array of applicable socioeconomic information, including (but not limited to):

- Age
- Gender
- Ethnicity
- Income
- Employment status
- Home ownership
- Internet access

When to Use It

Demographic information can be helpful when grouping individuals based on common characteristics, location, or potential priorities. Audience segmentation is often based on demographics, as are targeted offers, discounts, and campaigns.

Contextual data comprises information that provides perspective into a customer or their experience. This includes information such as:

- Customer intent (why they are calling)
- Last item purchased (and/or date of last purchase)
- Personal information (name, email, and address)
- Date of last customer service call (and whether it was resolved or not)
- Time on hold
- Customer's preferred communication method
- Attitudes about your company
- Last Web page viewed
- Last email opened or received

To be most effective, contextual data needs to be combined from multiple data points and touchpoints.

When to Use It

Contextual data is helpful when understanding either where a customer currently is (e.g., a Web page or a brick-and-mortar location) or what they have done (e.g., what types of products they have already purchased, if they just lodged a customer service request, or the last time they interacted with your company).

Behavioral data is data collected from a customer's intentional interactions and engagements with your company from the many channels you are listening from. This can include events such as:

- Website or mobile app interactions and where a user clicked, viewed, and converted
- Email sign-ups, opens, and clicks
- Subscription renewals
- In-store visits and purchases
- Customer service requests

Behavioral data is most useful when tied to a specific individual and the channel they were using (e.g., Web site, mobile app, call center, etc.). Behavioral data often feeds contextual data as well.

When to Use It

Behavioral data helps a company to understand the actions of an individual and their responses to specific campaigns and offers or other external events.

Ownership

These categories of data ownership are determined by their relationship to the company, how the information is collected, and the entity or "party" that can claim ownership over it.

Third-party data is not directly collected or owned by your company. It is data that an aggregator collects from various sources and sells as a package to augment an existing dataset or stand on its own.

- It may include anything from demographic to contextual and behavioral data.
- Traditionally, it has been used heavily in advertising segmentation and with Data Management Platforms (DMPs).

When to Use It

Third-party data is helpful to augment and enrich your existing customer data as long as you are using reliable sources of third-party information.

We're going to discuss this in a little more detail. Some of the challenges with third-party data include a lack of reliability and sometimes questionable methods of collection that can put at risk the privacy of consumers' information.

Second-party data is from channels you have a presence on but don't directly own, such as your company's social media profiles.

- It isn't owned directly by your company.
- Your company has the capability of using it within the bounds of the platform's capabilities and applicable regulations.

Second-party data can be defined as another organization's first-party data, as they gather it directly from their audience.

When to Use It

Second-party data is helpful to have access to because it is provided from a platform that customers generally both trust and interact with on a daily or weekly basis, which might be more frequent than they interact with your company's channels on average. Customers may also share more information with these sources than they would directly share with your company.

First-party data is information about your audience that you collect directly from their behaviors and interactions. It is often behavioral, as it is collected as a customer is taking actions such as signing up for emails, purchasing products, clicking on ads or emails, or other behaviors you can track, and can include a number of things:

- One example is data that your company owns because it is collected on something that you govern and manage data collection within.
- While data collection and governance must follow local regulations and legislative requirements, first-party data can be used by your company.

When to Use It

First-party data is critical to any marketer's work because it is directly gleaned from your customers' interactions with what you own, whether online or offline. Thus, first-party data is useful in many applications across a marketer's responsibilities.

Zero-party data is similar to first-party data in that your company directly owns it, but there are some key distinctions. The main distinction here is that this is information that a customer has intentionally provided rather than (in the case of first-party data) collected by a company based on a customer's behavior that is collected indirectly. Zero-party data can include:

- Information submitted in forms
- Survey answers
- Any other information individual customers explicitly provide to companies

Zero-party data is often demographic, though specifically communicating intent could be considered behavioral.

When to Use It

Similar to first-party data, zero-party data has broad applications across the work of marketing, advertising, and customer experience, and it has the added benefit of being explicitly provided to your company by your customers.

An Example: PB Shoes and Customer Data Ownership

All of these types of data and ownership can get a little convoluted. To make it easier, look at the following table (Table 11.1) to see a few examples of the types of data that PB Shoes uses and collects and what categories they fit within.

TABLE 11.1. An example of types of data by ownership type.

Type of Data	Examples	Definition
Third Party	A set of customer data acquired by a data broker	Third-party data is information collected and often sold by parties not directly affiliated with the customers whose information they have or the buyers of that information.
Third Party	Customer data for a list of potential customers who have been known to visit pickleball-related Web sites	This is an example of third-party data, where often large lists of consumer data with related interests are sold to interested parties.
Second Party	A customer's Facebook comments on PB Shoes products who posted on PB Shoes' profile on that channel	Second-party data is information a trusted party collects about its users that a company such as PB Shoes can access to a limited degree.
First Party	The last page on the PB Shoes Web site that a particular customer visited	First-party data is information a company measures and can collect about what its customers do and how they behave. Website interactions are a great example of this.
First Party	Information about the retail location a customer bought their last pair of PB Shoes at	First-party data isn't just relegated to digital interactions. Brands can also track when a customer visits and purchases from a brick-and-mortar store.
Zero Party	A customer's occupation as filled out in a form on the PB Shoes Web site	Remember, anything a customer intentionally fills out and submits to a company is considered zero-party data.

Business Data

This brings us to what we will refer to as business data, or the types of information that are related directly to the business, as opposed to data directly collected from or related to an individual customer.

Marketing and Sales

First, there is *channel and campaign data*, which is collected directly from various marketing channels, such as email, Web site, mobile app, in-store promotions, and advertising, or from an advertising or marketing campaign across one or more channels. This is critical for:

- Understanding the performance of a single marketing channel in the context of a larger campaign or simply as compared to the same channel during a previous period
- Understanding the performance of a campaign across one or more channels and one or more audience segments

Next, we have *customer segment data*, which looks at similar customer groups to identify areas of opportunity or challenges across groups with similar characteristics. This helps companies:

- Create tailored offers to customers who share similar interests and motivations.
- Better understand trends among customers who share similar backgrounds, product purchase behavior, or other similarities.

Finally, in the marketing and sales category, we have *sales data*, which helps us close the loop in an understanding that marketing has on acquiring new customers and retaining existing ones. In other words, in order to confirm a conversion, we often need to know that a purchase was made and fulfilled. Sales data helps us understand this.

Operational

The second category of business data is operational data, or information about the business that helps provide greater context for marketing performance and helps to paint a bigger picture of marketing's impact on the business itself.

First, we have *financial data*, which consists of revenue projections and actual numbers, plus profits and losses, and other information that helps marketers understand their efforts' impact on the bottom line. This data helps calculate customer lifetime value, can help you project revenue through a campaign over time, and more.

Then, we have *resource data*, which includes the internal time and costs associated with delivering sales or marketing. This can include everything from the cost of placing media for your advertising campaigns to the time it takes to create a new campaign or update content on a single channel. Resource data helps marketers create more realistic predictions and assessments about the value generated by their work.

Finally, we have *competitive data*, which consists of information obtained about the industries you compete in or publicly available information about competitors in your space. This information can be used to set benchmarks and to determine at a high level how your channels or campaigns are performing in the context of other companies that are doing similar work.

DETERMINING WHAT DATA IS NEEDED

So, how do we determine what we need? Trying to look at all that every time we measure is simply too much.

To do this, we can start with a few questions about our data that can help us prioritize what to look at. Remember that even though more data may *seem* like it is always a good thing, there is a cost to collecting, reporting on, and analyzing each new piece of information, whether that is the time to integrate systems, set up reports, or the effort needed to analyze a particular set of information. So, we want to limit our questions to the areas that will help us focus on data that will impact our work most.

You should ask whether the data is directly aligned to:

- The KPIs
- The channel
- The campaign
- The audience
- The work being done

It is often also helpful to design or mock up the report(s) that you want to use to analyze and share information about your marketing performance because it can often highlight the most useful information to have versus that which might simply be "nice to have."

The Data Collection Infrastructure

Effective marketing requires a strong infrastructure to collect and analyze data. One of the key components of this infrastructure is a Customer Data Platform (CDP), a technology platform that collects and manages customer data from various sources, such as Web sites, social media, and mobile apps.

CDPs allow marketers to create a unified view of their customers, which can be used to personalize and target their marketing efforts. Another important component is the analytics tools of each digital channel itself, or broader analytics tools collecting information from multiple channels, which are used to track and measure the performance of marketing campaigns. These tools can provide insights into customer behavior, such as Web site traffic, engagement, and conversion rates, and can be used to optimize campaigns and make data-driven decisions. Finally, Customer Relationship Management (CRM) systems are also important for collecting and managing customer data. CRM systems can be used to store customer information, track interactions, and manage customer relationships over time. By combining CDPs, analytics tools, and CRM systems, businesses can effectively collect and analyze marketing data to improve their marketing efforts.

Collecting vs Reporting

A note on "collecting" versus "reporting on": don't worry if the platforms you use collect a lot of information automatically. The key distinction to make is whether the data either requires time to integrate or will require a lot of effort to collect or analyze when it isn't directly related to the work at hand.

If, however, the data will be helpful in the long term and might be useful in the future to analyze, then it is fine to collect it. Just don't feel the need to report on every bit of data you collect in that case.

CONCLUSION

It is important to understand the different types of data you collect as a marketer because different types of data provide different insights and are suited to different purposes. By understanding the different types of data available, you can make more informed decisions about which data to collect, how to collect it, and how to use it to improve your marketing efforts.

With an understanding of the types of data in hand, the next chapter will now look at how to approach collecting those types of data in both single- and multi-channel scenarios.

CHAPTER 12

SINGLE- AND MULTI-CHANNEL DATA COLLECTION

N ow that we've explored the many types of data and how they can potentially fit into your marketing measurement, let's take a look at it on the channel level. We will do this in a channel-agnostic way; in other words, you should be able to apply these principles no matter the channel(s) you might be responsible for, whether it is a Web site, an email campaign, digital advertising, social media, or any other type of marketing effort.

SINGLE-CHANNEL MARKETING DATA COLLECTION

Single-channel marketing data collection is the process of gathering and analyzing data from one specific marketing channel, such as email campaigns, social media, search engine marketing, or a Web site. The focus here is on collecting insights related solely to the performance and customer interactions on that particular channel. For instance, if a marketer is running an email campaign, they may track metrics such as open rates, clickthrough rates, bounce rates, and conversions, all within the context of email performance.

As explored earlier in Chapter 5, some of the benefits of single-channel measurement are:

- It can often be easier to measure a single channel rather than reconcile or aggregate numbers from multiple channels.
- Analytics and reporting are often (for digital channels) built natively into the platforms themselves, which can simplify getting a quick view.
- A single channel can often be integrated into a more robust reporting tool more easily than multiple channels.

The simplicity of focusing on a single channel can be advantageous in certain situations. It allows marketers to gain deep insights into how one channel is performing and isolate variables that may be affecting its success. The limitation of this approach, however, is that it fails to capture the customer's entire journey, especially when consumers interact with multiple channels before making a purchase decision. For example, a customer might first see a product on social media, engage with it through an email, and then make a final purchase through the Web site. Single-channel data collection would miss these multi-touch interactions.

Challenges of Single-Channel Data Collection

One of the biggest challenges in single-channel marketing data collection is the risk of myopic analysis. Since the focus is exclusively on one channel, marketers might attribute too much importance to specific metrics within that channel without understanding how it fits into the broader customer journey. For instance, a campaign with high clickthrough rates on social media might not necessarily lead to conversions if the Web site landing page isn't optimized. A sole focus on social media performance metrics could create a false sense of success if Web site data is not considered.

Another challenge involves attribution. In a single-channel data collection strategy, it is difficult to determine the impact that other channels might have on the final result. If a customer both received an email and saw a display ad, attributing the conversion to the email alone can distort the overall effectiveness of that campaign. Without a holistic view, it becomes difficult to assign credit accurately, leading to suboptimal decision-making.

Data fragmentation is another potential pitfall. In single-channel data collection, it's harder to maintain a unified view of the customer. Each channel might provide its own set of data, but none offer the full picture. For example, a retail company may collect customer data from in-store visits but miss out on valuable online behavior that indicates product preferences or browsing habits. In such cases, decisions based on fragmented data may lead to misguided strategies that don't reflect true customer needs.

Some additional things to consider would be:

- How do you receive updates for results from the marketing channel? Is it automated? Are you relying on a third party to provide them, or do you have direct access to a tool or platform to get them yourself?
- Are you able to export the data you need to any other reporting tools or methods to visualize your channel's performance with the rest of your organization's marketing efforts?
- Is your channel a first-touch or last-touch part of the customer journey, or are you missing out on attribution opportunities?

Single-channel marketing data collection and measurement isn't good or bad, and sometimes it is necessary, regardless of whether it tells the full story or not. So consider the preceding for the best chance of success in your measurement activities.

That said, marketers need to recognize that relying on a single marketing channel for measurement can present significant challenges in understanding the full picture of a customer's multi-channel journey. To overcome these challenges, we need to invest in technology that can track customers across all channels and devices, understand how customers interact with each channel, use a multi-touch attribution model that can give credit to all channels that contributed to the conversion, identify areas of opportunity to optimize our marketing mix and maximize impact, and capture the full impact of our marketing efforts over time. By doing so, we can gain insights into the behaviors of our customers and drive marketing strategies that truly engage and connect with them.

DATA COLLECTION IN A MULTI-CHANNEL WORLD

Unlike single-channel data collection, multi-channel marketing data collection aggregates data from various touchpoints, including email, social media, Web sites, and paid ads. This provides a more comprehensive view of the customer journey, allowing marketers to understand how different channels work together to influence consumer behavior. In a multi-channel strategy, marketers track metrics such as cross-channel engagement, the sequence of interactions, and attribution across all platforms. This more holistic approach enables a more accurate measurement of how different channels contribute to conversions.

For example, a consumer might receive a promotional email, visit the Web site, and then finally make a purchase after seeing a retargeting ad on social media. A multi-channel data collection approach would capture this journey, allowing marketers to understand how each channel played a role in moving the consumer closer to conversion. This data can then inform future marketing strategies by identifying the most impactful touchpoints.

Single-channel data collection, while offering a focused approach to understanding a particular marketing channel, presents several challenges. It can lead to siloed insights, inaccurate attribution, and a fragmented understanding of the customer journey. By contrast, multi-channel data collection provides a more integrated view of customer interactions, making it easier to see how different touchpoints influence one another. Marketers should be mindful of these challenges and consider how their single-channel insights fit into the broader marketing ecosystem to optimize their strategies.

Thus, marketing in today's omnichannel, channel-switching world is more complex than ever, with customers' use of multiple channels to research, buy, and engage with brands the norm, not the exception. How does a single marketing channel fit into a larger multi-channel marketing mix, though, and why is it important?

Let's explore how a single channel fits into a sophisticated multi-channel marketing campaign, its contribution to multi-touch attribution, and how marketers should consider its contribution.

Understand Each Channel's Unique Contribution to the Customer Experience

Marketing today goes far beyond selling a product or service—it is about creating a cohesive and engaging customer experience that resonates with the target audience. In a world where customers are inundated with touchpoints from various channels, each one plays a specific role in shaping how consumers perceive and interact with a brand. To create a successful multi-channel campaign, marketers need to understand the unique contribution that each channel makes to the overall customer experience.

For example, email marketing is often a highly targeted channel that is used to nurture relationships, provide personalized offers, and re-engage customers who have already shown interest in a product or service. In contrast, a channel such as paid search is typically more transactional in nature, as it reaches consumers who are already actively searching for a solution to their needs. Social media might play a more passive role, focusing on brand awareness, engagement, and building long-term relationships with the audience. Each channel serves a distinct purpose, but when combined effectively, they contribute to a comprehensive customer journey that moves consumers closer to a purchase decision.

As an illustration of this, our hypothetical PB Shoes uses social media to introduce new product lines and build community engagement around the sport. Simultaneously, they run paid search ads targeting specific keywords such as "best shoes for pickleball players." Email marketing is then used to nurture relationships with customers who have expressed interest by offering them exclusive discounts and product recommendations based on their browsing behavior.

While each channel serves its own purpose, the combination of these touchpoints creates a seamless and comprehensive customer experience that leads to conversion.

Understanding the unique contribution of each channel also means recognizing that no single channel can carry the weight of a campaign alone. A brand might see significant traffic from social media, but without a strong Web site experience or compelling email follow-up, those social engagements may not lead to conversions. Similarly, a highly effective paid search campaign could generate new leads, but if the brand is absent on social media or lacks an engaging content strategy, it might struggle to build long-term loyalty with those leads.

Another key aspect of understanding channel contributions is recognizing how consumers move between channels throughout their journey. A customer might first learn about PB Shoes on Instagram, where they see an influencer wearing the shoes. Later, they might visit the PB Shoes Web site through a paid search ad to learn more about the product. Finally, they may receive an email with a promotional code that prompts them to make a purchase. Each channel in this scenario contributes something unique: social media builds awareness, paid search captures intent, and email drives conversion.

While a single marketing channel can have a significant impact, its role should be viewed in the context of the broader multi-channel strategy. Marketers must understand how each channel contributes to the overall customer experience and tailor their campaigns accordingly. By doing so, they can create a seamless, engaging, and valuable journey that aligns with consumer behavior and drives better results. For PB Shoes, this might mean continually optimizing the touchpoints at each stage of the journey, ensuring that every channel plays its part in moving customers closer to purchase.

Understand Each Channel's Contribution to a Conversion

For marketers working in a multi-channel environment, no single channel operates in isolation, as each serves as a piece of the larger puzzle, contributing in different ways to moving a customer from awareness to conversion. Multi-touch attribution is a powerful method that helps marketers understand how each channel and touchpoint plays a role in the customer's journey. Rather than focusing solely on the last touchpoint that resulted in a sale, multi-touch attribution assigns credit to all the interactions a customer had with the brand, providing a more holistic view of the marketing ecosystem.

MTA allows marketers to see how multiple channels work together to influence a customer's decision. For instance, a customer might first encounter a brand through a social media ad, then receive a promotional email, and later click on a paid search ad before making a purchase. Without multi-touch attribution, marketers might only credit the paid search ad with the conversion, overlooking the critical role that social media and email played in nurturing the customer throughout their journey. By understanding each channel's contribution, marketers can make better decisions about resource allocation and campaign optimization.

In the case of PB Shoes, they might run campaigns across several channels—social media, email, and paid search. Through multi-touch attribution, PB Shoes could analyze the entire customer journey and discover that while email marketing only directly contributes to a small percentage of sales, it plays a pivotal role in nurturing leads. For example, social media ads may be responsible for initial customer engagement, while follow-up emails provide product recommendations and exclusive discounts that nudge customers closer to a purchase. In this case, the role of email marketing, though not always directly linked to the final conversion, is vital to keeping potential customers engaged.

This level of analysis allows marketers to optimize campaigns more effectively. If PB Shoes finds that email plays a crucial role in educating and converting customers after their initial engagement through other channels, they can allocate more resources to optimizing email content, improving segmentation, and creating personalized messaging. Similarly, if the company sees that paid search ads are frequently the last touchpoint before conversion, they can refine the keywords and ad copy to ensure they resonate with users who are ready to purchase.

Another benefit of understanding each channel's contribution to a conversion is that it helps marketers tailor content and messaging to align with the customer's stage in the buying process. For instance, a prospect might interact with a brand's social media content early in their journey but later need more specific product information via email to make a decision. PB Shoes could create an email campaign that includes testimonials, product reviews, and case studies to address common questions or concerns raised by customers after initial engagement.

Understanding the contribution of each marketing channel to a conversion is essential for building a more cohesive, effective marketing strategy. MTA provides a detailed map of the customer journey, helping marketers see how different touchpoints influence consumer behavior. For a company such as PB Shoes, this means optimizing each channel's role—whether it's social media for awareness, email for nurturing, or paid search for final conversions—to create a seamless experience that drives better results across the entire marketing ecosystem.

Understand Which Channels Are Most Critical to Marketing Efforts and Which Are Not

In a multi-channel marketing strategy, not all channels carry equal weight. The importance of each channel depends largely on the campaign's objectives and the specific stage of the customer journey being targeted. Selecting the most appropriate channels is essential for ensuring that the marketing efforts are both efficient and effective. By focusing on the right channels for the right goals, marketers can optimize their resources and drive better results.

For example, if PB Shoes wants to increase brand awareness, they might focus on channels such as Search Engine Optimization (SEO), content marketing, and social media. These channels are effective at generating organic visibility and reaching a broader audience. SEO allows PB Shoes to appear in relevant search queries, while content marketing—through blogs, videos, and educational materials—helps position the brand as an authority in the niche of pickleball shoes. Social media, on the other hand, provides a platform to engage with customers and build a community around the brand.

If the goal of the campaign, however, is to generate leads or drive direct sales, PB Shoes would likely prioritize channels such as Pay-per-Click (PPC) advertising and email marketing. These channels are more performance-driven and targeted, making them suitable for reaching customers who are closer to making a purchase decision. PPC ads can capture consumers who are already searching for pickleball shoes or related products, while email marketing can nurture leads by offering personalized content, promotions, or exclusive offers based on customer behavior.

Each channel brings its own strengths and limitations. SEO, for instance, is highly effective in driving long-term, organic traffic, but it requires time and consistent effort to build. PPC, on the other hand, can deliver immediate results but at a higher cost, as every click incurs a fee.

Similarly, social media can be excellent for engagement and building brand loyalty but may struggle to drive direct conversions without a well-structured advertising strategy. Recognizing these nuances allows marketers to deploy each channel where it can provide the most value.

Using the right tool for the job, rather than simply relying on the tools that are most accessible, is a critical mindset shift for marketers. Too often, teams default to channels they are comfortable with, even if those channels may not be the most effective for achieving their objectives. For PB Shoes, understanding when to use SEO to build a long-term organic presence versus when to ramp up PPC campaigns to meet short-term sales goals is crucial for maximizing the Return on Investment (ROI) from each channel.

Finally, tracking and measuring the performance of each channel helps marketers understand which channels are truly critical to their marketing efforts. Data-driven insights can reveal which touchpoints are driving the most value and which ones may be underperforming. For instance, PB Shoes may discover that while social media engagement is high, it is not translating into conversions. In this case, the team may choose to allocate more resources to email marketing or paid search, where conversion rates are higher.

Thus, understanding which channels are most critical to your marketing efforts requires a clear grasp of the campaign's goals, the customer journey, and each channel's strengths and limitations. For a company such as our hypothetical PB Shoes example, this understanding translates to selecting the right combination of channels to drive brand awareness, lead generation, or direct sales, depending on their objectives. By using the right tools for the right job, they can create more targeted, effective campaigns that lead to better overall performance.

CONCLUSION

The success of a multi-channel marketing campaign depends on many factors, but one of the most important is the ability to measure and analyze the effectiveness of each channel. To do this, marketers need access to reliable data that can track the customer journey across all touchpoints. Without this data, it's impossible to determine which channels are driving conversions and which are not. By understanding how a single channel fits into a larger marketing mix, marketers can gain greater insights into their target audience and create more effective campaigns.

Marketing is not a one-dimensional discipline, nor has it ever been, and this is only growing more complex. Multiple channels are available to reach potential customers, and understanding how a single channel fits into a larger multi-channel marketing mix is crucial for success. By considering the contribution of each channel to the customer journey, utilizing multi-touch attribution, and selecting the right channels based on the desired outcomes, marketers can create more effective campaigns that drive conversions and increase revenue. The future of marketing is multi-channel—and omnichannel, even.

The next chapter will look at how to turn the data collection methods we've discussed in this chapter into a sustainable collection plan that can yield consistent results.

CHAPTER 13

CREATING A SUSTAINABLE DATA COLLECTION PLAN

I t is important to have a sustainable marketing data collection plan because it ensures that the data you collect is collected in a way that is ethical, responsible, and respectful of the privacy of your customers and other stakeholders. A sustainable data collection plan also helps ensure that the data you collect is accurate, reliable, and representative of your target audience, which is essential for making informed marketing decisions.

Additionally, sustainable data collection practices can help build trust and loyalty among your customers, as they are more likely to share their data with you if they feel that their privacy is being respected and that their data is being used responsibly and ethically. This, in turn, can help to improve the effectiveness of your marketing efforts and increase the ROI of your marketing budget.

There are several components to a sustainable data collection plan, including those influenced by external and internal factors. Let's start by talking about the external climate related to data collection, data privacy, and more.

THE CHANGING DATA PRIVACY LANDSCAPE

Data privacy has become a hot issue in today's digital marketing world. With the increasing number of high-profile data breaches—41.6 million accounts were leaked in the first quarter of 2023 alone[1]—and the growing concerns of consumers about how their data is being used, businesses need to be fully aware of the evolving data privacy landscape. From new privacy laws to an industry shift away from the usage of third-party Web browser cookies, marketers need to be well prepared and proactive to avoid legal or reputational risks.

Increasing Consumer Data Privacy Laws

One of the most significant changes in the data privacy landscape is the implementation of new regulations worldwide. The European Union enacted the General Data Protection Regulation (GDPR) in 2018[2], which has influenced a lot of legislation in other parts of the world, including the California Consumer Privacy Act (CCPA)[3] and the Brazilian General Data Protection Law (LGPD)[4].

Consumer data privacy laws such as GDPR came into existence as a response to growing concerns about how personal data was being collected, used, and shared by companies, particularly in the digital age. As technology advanced and more personal information became available online, incidents of data misuse and breaches became increasingly common. High-profile scandals, such as the Facebook-Cambridge Analytica incident[5], demonstrated the extent to which personal data could be exploited without the knowledge or consent of users, raising alarms about privacy and the need for stronger legal protections. Public demand for greater transparency and accountability in how companies handled personal data fueled the push for regulatory action.

GDPR set a new global standard for data privacy laws. It was designed to give consumers more control over their personal data, requiring companies to obtain explicit consent before collecting or processing information. The regulation also introduced strict penalties for non-compliance, compelling organizations to take data privacy seriously or face substantial fines. Additionally, GDPR established the right for individuals to access, correct, and delete their personal data, addressing a long-standing imbalance where companies had significant power over users' information.

Ultimately, laws such as GDPR emerged to address the increasing complexity of data ecosystems and the potential risks associated with unregulated data collection. By establishing clear guidelines and enforcing accountability, these laws aim to protect consumer rights in an era where data is an immensely valuable commodity. They also reflect the growing recognition that personal data is not just a business asset but a fundamental aspect of individual privacy and autonomy.

These laws require companies to obtain valid consent for data collection, allow consumers the right to access and delete their data, and be transparent about data processing. Marketers need to ensure that their data collection and storage practices comply with these regulations, or they risk facing hefty fines, lawsuits, and reputational damage.

Third-Party Cookie Deprecation

Third-party cookies are small pieces of data stored in a user's Web browser by a domain other than the one they are currently visiting. These cookies are typically used by advertisers and analytics platforms to track user behavior across different Web sites. For instance, if a user visits a Web site that displays ads served by an external advertising network, that network can place a third-party cookie in the user's browser. This allows the network to track the user's activity across various Web sites, building a detailed profile of their preferences and behavior, which advertisers can use to deliver targeted ads.

Third-party cookies have become a fundamental tool for online advertising, enabling marketers to deliver personalized ads, retarget users, and measure the effectiveness of their campaigns. They have, however, also raised significant privacy concerns, as many users are unaware that their browsing activity is being tracked across multiple Web sites. This has led to increased regulatory scrutiny and a shift in the industry, with major browsers such as Google Chrome and Apple's Safari taking steps to minimize or remove these cookies and their prevalence on the Web.

Google had originally announced that by 2024[6], it would stop supporting third-party cookies on its popular Chrome browser (the deadline has been revised several times since[7]). This statement has been revised as of July 2024 to reflect a shift away from full deprecation and towards a stance of providing greater access for consumers to choose to allow or disallow them[8]. This move has ignited concerns among marketers as cookies are essential for tracking user behavior, optimizing advertising campaigns, and retargeting.

In response, many ad tech companies are developing alternatives, including contextual advertising, device fingerprinting, and privacy-centric identifiers. Marketers, however, need to shift their strategies toward creating first-party data, which involves collecting data directly from their customers through consent-driven tactics, such as surveys, sign-ups, and preference centers.

Creating a First-Party Data Strategy

It should be noted that there is value in creating a first-party data strategy regardless of whether or not third-party data sources and browser cookies are allowed even in the longer term.

As discussed in greater detail in Chapter 11, first-party data is data that companies gather directly from their customers or prospects. By owning first-party data, marketers can understand their audience more effectively, tailor their campaigns based on individual preferences, and build long-term customer relationships. It is, however, essential to keep in mind data privacy concerns when collecting first-party data. Marketers need to be transparent about what data they're collecting, why they're collecting it, and how they are using it. They should also provide customers with clear options to opt out or manage their data preferences.

Data privacy is becoming an increasingly critical issue for marketers, and staying up to date with the changing landscape is essential. As governments across the world introduce new regulations and Google and others shift away from third-party cookies, marketers need to be proactive in protecting consumer data while still delivering effective marketing campaigns. Businesses can build more remarkable customer relationships and gain a competitive edge by implementing a first-party data strategy that balances data collection with transparency and consumer consent.

INTERNAL CHALLENGES AND OPPORTUNITIES

Now, let's turn our attention to internal obstacles and opportunities for data collection and utilization.

Collecting data is likely an essential part of your job as a marketer whether it is explicitly stated in your job description or not. With technology and regulations constantly evolving, however, it's imperative to future-proof your marketing data collection approach. By doing so, you can ensure your data is accurate, compliant with regulations, and provides valuable insights you can use to optimize your marketing strategy.

Future-Proofing Your Data Collection Approach

Let's explore four key strategies every marketer should know to future-proof their marketing data collection approach. These strategies include planning for new marketing channels or changes to existing ones, new types of data required to create better reporting, new data privacy regulations, and greater incorporation of Artificial Intelligence (AI) and Machine Learning (ML) tools.

Planning for New Marketing Channels or Changes to Existing Ones

Technology changes and consumer trends mean new marketing channels are constantly emerging, and existing channels can change quickly. To future-proof your marketing data collection approach, plan to adapt to these changes by building a flexible foundation for data collection.

For example, this could include the use of tag managers, which allow you to quickly add and remove tracking tags on your Web site or app, as well as investing in marketing analytics platforms that are equipped to handle a wide range of data sources.

Planning for New Types of Data That Is Required to Create Better Reporting

As marketers, we always look for new ways to optimize our campaigns and improve our reporting. This often requires collecting new types of data, however. To future-proof your marketing data collection approach, be proactive in identifying the data you need for better reporting and plan to collect it.

For example, this could include data from new sources such as social media or customer feedback surveys or more advanced data such as location data or purchasing behavior. By thinking ahead about the data you'll need, you can avoid scrambling to collect it later.

Planning for New Data Privacy Regulations

Data privacy regulations such as GDPR and CCPA have already affected how businesses collect and process data. With new regulations likely to emerge, it's essential to future-proof your marketing data collection approach by complying with current regulations and having a plan for new ones.

For example, this could mean implementing new tools or software that help you comply with regulations or planning to segment your data more effectively to ensure you only collect the data you need.

Planning for Greater Incorporation of AI and ML Tools

AI and ML are already transforming the marketing industry, and their impact is only set to grow. To future-proof your marketing data collection approach, plan to incorporate these tools into your strategy.

For example, this could include using AI and ML to analyze complex datasets, automate reporting processes, and identify new insights that could inform your marketing strategy. By planning to integrate these tools, you can stay ahead of the curve and make the most of the latest advances in marketing technology.

Data Requests: Working Well with Data and Technology Teams

Working with data and technology teams can be daunting for marketers. The data may be difficult to access, and the technology may not be user-friendly. Having access to the right data, however, is essential for creating effective marketing campaigns. Let's discuss three tips to help marketers work better with data and technology teams.

Communicate Effectively

The first tip for marketers working with data and technology teams is to communicate effectively. Ensure to clearly define what data you need and what you intend to do with it. Your request should be specific and actionable so that the technology team can provide that data to you quickly and easily.

It's also essential to understand the language of data. If you don't understand the terminology the technology team is using, ask for clarification. This will help bridge any communication gaps and ensure everyone is on the same page.

Build a Relationship with the Technology Team

The second tip is to build a strong relationship with the technology team. Develop a rapport with those in charge of the technology and data tools. Take the time to understand how these tools work so that you can better articulate what you need.

Clearly define how you want to use the data, but also be open to advice from the technology team. They may have insights into alternative data sources or tools to meet your needs better. Collaboration is key to ensuring that you get the data you need.

Maintain Flexibility

Lastly, be patient and flexible when working with the technology and data teams. You need to keep in mind that they are often dealing with a variety of requests from various departments. Therefore, provide sufficient lead times for request processing and fulfilling orders, and take into account that some types of data may be easier to retrieve than others. Still, more data requests may simply not be feasible continuously.

Understand the time and effort that goes into processing data requests, and be prepared to be flexible on timelines. If you have a hard deadline, communicate that to the technology team and see whether they can work to meet your request.

Working with data and technology teams may not always be easy, but it is essential for creating effective marketing campaigns. By communicating effectively, building a strong relationship with the technology team, and being patient and flexible, you can improve the process, making getting the data you need easier and faster. Following these tips will help you to become more efficient in your work and get the most out of your data.

CONCLUSION

Future-proofing your marketing data collection approach is essential for any marketer who wants to stay ahead of the curve and make the most of the latest trends in technology and regulation.

By planning for new marketing channels or changes to existing ones, new types of data, new data privacy regulations, and greater incorporation of AI and ML tools, you can ensure your data is accurate, up to date, and aligned with your business goals. So, take the time to think about your data collection strategy and how to future-proof it for success.

In the next chapter, we will explore the implications of data collection in an increasingly AI-driven marketing environment, and what this adds or might change from your existing approaches.

ENDNOTES

1 Surfshark. "Data breach statistics 2023 Q1 vs. 2022 Q4." Published May 10, 2023. Retrieved July 2023 from *https://surfshark.com/research/study/data-breach-statistics-2023-q1*

2 Insersoft Consulting. General Data Protection Regulation." Retrieved July 2023 from *https://gdpr-info.eu/*

3 State of California Department of Justice. "California Consumer Privacy Act (CCPA)." Retrieved July 2023 from *https://oag.ca.gov/privacy/ccpa*

4 Iapp Law. "Brazillian General Data Protection Law (LGPD, English Translation)." Retrieved July 2023 from *https://iapp.org/resources/article/brazilian-data-protection-law-lgpd-english-translation/*

5 Confessore, Nicholas. "Cambridge Analytica and Facebook: The Scandal and the Fallout So Far." The New York Times. April 4, 2018. Retrieved from *https://www.nytimes.com/2018/04/04/us/politics/cambridge-analytica-scandal-fallout.html*

6 Elias, Jennifer. "Google delays cookie-cutting to 2024." CNBC. July 27 2022. Retrieved July 2023 from *https://www.cnbc.com/2022/07/27/google-delays-cookie-cutting-to-2024.html*

7 Southern, Matt G. "Google Gives Third-Party Cookies Another Year." Search Engine Journal. July 28, 2022. Retrieved July 2023 from *https://www.searchenginejournal.com/google-gives-third-party-cookies-another-year/459412/*

8 Forrester. (2023, July 24). Google finally scraps its cookie deprecation plans. *Forrester Blogs*. *https://www.forrester.com/blogs/google-finally-scraps-its-cookie-deprecation-plans/*

CHAPTER 14

COLLECTING DATA IN AN AI-DRIVEN MARKETING ENVIRONMENT

Whille collecting high-quality data is always important, it is especially important in the context of Artificial Intelligence (AI). Good data is the raw material that powers AI systems and enables them to generate insights, automate tasks, and personalize interactions like never before. In this chapter, we will explore the evolving landscape of data collection in marketing, highlighting the critical role of data as the foundation of AI and Machine Learning (ML) technologies.

UNDERSTANDING AI AND ML DATA REQUIREMENTS

AI and ML models require specific types of data to learn and make predictions. First, we have structured data, such as sales numbers or clickthrough rates, which are quantifiable and easy for algorithms to interpret. Then, there is unstructured data, encompassing everything from social media comments to customer support call transcripts, which is rich in insights but requires more complex processing. For AI models to function effectively, they must be fed a balance of both, along with high-quality metadata that provides context and relevance to the data points.

Moreover, the data must embody diversity, representing the full spectrum of scenarios the AI or ML models are expected to encounter. For marketers, this means data should capture a wide range of customer interactions, market conditions, and potential influencing factors, ensuring the models are robust and applicable in real-world situations.

The Four Vs of Big Data

Of course, there are several aspects that marketers need to understand about the data that they collect. This is where some subcategorizations, such as the four Vs, as shown in Figure 14.1, are helpful.

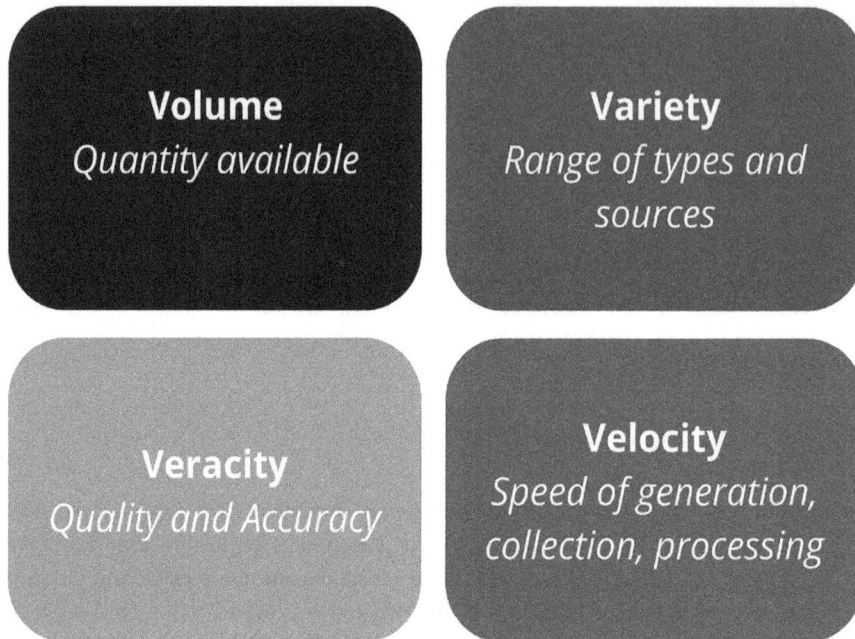

FIGURE 14.1. The four Vs of big data.

Since AI and ML thrive on big data, understanding the four Vs is critical for marketers:

- *Volume*: The quantity of data available for analysis. AI and ML models are particularly adept at digesting large volumes of data, uncovering patterns and trends that would be indiscernible to the human eye. For marketers, large volumes of data could mean millions of customer interactions across various touchpoints, from Web site visits to in-store purchases.
- *Variety*: The range of data types and sources. It's not enough to have a lot of data; the data must be from diverse sources and formats. This includes text, images, and videos, all of which can contribute to a more rounded understanding of the market and customer behavior.
- *Veracity*: The quality and accuracy of data. High veracity is crucial as it determines the reliability of the AI or ML model's output. Data must be truthful and reflective of true behaviors and preferences. Inaccurate or misleading data can lead to faulty insights, guiding marketers down the wrong path.
- *Velocity*: The speed at which data is generated, collected, and processed. In today's fast-paced digital world, the ability to process data in near real time can provide a significant competitive advantage. It allows for agile responses to emerging trends, customer needs, and market shifts.

For marketers utilizing AI and ML, attention to the four Vs ensures not just the creation of models but the deployment of ones that can deliver actionable, trustworthy, and timely insights to steer marketing strategies successfully. It's about harnessing the full potential of data to inform smarter, more responsive marketing efforts.

REAL-TIME DATA AND ITS RELEVANCE TO AI

Real-time data offers a wealth of information that brings a dynamic capability to AI model training. By leveraging data as it's generated, AI systems can provide up-to-the-minute insights and adapt to changes as they occur, keeping models current and highly relevant.

For example, for marketers at PB Shoes, this means having the ability to adjust campaigns on the fly based on the latest customer interactions. Real-time data allows for the immediate detection of patterns, such as a sudden spike in demand for a particular shoe size or style following a celebrity endorsement or a social media trend.

This agility can lead to more personalized customer experiences, as the AI can recommend products or services that align with instantaneous behavior and preferences. In turn, this responsiveness can significantly enhance customer satisfaction and conversion rates.

Capturing and Processing Data in Real Time

Capturing and processing real-time data necessitates robust tools and sophisticated techniques. Event stream processing software allows for the continuous ingestion of data as events occur. These technologies provide the infrastructure to handle large volumes of data at high velocity, enabling marketers to process and analyze data in real time. Furthermore, in-memory databases and data caching strategies can significantly reduce the time it takes for data to be available for analysis, ensuring that AI models can act on the most current data without delay.

Another crucial technique is the implementation of data orchestration layers that can pull in data from various sources, normalize it, and feed it into AI models without manual intervention. Coupled with ML algorithms designed for incremental learning, these systems can update the models' parameters in real time.

Marketers at PB Shoes, for instance, could use these techniques to detect emerging customer trends and respond with targeted promotions or content.

Real-time data is not without its challenges, though. It requires a robust IT infrastructure and a keen understanding of data flow management. Additionally, marketers must ensure that privacy regulations are adhered to when processing customer data in real time.

As you can see, real-time data enhances the nimbleness and accuracy of AI models, empowering marketers to make decisions that are as current as the data they are based on. By using sophisticated tools and techniques to capture and process this data, marketers can ensure that their AI-driven strategies are both effective and timely, capitalizing on opportunities as they unfold.

LEVERAGING AI FOR ENHANCED DATA COLLECTION

AI has the unique ability to not only analyze existing data but also to predict future trends and identify missing elements within datasets. By leveraging predictive analytics, AI can forecast upcoming consumer behaviors, market demands, and even product trends with remarkable accuracy.

For example, for marketers at PB Shoes, this could mean anticipating an increase in the popularity of certain shoe designs based on trending physical activities or health movements. AI's predictive capabilities allow for the proactive adjustment of marketing strategies, ensuring that PB Shoes stays ahead of the curve.

AI can also illuminate areas where data may be lacking, enabling marketers to conduct targeted data collection. For instance, if AI analysis reveals that certain demographic information is missing from a customer dataset, marketers can tailor their data collection efforts to fill these gaps, leading to more complete and useful datasets. This can significantly improve the personalization of marketing efforts, ensuring that every customer feels understood and valued.

Optimizing Data Collection Strategies for ML

ML can optimize data collection strategies by identifying the most valuable data points and the most efficient methods of gathering them. By analyzing the outcomes of different data collection approaches, ML algorithms can suggest adjustments to strategies, helping marketers to allocate resources more effectively. This could involve shifting focus to high-engagement channels, adjusting the frequency of data collection, or even refining the data points collected to enhance their usefulness.

ML models can also streamline the data collection process itself. For example, at PB Shoes, an ML system could automate the process of collecting customer feedback across various platforms, analyzing sentiment in real time, and integrating these insights into a central Customer Relationship Management (CRM) system. This automation not only saves time but also ensures that no valuable customer insights slip through the cracks.

In leveraging AI for enhanced data collection, marketers at PB Shoes or any other company can make their data work smarter, not harder. By predicting trends, filling dataset gaps, and optimizing collection strategies, AI transforms the way marketers approach data, making it a powerful ally in the quest for a deeper connection with customers and a more significant impact in the market.

Here is a checklist to ensure your data collection is optimized for potential analysis by AI and ML tools:

1. *Identify valuable data points*
   - Focus on collecting the most relevant data for your business goals and ML models.
   - Evaluate past data collection efforts to determine which data points drive the most insights.
   - Use AI to analyze data points that contribute to customer engagement and conversion rates.
2. *Leverage high-engagement channels*
   - Utilize ML to identify which channels (e.g., social media, email, or Web site) provide the most valuable customer data.
   - Shift focus toward channels where customers are most engaged to collect more actionable data.
3. *Automate data collection processes*
   - Implement AI-powered tools to automate data collection from multiple sources (e.g., feedback forms, customer interactions, and Web site behavior).
   - Ensure automated systems integrate collected data directly into your central CRM or analytics platform.
4. *Adjust data collection frequency*
   - Use ML to optimize how often data should be collected, balancing between over-collection and under-collection.

- Adjust data collection frequency to align with customer behavior patterns, ensuring data is both fresh and valuable.

5. *Refine data points for usefulness*
   - Focus on the most critical data points that ML models need for training, reducing data noise.
   - Continuously evaluate data points and remove those that are redundant or provide little predictive value.

6. *Fill dataset gaps with predictive insights*
   - Leverage AI to predict missing data or fill gaps in your dataset using historical data or patterns.
   - Ensure that dataset gaps are addressed so that ML models can function optimally.

7. *Optimize data collection strategy based on outcomes*
   - Use ML to analyze the outcomes of various data collection strategies and refine them over time.
   - Reallocate resources to more effective methods or channels for data collection based on AI-driven recommendations.

8. *Integrate real-time data analysis*
   - Incorporate real-time data collection and analysis using AI to capture customer feedback and sentiment instantly.
   - Ensure insights are immediately actionable by integrating real-time analysis into your marketing strategy.

By following these guidelines, a marketer can optimize their data collection processes to fully leverage the power of AI, ensuring data quality, relevance, and effectiveness in driving customer engagement and improving marketing outcomes.

CONCLUSION

While collecting good data is important in any marketing application, when teams rely heavily on AI and ML models, the quality and consistency of data become even more important. Remember the four Vs of data, as well as the real-time opportunities when working in an AI-based environment. Also, don't overlook the opportunity to use ML tools to help predict trends or fill in gaps in your datasets.

Part 3 Recap Quiz

We have now reached the end of the third section, where we have focused on the types of data we collect and ensuring that our data collection processes are robust enough to support our analysis efforts. Make sure you've mastered the ideas we've covered by answering the following three questions on the topics covered in the chapters in this section. To check your answers, refer to Appendix B, which lists all of the answers for the quizzes in the book.

Let's look at three questions on the content in Part 3.

Question 1
True or false: Alignment of metrics and KPIs to the strategy and goals of the business is a key reason to invest in a marketing measurement framework.

Question 2
Select the correct answer: The four Vs of big data are volume, variety, veracity, and:
a) Value
b) Velocity
c) Vivid

Question 3
Pick the correct answer: The following is a benefit of single-channel measurement:
a) It can often be easier to measure a single channel rather than reconcile or aggregate numbers from multiple channels
b) Analytics and reporting are often (for digital channels) built natively into the platforms themselves, which can simplify getting a quick view
c) A single channel can often be integrated into a more robust reporting tool more easily than multiple channels
d) All of the above

PART 4: MEASUREMENT AND TESTING

Marketing measurement and hypothesis-based testing are critical because they enable marketers to make data-driven decisions, improving the effectiveness and efficiency of campaigns. By measuring marketing activities, brands can assess the performance of various strategies, channels, and messages to see what works and what doesn't. This objective analysis allows marketers to optimize their efforts in real time, ensuring that resources are allocated to the most impactful initiatives. Hypothesis-based testing, such as A/B testing, provides a scientific approach to testing marketing ideas and validating assumptions before fully committing to a strategy, reducing the risk of wasted budget or missed opportunities.

Additionally, marketing measurement and testing help build a culture of accountability and continuous improvement. When marketers rely on data and structured testing, they can identify areas that need refinement and create evidence-based strategies to enhance their results. This iterative process allows brands to stay competitive in rapidly changing markets by adapting their marketing strategies based on real-world feedback. For example, PB Shoes could test different marketing messages or product offerings to determine what resonates best with their target audience, ensuring that future campaigns are more likely to succeed. Ultimately, this combination of measurement and testing drives better marketing outcomes, higher ROI, and stronger customer relationships.

To complicate this, though, marketing has never had such a multitude of platforms as it does today, with the 2023 Chiefmartec Marketing Technology Landscape Supergraphic containing 11,038 solutions classified as marketing technology platforms and solutions[1]—and that is only the digital ones! With so many possible channels available and new ones added daily, it can be overwhelming to know where to start optimizing your marketing channels. With the right approach, however, channel optimization can help you improve the effectiveness of your marketing campaigns and reach your desired audience more efficiently.

All of this relies on the marketing measurement framework we discussed earlier, so if you need a refresher on that, flip back to Part 2 of the book.

This also depends on how you report on the effectiveness of your marketing. HubSpot reported that 75% of marketers use their reports to show how campaigns are directly impacting revenue[2]. I highly encourage you not to be like the 25% of marketers who aren't reporting on how their marketing ties to business objectives!

WHAT WE WILL COVER IN THIS PART

In the chapters that follow, we will look at the following:

- How to create an effective marketing dashboard, including determining which channels to include and which metrics to use
- How to utilize hypothesis testing to achieve more effective marketing measurement
- How to incorporate artificial intelligence tools into measurement to allow the prediction and augmentation of hypothesis testing
- A further exploration of statistics that can be applied to your marketing measurement
- Constructing both single- and multi-channel marketing tests
- Multi-channel measurement approaches, including Media Mix Modeling (MMM) and Multi-Touch Attribution (MTA)

In this part of the book, we'll discuss how marketers can approach marketing channel optimization and where to start. Then, in the chapters that follow, we will focus on optimizing a single channel, regardless of which (of the many potential channels available) that may be.

ENDNOTES

1   Brinker, Scott. "2023 Marketing Technology Landscape Supergraphic: 11,038 solutions searchable on martechmap.com." Retrieved July 2023 from *https://chiefmartec.com/2023/05/2023-marketing-technology-landscape-supergraphic-11038-solutions-searchable-on-martechmap-com/*
2   HubSpot. "The Ultimate List of Marketing Statistics for 2022." HubSpot Blog. Retrieved July 2023 from *https://www.hubspot.com/marketing-statistics*

CHAPTER 15

CREATING A MARKETING DASHBOARD

E ven though you don't yet have metrics to report on, a helpful step in the measurement process is to design the view you want to see your data in rather than relying on the stand-ard dashboards a platform may provide. If you only rely on what is provided, you may be forced to compromise on what you want to see and how you want to see it.

Thus, designing your dashboard *before* you start to work with data is a good step to ensure you have a clear picture of what you want. This doesn't have to be anything more than a sketch or a document with a bullet list of information if you lack the time or resources to create a full mockup of a dashboard. The most important aspect at this stage is ensuring that the important metrics tell the right story in your dashboard, not the fidelity of your mockup.

DETERMINING WHICH CHANNEL(S) TO MEASURE

While you want to design your dashboard early in the process, you do need to first have an understanding of the channels and behaviors you would like to measure first. Thus, having an understanding of the marketing channels available to you is helpful.

This brings us back to looking at whether you want your dashboard to measure a single chan-nel or multiple channels. For instance, some challenges of measuring a single channel on its own might be:

- A single channel rarely tells the "full story" of a campaign or other efforts, where success on a single channel may give the appearance of overall success when an overall effort is less than successful.
- Another challenge with relying on a single marketing channel for measurement is that it can lead to incorrect assumptions about customer behavior. For instance, a customer may click on a Google ad and then return to your Web site a few times before making a pur-chase. If we measure the effectiveness of the Google ad based on a last-click attribution model, we might assume that the ad was more effective than it actually was.
- A third challenge with relying on a single marketing channel for measurement is that it can result in missed opportunities to optimize marketing strategies. For instance, if we see that a particular channel is driving the most conversions, we may be inclined to invest all our resources in that channel.

- An additional challenge with relying on a single marketing channel for measurement is that it can obscure the long-term impact of marketing efforts. For example, a customer who clicks on a Facebook ad may not convert right away. They may, however, still interact with your brand across other channels before ultimately making a purchase. If we only measure the effectiveness of the Facebook ad, we may not give credit to the other touchpoints that contributed to the conversion. By measuring across all channels and tracking the entire customer journey, we can capture the full impact of our marketing efforts over time.

Of course, multi-channel measurement can pose its own challenges, such as greater complexity in both collection and integration for reporting. This complexity often means longer lead times and assistance from external teams, such as a data science team or IT, with data integration. Ultimately, you and your marketing team will need to determine the cost-benefit of handling greater complexity in your dashboards.

GETTING STARTED WITH YOUR DASHBOARD

Designing your marketing dashboard before diving into data collection and measurement is critical to maintaining objectivity and ensuring that the final output is purpose-driven and aligned with your strategic marketing goals and KPIs. If you start measuring without a clear plan, there's a risk of being swayed by interesting but non-essential data, which can lead to "vanity metrics" that don't truly align with your objectives. A well-thought-out dashboard design acts as a blueprint, focusing on the metrics that matter and providing a direct line of sight to your original goals, thus supporting strategic decision-making.

Here are a few things to consider before you start designing your marketing dashboard:

- *Frequency of reporting*: Consider how easy it is to update your dashboard, particularly if you need to make manual updates on a frequent basis, such as weekly or even daily. You may want to prioritize simplicity for a frequently updated dashboard, but add some more complexity for one that is shown to a key stakeholder audience on a quarterly basis.
- *Usability and accessibility*: Ensure that the dashboard is user-friendly and accessible to all stakeholders. The design should facilitate quick understanding and ease of interaction.
- *Customization and flexibility*: Account for the need to customize views for different users and the ability to drill down into more detailed data where necessary.
- *Scalability*: Design with the future in mind. The dashboard should be able to evolve and scale as new data and metrics become relevant.
- *Integration*: Consider the integration capabilities with various data sources to ensure that your dashboard can pull in real-time data from across all marketing channels.

Choosing the Right Charts and Graphs

The visual representation of data on a marketing dashboard is as crucial as the data itself. Selecting the appropriate chart or visual can significantly enhance the understanding and actionable insights derived from the dashboard. Here's guidance on choosing the right types of visuals.

Line Charts

Line charts are ideal for displaying data trends over time. They help in tracking the progression of key metrics such as Web site traffic, lead generation, and sales figures across different timeframes. For instance, a marketer could use a line chart to visualize the month-over-month increase in email signups following an SEO campaign, such as the one shown in Figure 15.1.

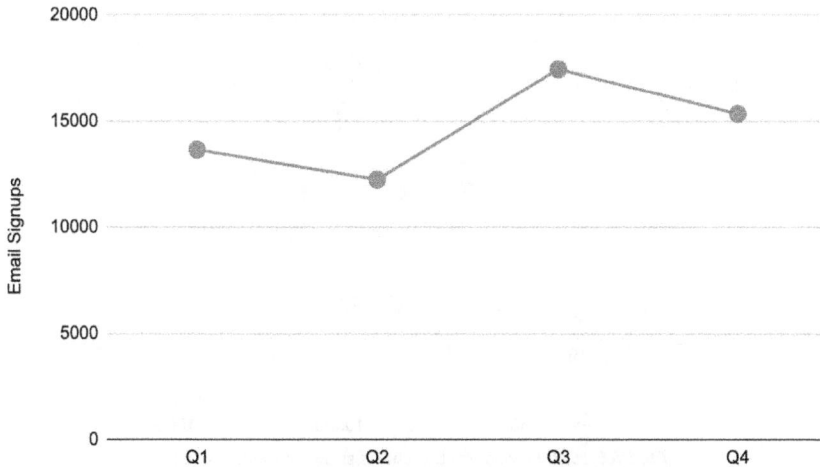

FIGURE 15.1. A line chart showing email signups by quarter.

Bar and Column Charts

Bar charts are effective for comparing quantitative data across different categories, such as the chart shown in Figure 5.2, which uses the same data as the previous line chart.

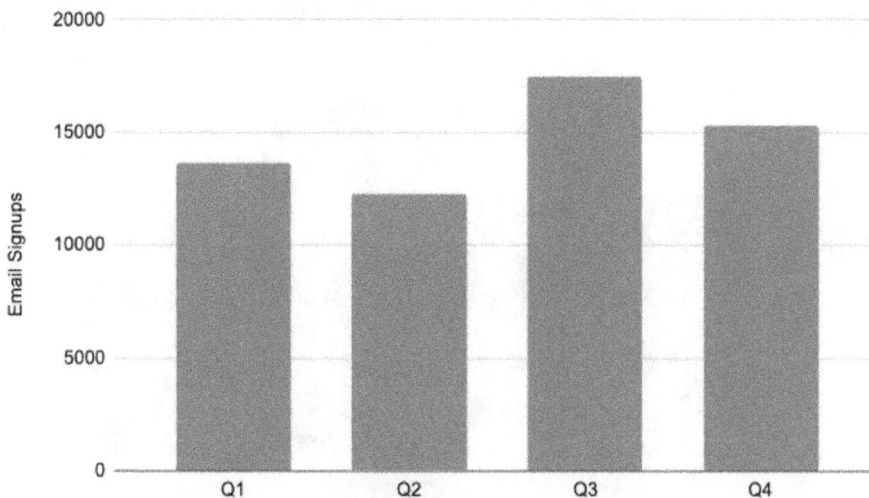

FIGURE 15.2. A bar chart showing email signups by quarter.

Use horizontal bars for comparisons where the categories are text-heavy, thus increasing legibility, such as the chart in Figure 15.3, where we illustrate sales of particular types of pickleball shoes that have 3–4 words in their descriptive name.

Sales of Pickleball Shoes Q1-4

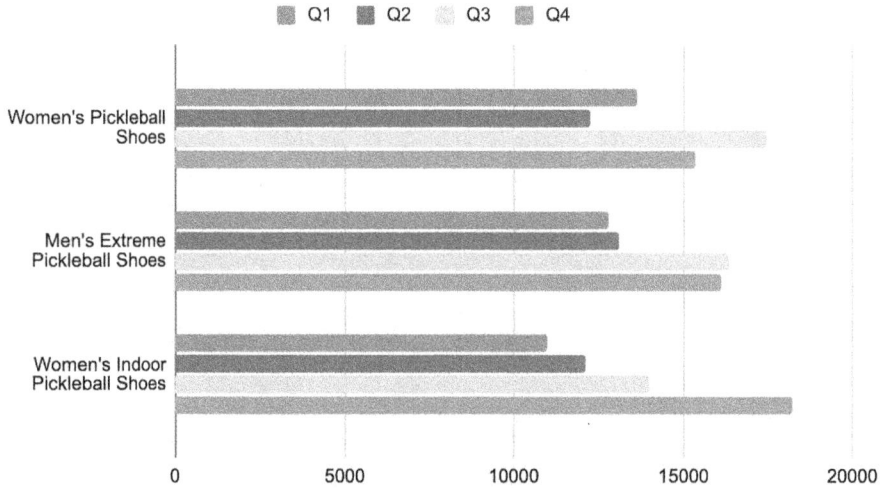

FIGURE 15.3. Horizontal bar charts showing longer labels.

Use vertical columns when there are fewer categories or when displaying a time series. These are particularly useful for showing comparative performance, such as Figure 15.4, which shows a comparison of sales of women's and men's pickleball shoe sales over the past four quarters.

Women's Shoes and Men's Shoes

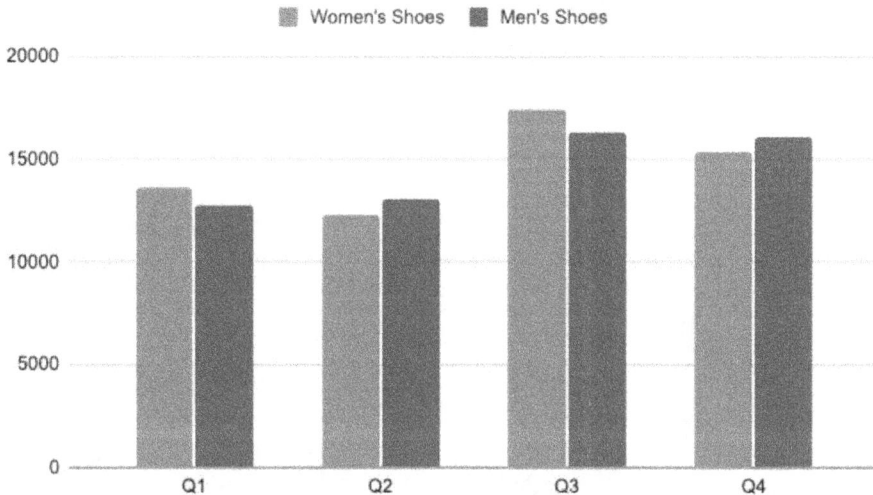

FIGURE 15.4. Vertical bar charts comparing shoe sales by quarter.

Pie Charts and Donut Charts

Pie and donut charts are best suited for illustrating proportions within a dataset, such as market share or the distribution of marketing budget across different initiatives. An example is shown in Figure 15.5, which illustrates the percentage of shoe sales by marketing channel.

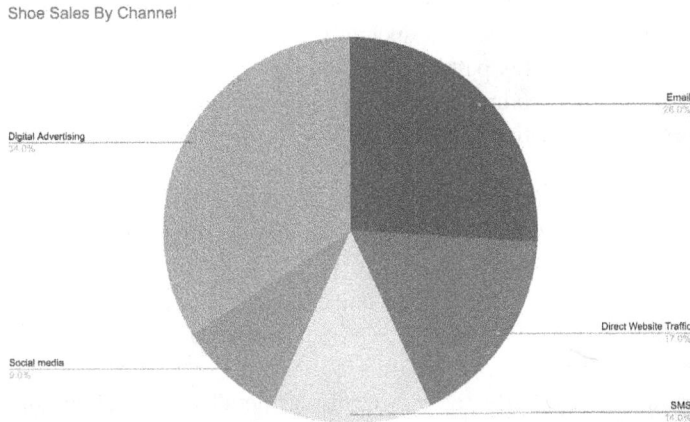

Shoe Sales By Channel

Email
26.0%

Digital Advertising
34.0%

Direct Website Traffic
17.0%

Social media
9.0%

SMS
14.0%

FIGURE 15.5. A pie chart illustrating the percentage of shoe sales by marketing channel.

Despite pie charts' usefulness in select instances, they should be used sparingly and only when the number of categories is limited to avoid clutter and confusion.

Area Charts

Area charts are a variation of line charts with the area below the line filled in, emphasizing volume. They are useful for showcasing accumulated growth over time, such as the total number of active subscribers to a service or, in the case of Figure 15.6, the overall growth of pickleball shoe sales across four product lines over the last four quarters.

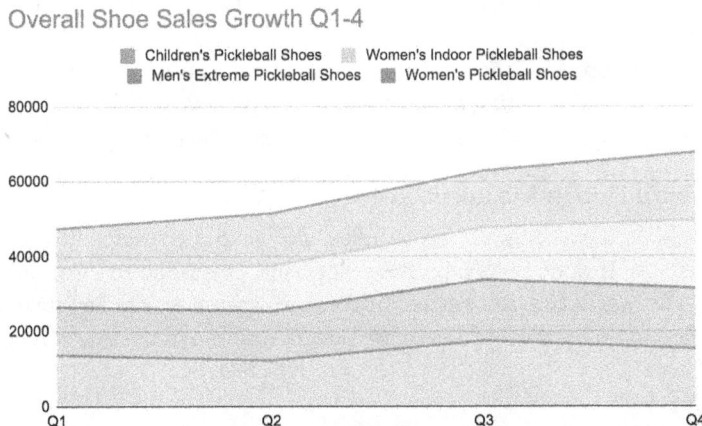

Overall Shoe Sales Growth Q1-4

Children's Pickleball Shoes   Women's Indoor Pickleball Shoes
Men's Extreme Pickleball Shoes   Women's Pickleball Shoes

FIGURE 15.6. Area chart showing combined product line sales over a four-quarter period.

Other Charts to Consider

Of course, different measurements and findings require different approaches. Here are some additional types of charts to consider, and most are available through standard office applications such as Microsoft Excel or Google Workspace:

- *Scatter plots* show the relationship between two quantitative variables. Marketers might use these to explore correlations, such as the relationship between ad spend and Web site conversions, or to identify patterns in customer behavior.
- *Heat maps* use color coding to display complex data in an easily digestible format. They can be used to show activity across a Web site or the concentration of sales across different regions.
- *Histograms* are used to display the distribution of a dataset and are useful for marketers looking to understand the frequency of purchase amounts or the distribution of customer engagement times.
- *Gauges and scorecards* provide at-a-glance indicators of performance against targets, such as progress toward a sales goal. They should be used for key metrics where immediate awareness is crucial.
- *Tables* are a simple yet effective way to display detailed data. They can be used when specific numerical values are necessary for decision-making, such as listing individual campaign costs and ROIs.
- *Infographics* combine visuals and text to tell a story with data. They can be used in marketing dashboards to summarize campaign results or to explain complex data in a narrative format. They are best suited when information requires more visual storytelling and can sometimes be a distraction if a simple set of information needs to be illustrated.
- *Bullet graphs* provide a rich display of data in a small space and are used to show performance data such as current versus target results. They are especially effective on executive dashboards where space is at a premium.

When designing a dashboard, marketers should choose visuals that not only convey information effectively but also resonate with the audience. Simplicity, clarity, and context should be the guiding principles in visual selection to ensure the dashboard communicates the right information in the right way.

For instance, Figure 15.7 shows a simple dashboard that gives a marketing team statistics about their Web site visitors using data from a source such as Google Analytics. As you can see, there are a variety of types of charts, chosen to represent the given type of measurement.

Common Dashboard Design Mistakes

A great dashboard can simplify the complex and make the results of your marketing efforts easy to understand. If done poorly, on the other hand, it can fail to illustrate the effectiveness of your work—or, just as bad, send mixed or conflicting messages to key stakeholders who need vital information to do their work. If you are new to dashboard design, here are a few things to consider and avoid:

- *Overcomplication of information*: Avoid cluttering the dashboard with too much information, which can overwhelm users.

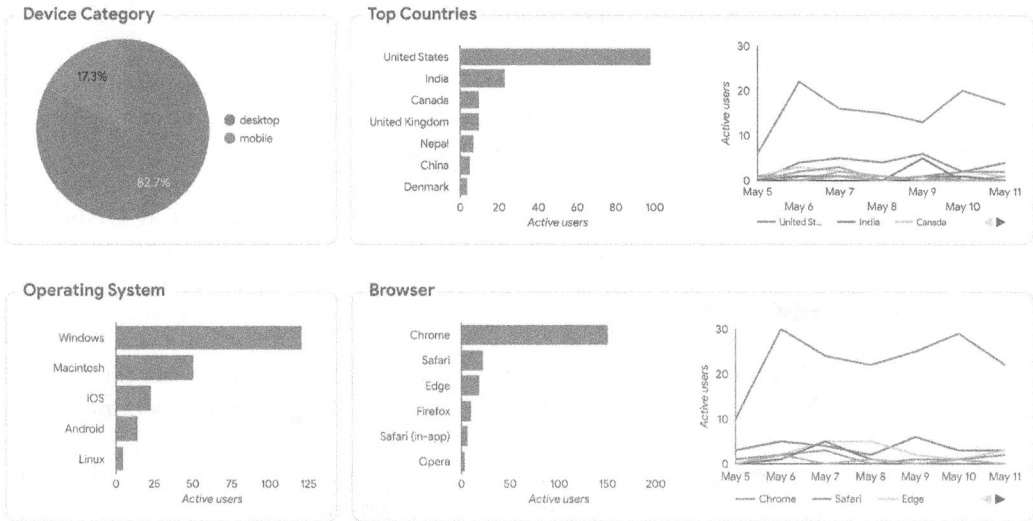

FIGURE 15.7. A Web site analytics dashboard with a variety of chart types.

- *Overcomplication of design*: Avoid distracting 3D effects that can make it difficult to imme-diately understand how the data is being presented.
- *Ignoring mobile users*: Failing to optimize for mobile devices can limit the dashboard's usefulness for stakeholders on the go.
- *Neglecting the narrative*: The dashboard should tell a story about the data; missing this nar-rative can make it harder to draw actionable insights.

A well-designed marketing dashboard is a vital tool that reflects and supports your marketing strategy. By pre-designing your dashboard, considering usability, visualization, and audience needs, and avoiding common pitfalls, you can ensure it remains a valuable asset. Remember to revisit and refine your dashboard regularly to keep it aligned with your evolving marketing landscape.

CONFIRM YOU ARE CAPTURING THE METRICS YOU'VE DEFINED

With the reporting and tracking capabilities within most modern marketing platforms, you can track a range of metrics. The metrics you need to measure and map to your goals, however, are not always available in the "out-of-the-box reports" provided.

We talked in more depth about data collection in Part 3 of this book, so please refer to that section for more ideas. This step, however, is important because many times, once marketing teams go through the design process, they may add metrics or calculations that require addi-tional effort than originally planned.

This includes performing more complex measurements that require combining multiple metrics and performing calculations. For instance, customer lifetime value is calculated as:

Customer Lifetime Value (CLV) =
(Purchase Frequency [PF] × Average Order Value [AOV]

× Gross Margin [GM] × Customer Lifespan [CL]) /
Number of New Customers

It is unlikely that there will be a single source of information for the data required to perform this calculation. Thus, there needs to be an additional step in the dashboard setup process to perform this calculation so it can be added to a dashboard.

Thus, you need to take the extra step of ensuring that what you need to report on your goals is either easily provided or can be provided with additional integrations. You may need to work with a data team or a platform vendor to determine this in some cases.

CREATE THE DASHBOARD

Using the dashboard you designed earlier, plus the analytics and other data you have collected, you should now be able to see a full picture of your marketing channel performance at a glance. This is a key step in optimizing your channel.

There are many tools available to create a marketing dashboard, including anything from a spreadsheet application such as Microsoft Excel to more specific tools such as Tableau or Google's Looker Studio. While many of these tools may vary in the way they operate, the following should give you a general guide to creating a dashboard, assuming you have your data sources defined and ready and your dashboard designed.

Connect to Your Data Source

To start, you will want to connect your dashboard application to one or more data sources. This could be things such as your Web site analytics or social media metrics; or, if you are using a spreadsheet to track information, you should verify your data is accurately formatted in that sheet.

Design the Layout

With one or more data sources connected, it is time to design the overall layout of the dashboard. You should have done most of this work previously, but there may be some slight differences in either the available chart types or the exact layout requirements between what you and your team designed earlier and what the platform you are using requires.

Ideally, these differences will be minimal, or else you may want to revisit the overall design. It is also recommended to gain familiarity with the reporting tool that you will be using to create a dashboard before you begin the design process to ensure there are minimal modifications needed.

Choose the Metrics

Having already connected the data sources, you will now need to choose the specific metrics that you want to show in your report. For instance, if you want to create a dashboard that shows Web site visits to your online store, you will need to filter overall Web traffic to only show the subset that you are interested in viewing.

Choose and Build the Charts

Now it is time to choose the visualization for your data, using the metrics from the data sources you've connected. Make sure to follow your original design for the dashboard and use the most appropriate charts to display the information.

If the type of chart you had originally planned on using is unavailable, you might either choose the next best available option or rethink your approach altogether.

This is also the step where you might choose to build in some types of interactivity, such as providing the ability to choose specific date ranges to report on your marketing efforts or rollover effects, if your reporting application allows.

Test and Style

With the charts set up, it is important to test the dashboard and make sure everything is working properly. You should compare the data that is showing in your dashboard with the data you get from a native application.

For instance, for search advertising clicks, you might want to compare the data that is displayed on your dashboard with what you see directly in the Google Ads interface.

Preview and Refine

You are now ready to preview your dashboard and show it to your team and other stakeholders. Make sure to get feedback before proceeding to share it widely.

Over time, you will want to refine it as you either get feedback or you and your team use it and find areas where it can be improved. This is a necessary part of the process, but be careful as any large-scale changes might make it difficult to compare one date range's data to another.

CONCLUSION

Ensuring that your marketing data maps to your goals and KPIs is essential to any marketing strategy. Remember, data is only valuable if it's used correctly, so take the time to align it with your goals. With these points as your guide, you're well on your way to success.

Now that we have explored how to visualize your measurements effectively, the next chapter will discuss how to create a strong hypothesis to begin your testing.

CHAPTER 16

BEGINNING WITH A STRONG HYPOTHESIS

Now that you have your KPIs translated to measurements, you are collecting data properly, and you've created a dashboard to visualize your measurements, it is time to start measuring and testing your marketing efforts.

To do this well, it's important to create a hypothesis around your goals. A hypothesis is a clear statement that defines what you want to test and why.

Hypothesis testing is a method used to decide whether there is enough evidence in a sample of data to infer that a certain condition is true for the entire population. In marketing, hypothesis testing might be used to determine whether a new campaign led to a higher conversion rate.

NULL AND ALTERNATIVE HYPOTHESES

Two critical components of hypothesis testing are the null and alternative hypotheses. The null hypothesis (H0) typically asserts that no effect or difference is expected in the study. The alternative hypothesis (HA) is what the researcher wants to prove—for example, that a new banner ad has a higher clickthrough rate than the old one.

Developing a strong hypothesis sets the foundation for a successful campaign and helps you to determine the appropriate testing methods. Let's look at some best practices for developing a strong hypothesis.

START WITH A QUESTION OR PROBLEM STATEMENT

The foundation of any strong hypothesis begins with a clear question or problem statement. In marketing, this question typically stems from a specific challenge or opportunity that the team is looking to address. It could be about improving conversion rates, optimizing ad performance, or understanding customer behavior better. The key is to pinpoint an issue that, when solved, will have a significant impact on your marketing strategy. Starting with a well-defined question ensures that the hypothesis remains relevant and focused on real business objectives, giving the testing process clear direction and purpose.

For example, if your Web site's bounce rate is unusually high, the question might be, "What factors are contributing to users leaving the Web site quickly?" Alternatively, if a certain ad campaign isn't delivering results, the question could focus on why the campaign isn't resonating with the target audience. By defining the problem clearly, you can start to formulate a hypothesis that will allow you to test different variables and gather actionable insights. Without a clearly defined question or problem, the testing process can become unfocused, wasting time and resources on irrelevant factors.

Moreover, a good problem statement helps you prioritize what needs to be addressed first. Not every marketing challenge will have equal importance, and the goal of hypothesis testing is to focus on areas that will deliver the most impactful improvements. By asking the right questions, you ensure that your hypothesis is not only solving immediate problems but also contributing to the long-term success of your marketing efforts. This approach forces marketers to think strategically, ensuring that the testing process is aligned with overall business goals.

Some Example Questions and Problem Statements

Let's take a look at a few example questions and problem statements as well as what makes them well formed:

- *Why is our Web site's conversion rate lower on mobile devices compared to desktop devices, and how can we optimize the mobile experience to improve conversions?*
  This question is good because it is specific, focused on a key performance metric (conversion rate), and targets a clear comparison between two platforms. It also sets up actionable next steps by identifying optimization opportunities for mobile, which is critical for many businesses today.
- *What factors are contributing to the low open rates of our email campaigns, and would changing the subject line or send time increase engagement?*
  This is a strong problem statement because it not only identifies a clear performance issue (low open rates) but also suggests variables to test (subject line and send time). It's actionable and focused and allows for easy hypothesis development to test changes and measure results.
- *Why are our Facebook ads underperforming compared to our Google ads, and how can we adjust our targeting or creative decisions to improve Facebook ad ROI?*
  This question works well because it compares two specific channels, allowing for a focused analysis of why one is underperforming. Highlighting both targeting and creative decisions as potential factors opens the door to testing multiple hypotheses for improvement.
- *Why do visitors to our landing page leave without interacting, and would simplifying the design or adjusting the messaging reduce the bounce rate?*
  This is a good problem statement as it directly addresses a clear user behavior issue (bounce rate). It also proposes actionable solutions—simplifying the design or tweaking messaging—making it easy to test different variables to improve user engagement.
- *What are the key factors leading to customer churn within the first 3 months of purchase, and would a post-purchase email series improve customer retention rates?*
  This is a strong question because it focuses on an important business challenge—customer churn—and sets the stage for actionable testing. It also identifies a specific solution to test (post-purchase email series), which is measurable and directly connected to the issue of retention.

Back to our example

If PB Shoes wants to find out whether changing the color of its Call-to-Action (CTA) button in an email will increase conversions on an upcoming line of pickleball shoes for kids, your hypothesis could be, "If we change the color of the CTA button to red on the PB Shoes kids page, we will see an increase in conversions." Remember that this hypothesis should be based directly on one of the marketing objectives and goals that you previously identified.

Starting with a question or problem statement ensures that your hypothesis is built on a strong foundation. It guides the entire testing process, ensuring that every experiment you conduct is designed to answer a meaningful question that could influence your broader marketing strategy. Without a clear problem to address, even the most carefully designed tests may lack relevance and fail to deliver actionable results. This first step sets the stage for a successful, data-driven hypothesis that can significantly improve marketing performance.

BE SPECIFIC

When developing a hypothesis for marketing testing, it is crucial to be specific. A vague hypothesis will not provide a clear direction for the experiment or yield actionable insights. The more detailed and focused your hypothesis, the easier it will be to design a test and measure the outcomes accurately. Specificity ensures that you are examining a well-defined variable or aspect of your marketing strategy, which simplifies both the execution and evaluation of the test. For example, rather than hypothesizing "Changing our Web site will improve conversion rates," a more specific statement would be, "Reducing the number of form fields on the sign-up page will increase the conversion rate by 10%."

A specific hypothesis also allows for measurable outcomes, making it easier to confirm whether your predictions were correct. When crafting a hypothesis, include concrete figures or metrics that will allow you to gauge success. In the preceding example, you aren't just expecting an improvement in conversion rates, but a quantifiable change—a 10% increase. This type of measurable outcome provides a clear benchmark that allows for a definitive answer when analyzing the test results. Additionally, having a clear hypothesis helps in isolating variables and avoiding extraneous factors that could skew the data.

Finally, specificity in your hypothesis is essential for drawing meaningful conclusions. When your prediction is clearly stated, it becomes easier to validate or invalidate the hypothesis based on the data. This approach not only streamlines the process but also improves the quality of insights generated, helping marketers make more informed decisions. For example, if the goal is to reduce bounce rates by improving the Web site's mobile responsiveness, the hypothesis should clearly define what kind of responsiveness improvements will be made and how much of a bounce rate decrease is expected. This kind of clarity leads to stronger, data-backed conclusions that directly inform your marketing strategy moving forward.

Examples of Specificity

Let's look at a few examples of this and why they are specific enough:

- *"Reducing the number of form fields on our sign-up page from 5 to 3 will increase the conversion rate by 15% over the next 30 days."*

This is a good example because it specifies both the action (reducing form fields) and the expected outcome (15% increase in conversion), along with a clear timeframe for measurement.

- *"Changing the subject line of our weekly email to include the recipient's first name will increase open rates by 10% in the next two campaigns."*
  This is specific because it focuses on a single variable (personalizing the subject line) and predicts a measurable change in open rates within a defined scope (two campaigns).

- *"Increasing our Facebook ad budget by 20% for the next month will generate a 25% increase in Web site traffic from paid ads."*
  This example clearly outlines the action (increasing the ad budget), the expected result (25% increase in traffic), and the channel being tested (Facebook ads), making it easy to track and measure.

- *"Offering a 10% discount in the first week of launching our new product will increase first-week sales by 30% compared to similar product launches without a discount."*
  This is specific because it isolates a single action (offering a discount) and compares the result to a defined baseline (previous launches), providing a clear benchmark for success.

- *"Testing two versions of our landing page—one with a video and one with static images—will increase the average time spent on the page by 20% for the version with the video."*
  This is a strong example of specificity because it clearly defines the variable being tested (video vs static images) and sets a measurable outcome (20% increase in time spent on the page).

Back to our example

For PB Shoes to construct a hypothesis around their advertising for those kids' pickleball shoes, saying "If we increase our advertising budget for kids' pickleball shoes, we will see an increase in Web site traffic" is too broad. A more specific hypothesis could be, "If we increase our advertising budget by 20%, we will see a 15% increase in Web site traffic from our target audience."

Being specific in your hypothesis is essential for achieving clear, measurable results. A well-defined hypothesis allows marketers to focus on a single variable, predict the expected outcome, and measure success against a clear benchmark. By narrowing down the scope and including precise metrics, you can more easily validate or invalidate the hypothesis, leading to actionable insights that directly inform future marketing strategies. Specificity not only improves the accuracy of your testing but also ensures that your conclusions are meaningful and impactful.

CONSIDER THE VARIABLES

When crafting a hypothesis for marketing testing, it's important to identify and account for all the variables that could influence the outcome. Variables are the factors that will either change or be measured during the experiment, and they play a central role in how the test is structured. A thorough understanding of these variables ensures that your hypothesis is well constructed and that the testing process will produce meaningful results. There are three types of variables to consider: independent, dependent, and confounding variables.

The **independent variable** is the factor you are intentionally manipulating to observe its effects. For example, in an email marketing experiment, the independent variable could be the email subject line. You might change the subject line to see how it impacts open rates. This is the primary focus of your test, as the independent variable is what you're actively changing to understand its influence on customer behavior or other outcomes.

The **dependent variable** is what you are measuring in response to the changes made to the independent variable. In the email marketing example, the dependent variable could be the email open rates or clickthrough rates. This is the outcome you're interested in tracking to assess whether the change you made to the independent variable (the subject line) had the desired effect. The dependent variable is central to validating or disproving your hypothesis, as it provides the data necessary to draw conclusions.

Finally, it's critical to account for any *confounding variables*—factors that might unintentionally influence the results of your test. Confounding variables can obscure the relationship between the independent and dependent variables, making it difficult to determine whether the changes in the dependent variable were truly due to the independent variable or something else. For instance, if you're running an A/B test on landing page designs, a confounding variable could be the timing of the test (such as running one variant during a holiday season when traffic naturally increases). Identifying and controlling for these variables ensures that your results are accurate and reliable.

Some Examples of Considering Variables

Here are some examples of considering variables in marketing experiments:

- *Changing the CTA button color on a landing page*
  - Independent variable: The color of the CTA button.
  - *Dependent variable*: The number of clicks or conversions.
  - *Confounding variable*: The time of day the test is run, as traffic could fluctuate based on external factors.
  - This clearly identifies the independent (button color) and dependent (conversions) variables and accounts for potential confounding factors (time of day), which could skew the results.
- *Testing two different email subject lines*
  - Independent variable: The email subject line.
  - *Dependent variable*: Open rate.
  - *Confounding variable*: The day of the week the emails are sent (e.g., emails sent on Monday might perform better than those sent on Friday).
  - The specific manipulation of subject lines provides a clear focus, while accounting for confounding factors (such as send times) ensures that the results are valid.
- *Experimenting with discount offers in retargeting ads*
  - Independent variable: The type of discount offered (10% off vs free shipping).
  - *Dependent variable*: Clickthrough rates or conversion rates.
  - *Confounding variable*: The time of the campaign (e.g., during a sales event or major holiday, consumer behavior may be different).
  - This example uses a clear independent variable (the type of discount) and shows how testing during a holiday or special event could confound results, making it necessary to control for timing.

- *Testing blog titles for SEO performance*
  - Independent variable: The wording of the blog title (informational vs keyword-focused).
  - *Dependent variable*: Organic search traffic.
  - *Confounding variable*: Changes to search engine algorithms during the test period.
  - By focusing on blog title wording and carefully monitoring traffic over a controlled period, you isolate the effect of the title. Acknowledging algorithm updates as a potential confounding variable helps keep results accurate.
- *Running a social media ad with different images*
  - Independent variable: The image used in the ad (image of a product vs lifestyle image).
  - *Dependent variable*: Engagement rate (likes, comments, and shares).
  - *Confounding variable*: The time of day the ad is displayed, as audience activity may fluctuate.

The experiment isolates the impact of ad imagery while recognizing that user activity patterns may differ depending on when the ad is shown, ensuring more valid conclusions.

Back to our example

Suppose you're testing the effectiveness of a new email campaign for PB Shoes' kids' pickleball shoes. In that case, you should consider variables such as the time of day the email is sent, the subject line, and the content, and those considerations might be based on when the kids' parents can check their email since the kids themselves are likely not old enough to receive emails from your marketing efforts. These variables can impact the outcome of your test and should be accounted for in your hypothesis.

By carefully considering all the variables involved in your experiment, you set up a structured and scientifically sound test. This approach helps ensure that the changes in your results are truly due to the variable you're testing, leading to more confident decision-making based on the outcomes.

MAKE IT FALSIFIABLE

For a hypothesis to be valuable in marketing testing, it must be falsifiable. This means that it should be structured in a way that allows the possibility of it being proven false. In scientific terms, this is often referred to as the "null hypothesis"—the assumption that there is no relationship or effect. If your hypothesis can't be proven false, it's not scientifically valid, nor is it useful for decision-making. This ensures that the hypothesis is clear and testable, and it makes the results of your test more meaningful.

In marketing, a hypothesis such as "Changing the headline on our landing page will increase conversions by 10%" is a good example of falsifiability. If you run the experiment and conversions either don't increase or don't reach the 10% threshold, you can conclude that the hypothesis was false. This clarity is crucial because it allows you to take action based on concrete evidence. If the hypothesis is validated, you can move forward with confidence, but if it's disproven, you have a clear starting point to iterate on your strategy.

A hypothesis that isn't falsifiable is often vague or overly broad. For example, a hypothesis such as "Our new product launch will be successful" is not falsifiable because it doesn't define what "successful" means, nor does it establish clear metrics to measure that success. Without the ability to prove it false, there's no way to know whether your marketing efforts are truly working. A more effective hypothesis would specify measurable outcomes, such as "Our new product launch email campaign will result in a 15% increase in open rates compared to previous campaigns." This is a clear, testable hypothesis that can be validated or disproven with actual data.

Some Examples of Falsifiable Hypotheses

Here are five examples of effectively falsifiable hypotheses:

- *"Changing the color of our Web site's CTA button from blue to red will increase clickthrough rates by 20%."*
  This is a good hypothesis because it clearly states a measurable change (CTA button color) and specifies the expected result (20% increase in clickthrough rates). If the change doesn't result in a 20% increase, the hypothesis is falsified.
- *"Sending promotional emails at 9 a.m. will lead to a higher open rate compared to emails sent at 12 p.m. by at least 15%."*
  This hypothesis is falsifiable because it directly compares two variables (email send times) and predicts a specific result (15% higher open rate). It can be proven false if the 9 a.m. send time doesn't outperform the 12 p.m. send time by the expected margin.
- *"Reducing the number of form fields on the lead generation page from six to three will result in a 25% increase in form submissions."*
  This is a good example because it involves a specific change (reducing form fields) and a measurable outcome (25% increase in form submissions). The hypothesis can be proven false if form submissions do not increase by the stated percentage.
- *"Adding customer testimonials to our product page will increase the average time spent on the page by 10%."*
  This hypothesis is strong because it defines a clear action (adding testimonials) and links it to a specific, measurable outcome (10% increase in time spent). If the testimonials do not lead to a 10% increase, the hypothesis is falsified.
- *"Introducing a new rewards program will decrease customer churn by 5% within the first 3 months of its implementation."*
  This is a good falsifiable hypothesis because it specifies an action (introducing a rewards program) and sets a clear target (5% reduction in churn). The hypothesis can be proven false if customer churn does not decrease by the expected amount within the given timeframe.

Back to our example

If your hypothesis is "If we improve our Web site design, we will see an increase in conversions," you should be able to design a test that could potentially show that improving your Web site design does not result in an increase in conversions.

As you might be thinking already, that hypothesis is not nearly specific enough, so adding some variables and making a better hypothesis from the start would be helpful. For instance, PB Shoes could say, "By showing more images of kids actively using our kids' pickleball shoes on key landing pages and making the CTA clearer and easier to see, we should see an increase in conversions."

Making your hypothesis falsifiable ensures that your testing process is scientifically sound and provides clear, actionable insights. A strong hypothesis sets up an experiment where you can learn something valuable, regardless of whether the results confirm or reject your original prediction. Without falsifiability, your testing will lack rigor and could lead to ambiguous or unhelpful conclusions.

TEST AND LEARN

After developing a strong, testable hypothesis, the next step is to design and execute your experiment. It's essential to structure your test around the hypothesis and clearly define how you will measure the results. The goal is to create a well-controlled environment where the variables you've identified are accurately manipulated and measured. This involves choosing appropriate tools and methodologies, such as A/B testing, multivariate analysis, or user surveys, and ensuring that your metrics are both reliable and valid for the research question at hand. By carefully planning how you will gather and interpret the data, you ensure that the results will provide meaningful insights that can be used to either validate or disprove your hypothesis.

It's also important to remember that testing is part of a continuous learning process. The real value of testing lies in the insights gained from the results, regardless of whether your hypothesis is proven correct or not. A negative result does not mean failure—it is simply part of the learning process that helps you refine your marketing strategies. For example, if a new ad creative doesn't drive the expected increase in clickthrough rates, you now know that this particular variable isn't as impactful as you predicted, allowing you to pivot and try different approaches.

In every test, the goal is to gather actionable data that can be used to inform future decisions. You're not just testing for the sake of testing; you're using a systematic approach to improve your marketing outcomes over time. With each test, whether the results are positive or negative, you learn something valuable about your audience, your strategies, or your product. This iterative process of testing, learning, and refining is key to making data-driven marketing decisions that continually improve performance. The more tests you run, the more insights you accumulate, which ultimately leads to smarter and more effective marketing strategies.

SOME MORE HYPOTHESIS EXAMPLES

To further illustrate what makes a good hypothesis, or one that needs improvement, look at the following table for additional ideas.

TABLE 16.1. Hypothesis examples

Hypothesis	Is it good or does it need improvement?	Explanation
If we add customer reviews to product pages, our conversion rate will increase by at least 15%.	Good	This hypothesis is clear and measurable and establishes a specific expected outcome.
Changing the background color on our landing page will make it more attractive.	Needs improvement	This hypothesis is vague ("more attractive" is not measurable) and lacks a specific outcome.

Continued

TABLE 16.1. (*Continuted*) Hypothesis examples

Hypothesis	Is it good or does it need improvement?	Explanation
Offering a 10% discount on first-time purchases will increase customer acquisition by 20% in Q2.	Good	The hypothesis is specific, ties a particular action to a measurable result, and sets a timeframe for evaluation.
Social media influencers will improve brand recognition.	Needs improvement	"Improve brand recognition" is not quantifiable without specific metrics, and no timeframe is set.
Implementing a chatbot for customer inquiries will reduce average resolution time by 50%.	Good	It is a good hypothesis as it predicts a precise, quantifiable impact on a KPI (average resolution time).

As you can see, the "good" hypotheses are actionable, have clear metrics for success, and are directly tied to the company's strategic goals. In contrast, the hypotheses that "need improvement" are too broad, lack specificity, and do not provide a solid basis for measurement or action.

CONCLUSION

Developing a strong hypothesis is essential for a successful marketing campaign. By starting with a clear question, being specific and measurable, considering the variables, making it falsifiable, and testing and learning, you can create a hypothesis that sets the foundation for a well-executed campaign. Remember that hypothesis testing is an ongoing process and that with each iteration, you'll gain valuable insights that can help you achieve your campaign goals.

As we have explored in the other parts of the book, artificial intelligence is playing an increasingly large role in marketing measurement, and hypothesis creation is one of those areas. The next chapter will explore some AI-based approaches to developing your hypotheses as well as some initial exploration of predictive analytics.

CHAPTER 17

AI-BASED APPROACHES TO PREDICTION AND HYPOTHESIS DEVELOPMENT

The ever-increasing adoption and proliferation of Artificial Intelligence (AI) tools have opened up new opportunities for marketers in predictive analysis and hypothesis development. This chapter delves into the ability of AI-based tools and platforms to analyze vast datasets with incredible speed and accuracy, as well as to predict future trends and generate hypotheses that were previously beyond the reach of human cognition. AI's predictive prowess stems from its Machine Learning (ML) algorithms, which can identify patterns and relationships in data that are invisible to the naked eye, paving the way for more precise and informed marketing strategies.

THE BASICS OF AI IN PREDICTION

Earlier in the book, we looked at how AI-based tools used in marketing can augment work done by those teams in general, but now it is time to look at how AI, and ML in particular, can be used to help in measurement and testing. At its core, AI utilizes ML models that can analyze vast amounts of data and identify patterns that would be imperceptible to human analysts. These models are trained on historical data but are uniquely adept at adapting to new information, making them highly effective for dynamic market environments.

As these models operate by learning from the data they are fed, data quality is of utmost importance, and in addition to quality, we need to make sure we are collecting the right types of data.

In the context of forecasting, this often involves time-series data, which helps the models understand how certain variables evolve over time. For marketers, this capability means they can predict future consumer behaviors based on past actions. For example, by analyzing past sales data, social media engagement, and search trends, AI can predict future product demands and consumer responses to marketing campaigns. This predictive power enables marketers to allocate resources more efficiently, tailor marketing messages to meet anticipated needs, and adjust strategies in real time based on predicted market conditions.

Case Study: Predicting the Next Big Trend in Pickleball Shoes

Let's look at a hypothetical scenario with PB Shoes, where the company leverages AI to both track and predict the evolving preferences of their market segment.

By inputting historical sales data, customer reviews, and online engagement metrics into their AI system, PB Shoes could forecast upcoming trends in shoe preferences. The AI algorithms analyzed patterns such as changes in color preferences, preferred types of shoe closures, and traction needs based on customer feedback and broader market analysis.

This predictive insight allowed PB Shoes to adjust their production schedules, streamline inventory management, and optimize marketing campaigns to capitalize on these trends before they fully materialized. By utilizing these AI-driven insights, they were able to stay ahead of the competition by introducing innovative products right as the emerging trends gained momentum. Moreover, by using AI to continuously update their predictions based on real-time data, PB Shoes maintained a proactive stance in market trend utilization, ensuring that their products always resonated with current customer desires.

AI's role in prediction is not just about foreseeing the future but creating a dynamic framework where businesses can remain agile and responsive. As AI technology evolves, the depth and accuracy of predictive insights will continue to grow, further enhancing the strategic capabilities of marketers and businesses alike.

FROM HISTORICAL DATA TO PREDICTIVE INSIGHTS

Harnessing historical marketing data for predictive insights is a cornerstone of modern AI and ML strategies in marketing. The process involves several sophisticated techniques that transform raw data into valuable forecasts and trends, enabling businesses to anticipate future outcomes based on past patterns.

Data Preprocessing

The first step in making historical data usable for AI and ML is preprocessing. This involves cleaning the data to remove errors and inconsistencies, normalizing data formats, and filling in missing values. Effective preprocessing enhances the quality of data, which is crucial for the accuracy of AI predictions. Techniques such as feature scaling and transformation are also employed to ensure that the data is in a suitable format for analysis.

Feature Selection and Engineering

AI models require relevant features to make accurate predictions. Feature selection involves identifying the most important variables that influence the outcome, while feature engineering is about creating new variables from existing data. Both processes are vital because they directly impact the model's ability to learn from historical data. For example, from raw sales data, new features such as month-on-month growth percentage, seasonality adjustments, and promotional impacts can be engineered to enrich the model's inputs.

Model Training and Validation

With features prepared, the next step is to train predictive models. Supervised learning models, such as regression analysis, decision trees, and neural networks, are common in this phase. These models learn from the historical data, where the past outcomes are known, to predict future results. Validation, typically done through techniques such as cross-validation, helps in assessing the model's performance and ensuring that it generalizes well to new, unseen data.

PREDICTIVE ANALYTICS

Once validated, the AI models are used to perform predictive analytics. This involves running the models on current data to forecast future outcomes. Predictive analytics can identify trends, detect anomalies, and suggest probable future scenarios based on historical data patterns.

Case Study: How PB Shoes Uses Past Sales Data to Anticipate Future Demand Spikes

Our hypothetical company, PB Shoes, exemplifies the application of these techniques. By analyzing historical sales data, including variables such as sales volumes, customer demographics, and promotional calendars, PB Shoes trained AI models to recognize patterns associated with demand spikes. For instance, they discovered that certain promotional activities or seasonal changes led to significant increases in demand.

Using regression models and time-series analysis, PB Shoes can forecast demand trends with remarkable accuracy. The models take into account not just the direct sales data, but also derived features such as the rate of sales increase leading up to holidays or special events. This enables PB Shoes to prepare adequately by adjusting inventory levels, aligning production schedules, and tailoring marketing efforts to capitalize on anticipated demand increases.

As we've seen, converting historical marketing data into predictive insights using AI involves meticulous data preparation, strategic feature engineering, and sophisticated modeling techniques. By implementing these methods, marketers can not only understand past behaviors but also proactively respond to future market dynamics. PB Shoes' success in forecasting demand spikes underscores the transformative power of AI in turning historical data into a strategic asset for anticipating market trends.

DEVELOPING HYPOTHESES WITH AI

Integrating AI into the hypothesis development process can prove beneficial to teams when creating their marketing strategies. AI can play a dual role, enhancing the efficiency of this process while also improving the precision of the hypotheses formulated.

The initial step of AI-driven hypothesis development involves data aggregation, where AI systems collect and assimilate vast amounts of varied data sources. Next comes the application of data mining techniques, where AI algorithms identify patterns, trends, and correlations within the data that may not be immediately apparent to human analysts.

Once potential influences on consumer behavior or market dynamics are identified, AI-based data analysis tools can help simulate different scenarios based on these insights. This involves using sophisticated modeling techniques such as ML and predictive analytics to forecast the outcomes of various strategic changes or marketing interventions. The hypotheses are then refined through iterative testing, where AI systems quickly process feedback from each test to enhance the accuracy and relevance of the hypothesis.

Case Study: Hypothesis Development at PB Shoes: Using AI to Test New Market Entry Strategies

At PB Shoes, AI plays a pivotal role in formulating hypotheses for new market entry strategies. The process begins with AI's analysis of global sales data, consumer behavior analytics, social media sentiment, and competitive landscape data. By leveraging natural language processing and ML, PB Shoes can identify emerging trends and consumer needs across different geographical regions.

For instance, if AI analysis reveals a growing interest in eco-friendly athletic wear in Europe, PB Shoes may hypothesize that entering this market with a line of sustainably produced pickleball shoes could meet an unfulfilled consumer demand. To test this hypothesis, AI simulations predict consumer responses based on historical data from similar product launches and market responses to sustainability initiatives within similar demographics.

These AI-driven insights enable PB Shoes to not only formulate targeted hypotheses but also prioritize resources effectively when exploring new markets. By predicting potential outcomes, AI reduces the financial risk associated with market expansion and allows PB Shoes to tailor their entry strategies to maximize market impact.

Incorporating AI into hypothesis development transforms the traditional approach by allowing for a more data-driven, analytical process that can adapt dynamically to new information and feedback. At PB Shoes, this capability ensures that strategic decisions are both forward-looking and grounded in empirical evidence, thereby enhancing the company's agility and effectiveness in responding to new market opportunities. As AI technology continues to evolve, its integration into hypothesis development is set to become a standard practice, revolutionizing how marketing strategies are conceived and implemented.

AI AND MARKET SEGMENTATION

Dynamic market segmentation involves continuously analyzing and categorizing consumers based on a multitude of variables, including behavior, demographics, and interactions. AI excels in this area by utilizing ML algorithms to sift through large datasets, identifying patterns and clusters that might not be evident through traditional analysis.

Adaptability Is Key

AI-driven segmentation tools can adapt in real time to changes in consumer behavior, ensuring that segmentation models remain relevant and highly targeted. This adaptability is crucial for developing precise marketing strategies and hypotheses that are tailored to specific consumer segments. For instance, AI can help hypothesize which product features or marketing messages are most likely to resonate with different segments based on emerging trends and changing preferences. This targeted approach not only enhances the effectiveness of marketing campaigns but also increases efficiency by allocating resources to the most promising opportunities.

Case Study: PB Shoes' Approach to AI-Powered Audience Segmentation

PB Shoes harnesses the power of AI to segment its audience with precision, thereby crafting highly effective personalized marketing strategies. By integrating AI with their Customer Relationship Management (CRM) system, PB Shoes analyzes customer purchase history, online browsing behaviors, and feedback to create detailed customer profiles.

For example, AI helps PB Shoes segment their customers into distinct groups, such as competitive athletes, recreational users, and fashion-focused consumers. Each segment is analyzed to determine specific needs and preferences, such as the importance of shoe performance versus aesthetic design. Using this segmented data, PB Shoes can hypothesize and implement targeted marketing campaigns. For competitive athletes, they might focus on durability and performance enhancement, while for fashion-focused consumers, style and trendiness might be emphasized.

Furthermore, AI enables dynamic segmentation by updating customer profiles in real time as new data comes in. This means that PB Shoes can quickly adapt their strategies in response to new information, such as a sudden rise in interest in eco-friendly materials or a shift in consumer demographics. This responsiveness not only improves customer satisfaction but also boosts loyalty and engagement by delivering more relevant and timely content and offers.

AI-powered market segmentation represents a significant advancement in how businesses understand and interact with their customer base. For PB Shoes, leveraging AI not only sharpens the accuracy of their market segmentation but also enhances the development of targeted hypotheses, leading to more successful marketing outcomes. As AI tools and technologies continue to evolve, they offer profound possibilities for personalized marketing that meets consumers at the point of their needs and preferences, setting a new standard for what is achievable in market segmentation.

TESTING HYPOTHESES WITH AI-ENHANCED TOOLS

AI significantly enhances the efficiency and effectiveness of hypothesis testing in marketing, particularly through advanced A/B testing and multivariate experiments. AI tools can automate the process of setting up and running these tests, ensuring that the most relevant variables are included and that the data collected is robust and significant.

Rapid Analysis Increases the Pace of Optimization

AI enhances traditional A/B testing by optimizing the selection of variables and rapidly analyzing results to identify patterns that might not be immediately obvious. This allows for more precise segmentation of test groups and customization of the variables being tested. Furthermore, AI can manage multiple variations at once, scaling up the complexity of multivariate testing far beyond what could be feasibly managed manually. This capability enables marketers to test various combinations of elements on a Web page, email campaign, or digital ad and quickly determine which combinations perform best.

Case Study: PB Shoes' AI-Assisted A/B Testing on Digital Ad Effectiveness

At PB Shoes, AI-assisted A/B testing has revolutionized their approach to evaluating digital ad effectiveness. For a recent campaign, PB Shoes utilized AI tools to design and execute a series of A/B tests aimed at determining the most effective ad formats, messaging, and visuals for different customer segments.

The process began with the AI analyzing historical data to hypothesize which elements are likely to influence customer engagement and conversion rates. The AI then set up multiple test scenarios, automatically adjusting variables such as image placement, call-to-action wording, and layout designs across different demographic and psychographic audience segments. The system monitored user interactions in real time, using advanced algorithms to adjust the weighting of different tests dynamically based on early feedback.

For instance, if initial data showed that younger audiences responded more positively to a casual tone and dynamic images, the AI quickly shifted more resources to test variations of this theme more extensively. Conversely, it reduced exposure to less effective variants, thereby optimizing the overall resource allocation and increasing the speed at which optimal ad configurations were identified.

AI-assisted tools offer a powerful advantage in hypothesis testing by allowing marketers to conduct more complex, personalized, and effective experiments. In the case of PB Shoes, AI-enhanced A/B testing not only improved the efficiency and effectiveness of their digital advertising but also provided deeper insights into customer preferences and behaviors. This level of testing is invaluable for refining marketing strategies and ensuring that campaigns are precisely targeted to meet the evolving expectations of the market. As AI technology continues to advance, its integration into hypothesis testing will further empower marketers to innovate and adapt with unprecedented agility and informed confidence.

OVERCOMING BIASES AND LIMITATIONS

As powerful as AI tools are in transforming marketing analytics, they are not immune to biases, which can stem from skewed data inputs, flawed algorithmic design, or even the unintentional prejudices of the developers. These biases can significantly distort AI predictions and lead to the development of ineffective or unfair marketing strategies. Identifying and mitigating these biases is crucial to ensure the accuracy and fairness of AI applications in marketing.

Getting to the Source

The first step in this process involves understanding the source of the data. Biases often enter AI systems through the data they are trained on. For example, if an AI model is trained predominantly on data from urban, tech-savvy consumers, it may not perform well for rural markets or those with less robust infrastructure. To counter this, it's essential to ensure data diversity and representativeness in the training sets. Furthermore, regular audits of AI algorithms are necessary to identify any patterns of bias, such as preferential treatment of certain demographics or behaviors.

Ensuring Timeliness

Another important aspect of overcoming bias when using AI in your hypotheses and testing is the frequent updating of AI models to reflect new data and emerging trends, preventing them from becoming outdated and biased toward historical patterns. Involving domain experts in the development and training phases of AI tools can also provide additional oversight and ensure that the models consider all relevant variables fairly.

Case Study: How PB Shoes Ensures Unbiased AI Applications

PB Shoes has implemented several strategies to ensure that their AI applications remain objective and free from biases. First, the company maintains a diverse dataset that accurately reflects its entire customer base, including various age groups, geographic locations, and socio-economic statuses. This diversity helps in training AI models that are robust and applicable to all segments of their market.

To further enhance objectivity, PB Shoes employs ensemble learning techniques where multiple AI models are used in tandem to make predictions. This approach helps in averaging out individual model biases, leading to more accurate and balanced outcomes. PB Shoes also conducts periodic reviews of their AI models with external consultants who specialize in ethical AI to audit and review their systems for any signs of bias.

Additionally, PB Shoes has established an AI ethics board that oversees all AI initiatives. This board ensures that every application of AI in the company adheres to ethical guidelines and is transparent to stakeholders about how data is being used and decisions are being made. The board also engages with customers to gather feedback on AI-driven interactions, using this information to make continuous improvements.

Overcoming biases in AI is essential for developing effective and equitable marketing strategies. By ensuring data diversity, conducting regular audits, and employing ethical oversight, marketers can mitigate biases in AI applications. PB Shoes exemplifies how a conscientious approach to AI can lead to more objective, fair, and successful marketing outcomes. As AI continues to evolve, maintaining vigilance against biases will remain a crucial challenge for marketers aiming to leverage this technology responsibly.

CONCLUSION

The integration of AI into marketing analysis provides marketing teams with opportunities for more robust prediction and hypothesis development. As we have explored throughout this chapter, AI's ability to process vast quantities of data rapidly and with high accuracy enables marketers to not only understand past consumer behaviors but also anticipate future trends and react proactively. This predictive capability is critical in a rapidly changing market environment, where staying ahead of trends can be the difference between leading the market and lagging behind.

AI's role extends beyond mere analysis; it is a transformative tool that redefines how marketing strategies are conceived and implemented. Through dynamic market segmentation, effective hypothesis testing, and the mitigation of biases, AI empowers marketers to make informed, data-driven decisions. The case studies and examples discussed, particularly the innovative strategies employed by PB Shoes, illustrate how AI can be leveraged to gain a competitive edge and tailor marketing efforts to meet the precise needs of the target audience.

The adoption of AI offers a path toward more scientific marketing practices, where decisions are guided by data and machine-learned insights rather than intuition and conjecture. It is also important, however, to approach AI with a critical mind, understanding its limitations and ensuring ethical usage, especially in terms of data handling and consumer privacy.

Integrating AI into marketing practices involves both excitement and responsibility. For marketers willing to invest in AI and develop their capabilities in this area, the potential rewards include not only improved efficiency and effectiveness in their campaigns but also a deeper connection with their customers. As AI technology continues to evolve, staying informed and adaptable will be key to harnessing its full potential, ensuring that marketers can continue to thrive in an increasingly digital and data-driven world.

We touched on some of the statistical concepts discussed earlier in the book in this chapter. In the next chapter, we will look more deeply at some statistical considerations as you engage in marketing measurement and testing.

18

STATISTICAL CONSIDERATIONS FOR TESTING

While much of what has been discussed in this book does not require statistics, there can be benefits to employing statistical methods when analyzing your marketing efforts. In this chapter, we are going to look at the core principles of statistical testing in marketing, exploring how these techniques can be used to validate hypotheses, measure campaign effectiveness, and optimize marketing strategies based on quantitative data.

Statistical testing provides a robust framework for marketers to assess the success of their campaigns against specific objectives and metrics. Whether it's determining the impact of a new advertising approach, evaluating customer segmentation strategies, or measuring the ROI of different marketing channels, statistical testing offers a systematic way to derive meaningful conclusions from complex datasets.

If you are new to statistics, some of the concepts in this chapter might be a little advanced, but most of what will be covered builds on some of the statistical concepts that have already been discussed. While at least a foundational understanding of basic statistical concepts, such as hypothesis testing, significance levels, and confidence intervals, will be helpful, the content should at least provide some starting points for areas to research further.

PRINCIPLES OF STATISTICAL TESTING

Statistical testing leads to a more robust quantitative analysis of marketing data, providing a methodical approach to validating hypotheses and making informed decisions based on data. Understanding these principles is essential for any marketer looking to evaluate the effectiveness of their strategies scientifically.

Fundamental Statistical Concepts

Let's start by reviewing some of the fundamental statistical concepts and demonstrate how they apply to common marketing scenarios.

P-Value

The p-value indicates the probability of observing the test results under the null hypothesis.

A p-value is a measure that helps us decide whether the effect we are seeing in our data (such as an increase in sales after a new advertising campaign) is likely due to chance or the actual impact of the campaign.

Imagine flipping a coin 10 times to test whether it's fair, and it lands on heads 9 times. The p-value tells you how surprising this outcome is under the assumption that the coin is fair. In statistical testing, if this p-value is very small (typically less than 0.05), it means the result is surprising enough under the assumption (null hypothesis) that we reject the idea of "chance" and conclude there's an actual effect (such as the coin being biased, or the marketing campaign being effective).

Significance Level

A p-value lower than the significance level (represented as , often set at 0.05) suggests that the observed data are inconsistent with the null hypothesis, leading to its rejection in favor of the alternative hypothesis.

This means there is less than a 5% probability that the observed results are due to chance, thus affirming the effectiveness of the marketing strategy.

For example, if you run a campaign to increase brand awareness and the p-value associated with the increase in brand engagement metrics (such as survey scores or social mentions) is below 0.05, you can claim with confidence that the campaign caused the increase.

When evaluating the effectiveness of a marketing campaign, statistical significance helps marketers avoid drawing false conclusions from random fluctuations in data. It is essential for validating the impact of new marketing tactics before rolling them out broadly.

It's also important to consider the practical significance of your results. Even if a result is statistically significant, it's worth considering whether the size of the effect is large enough to be of practical value. For example, a statistically significant 0.5% increase in customer conversion rate might not justify the cost of a costly advertising campaign.

Confidence Interval

This statistical concept provides a range of values, calculated from the data sample, that is likely to contain the true population parameter. In marketing, a 95% confidence interval for an average increase in sales due to a campaign gives a range from which the true increase can be asserted with 95% confidence.

A confidence interval gives an estimated range of values, which is likely to include an unknown population parameter, the estimated range being calculated from a given set of sample data.

In marketing, if you're measuring the increase in traffic to your Web site after launching a new ad, a 95% confidence interval might be from a 10% to a 20% increase. This means you can be 95% confident that the true increase in traffic, across all potential Web site visitors, is between 10% and 20%.

Sample Size

Understanding the concepts of sample size and statistical power is essential for conducting reliable marketing tests that produce valid results. These elements are critical in planning your studies so that they are capable of detecting the effects you are interested in observing. This section will explore how to determine an appropriate sample size and discuss the importance of statistical power in marketing research.

Basics of Sample Size Determination

- *Objective assessment*: The first step in determining the sample size is to define what you want to test and your desired accuracy level. This might include estimating a population parameter (such as average customer spend) or testing a hypothesis (such as whether new packaging increases sales).
- *Variability and effect size*: The more variable your data, the larger the sample size needed to detect a given effect size. The effect size is a measure of how strong a signal you are trying to detect, such as the difference in response rates between two marketing campaigns.
- *Confidence level and margin of error*: Decide on your confidence level (commonly 95%), which reflects how sure you want to be about your findings. The margin of error indicates the range within which the true value lies. Smaller margins of error require larger sample sizes.
- *Formula and software*: Use established statistical formulas to calculate sample size, taking into account the preceding factors. Many statistical software packages and online calculators can automate this calculation based on your inputs.

Example in a Marketing Context

Suppose a marketer wants to test whether a new product's launch campaign increases brand awareness. If previous campaigns show a 30% awareness level with high variability, and the marketer wants to detect a 5% increase in awareness with 95% confidence and a 5% margin of error, the required sample size would be calculated to ensure these conditions are met.

Statistical Power

- *Definition*: Statistical power is the probability that a test will correctly reject the null hypothesis when it is false. In simpler terms, it's the test's ability to detect an effect if there is one.
- *Influencing factors*: Power is influenced by the sample size, the effect size (the magnitude of the effect), the significance level (the threshold for rejecting the null hypothesis, typically set at 0.05), and the variability of the data.
- *High power benefits*: A high-powered study is more likely to detect meaningful differences or changes brought about by a marketing strategy. This reduces the risk of Type II errors (falsely accepting the null hypothesis when it should be rejected).

Example for Marketers

Statistical power is crucial for making informed decisions in marketing. For example, if a company is testing two versions of an ad to see which one generates more clicks, a high-powered test ensures that if one ad truly performs better, the test is likely to detect this difference. This prevents the company from mistakenly continuing with a less effective ad due to inadequate test power.

Determining the right sample size and ensuring sufficient statistical power are foundational elements of designing effective marketing tests. By carefully planning these aspects, marketers can increase the reliability of their conclusions, making the most of their research efforts and resources. These statistical considerations help ensure that the decisions made based on test results truly reflect the preferences and behaviors of the target market, thereby optimizing marketing strategies and outcomes.

EXAMPLES: USING STATISTICAL PRINCIPLES IN MARKETING SCENARIOS

With some definitions of statistical principles under our belt, let's walk through a few examples of how to put these statistical principles into practice.

Example 1: Evaluating Campaign Effectiveness

- *Scenario*: A marketer wants to test whether a new online advertisement is more effective than the existing one.
- *Application*: The marketer sets up an A/B test where each version of the advertisement is shown to a different group of Web site visitors. The null hypothesis states that there is no difference in the Clickthrough Rates (CTRs) for the ads. After collecting the data, a hypothesis test is performed. If the p-value is less than 0.05, the marketer can reject the null hypothesis, concluding that the new ad performs better.

Example 2: Product Pricing Strategy

- *Scenario*: A company considers two different pricing strategies for a new product and wants to determine which strategy yields higher sales.
- *Application*: The company uses a split-test approach, applying different pricing strategies to similar demographic groups over a specific period. Statistical testing can then be applied to compare the sales data from the two groups. Confidence intervals for the average sales under each strategy can help determine whether one pricing strategy consistently leads to higher sales than the other.

Example 3: Customer Satisfaction Analysis

- *Scenario*: After implementing changes in customer service protocols, a company wants to assess the impact on customer satisfaction.
- *Application*: Customer satisfaction scores before and after the implementation are compared using a paired t-test (if the data distribution is assumed to be normal). This test will help determine whether the changes in protocol led to a statistically significant improvement in customer satisfaction.

TABLE 18.1. Some common statistical tests for marketers.

Type of Test	When to Use	When Not to Use
T-test	Comparing the means of two groups on a continuous data scale.	Data does not meet the assumptions of normality or when you have more than two groups to compare.
Chi-square test	Examining the relationship between two categorical variables.	Expected frequencies are very low (less than 5) or when dealing with numerical data.
ANOVA	Comparing the means of three or more groups.	Groups do not have equal variances or when you need to compare only two groups.
Correlation coefficient	Measuring the strength and direction of the relationship between two continuous variables.	Variables are categorical, or you're trying to establish causation, not just correlation.
Logistic regression	Predicting the probability of a binary outcome based on one or more predictor variables.	The dependent variable is not binary or the relationship between variables is non-linear.

Understanding these principles enables marketers to apply statistical testing methods effectively to various marketing questions, ensuring that decisions are data-driven and reflect true market conditions rather than random variations. With these tools, marketers can objectively assess the success of their strategies and refine their approaches based on solid evidence.

CHOOSING THE RIGHT STATISTICAL TEST

If you are already familiar with statistical testing, you are likely aware that there are many types of potential tests that can be performed. The following is an overview of five types of tests and when they should (or shouldn't) be applied.

SOME COMMON STATISTICAL TESTS THAT MARKETERS USE

The following are some common statistical tests used by marketers.

T-Test

A t-test is a statistical test used to compare the means of two groups to see whether they are statistically different from each other. This test assumes that the data is normally distributed and the variance between the two groups is equal.

How to Conduct

To perform a t-test, you calculate the difference between the two group means and divide this by the standard error of the difference. A t-distribution is then used to find the t-value, which can be compared against a critical value from the t-distribution table to determine significance.

Example

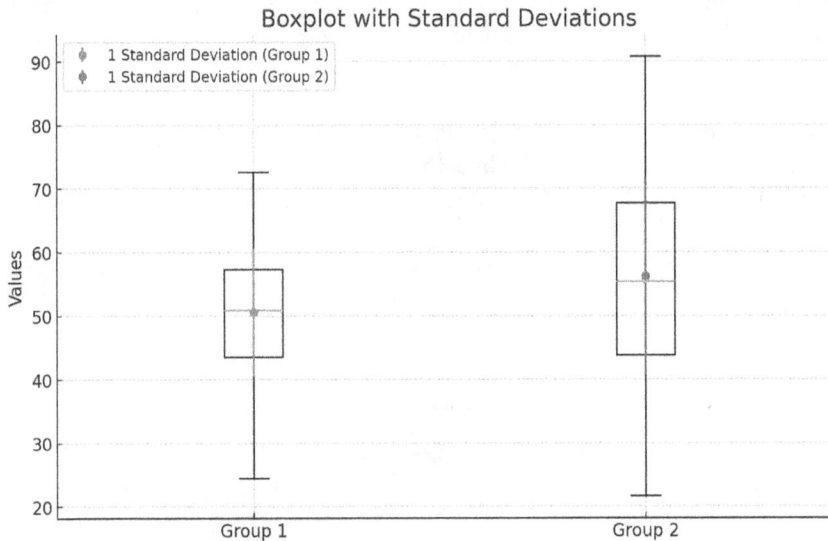

FIGURE 18.1. A t-test using a boxplot visualization.

As you can see in Figure 18.1, we have a boxplot visualization for two groups of data, which is a common way that a t-test is plotted. Each boxplot displays the median, quartiles, and outliers of the data distributions. There are also markers showing the mean and one standard deviation above and below the mean for each group.

The red marker (on the left) represents the mean and standard deviation of group 1. The green marker (on the right) represents the mean and standard deviation of group 2. This visualization helps to compare the central tendency and variability of the two groups, which are common aspects examined in a t-test.

When to Use

Use a t-test when you want to compare the average performance between two groups on a continuous data scale. It's ideal for assessing things such as the difference in average sales before and after a specific marketing campaign for a similar time of year.

When to Avoid

Avoid a t-test when your data does not meet the assumptions of normality. This refers to the presumption that the data being analyzed is drawn from a population that follows a normal distribution, sometimes known as a Gaussian distribution or bell curve. This distribution is symmetric about the mean, meaning that the mean, median, and mode of the data are equal, and it follows a specific bell-shaped curve when graphed.

A t-test should also be avoided when you have more than two groups to compare. It's also not suitable for categorical data or paired observations.

The t-test is best used when comparing the means of two groups to find out whether there's a significant difference. Ensure the data is normally distributed and variance is equal before proceeding, and do not use for categorical data or more than two groups.

Chi-Square Test

The chi-square test is used to determine whether there is a significant association between categorical variables. It's a non-parametric test that doesn't assume a normal distribution.

How to Perform

To perform a chi-square test, an observed frequency table is compared to an expected frequency table, calculated based on the hypothesis of no association. The sum of the squared difference between observed and expected frequencies, divided by the expected frequencies, gives the chi-square statistic.

For instance, let's say we wanted to compare sales results from two different channels used within a marketing campaign: email and social media.

We have the following data.

TABLE 18.2. Sample results from an email and social media campaign.

Channel	Successful (Bought)	Not Successful (Did Not Buy)
Email	120	150
Social Media	80	200

Using statistical software, we will perform a chi-square test to determine whether there is a statistically significant difference in the success rates between those two marketing channels.

The results of our test are the following:

- Chi-square statistic: 14.29
- P-value: 0.00016
- Degrees of freedom: 1
- Expected frequencies:
  - Email:
    - 98.18 (successful)
    - 171.82 (not successful)
  - Social media:
    - 101.82 (successful)
    - 178.18 (not successful)

Interpretation of the Results of the Chi-Square Test

We are going to leave some of the terms used previously to you to do some further exploration of, but we will highlight the most relevant here.

The p-value is 0.00016, which, being less than 0.05, indicates that there is a statistically significant difference in the success rates between email and social media marketing channels. This means that the channel used (email or social media) is likely to influence the success of the sales in this hypothetical marketing campaign.

You can also see this in a chart, as shown in Figure 18.2, which shows the observed (what actually occurred) as well as the expected (what is predicted based on the previous observations) results.

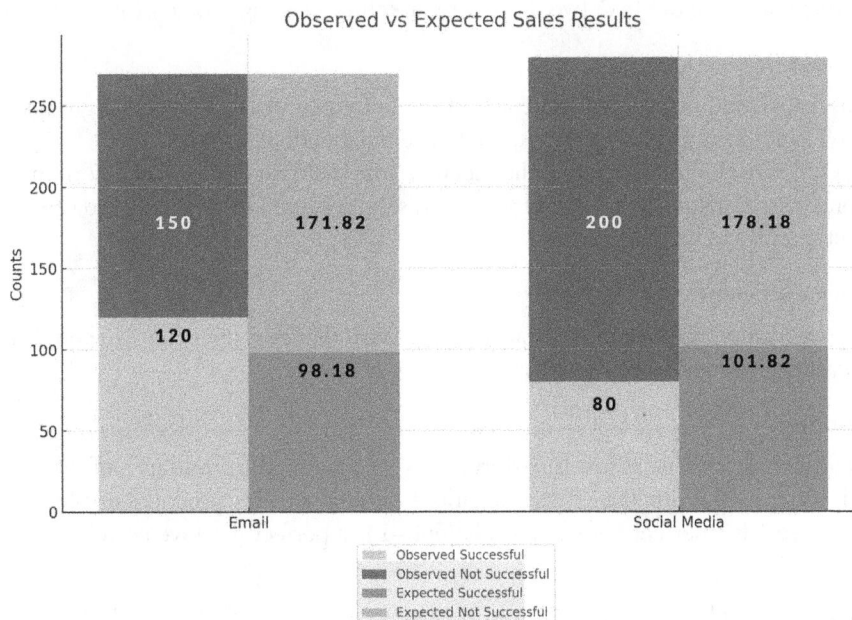

FIGURE 18.2. A chi-square test based on a comparison of two channels (email and social media) used to run a marketing campaign.

When to Use

This test is suitable when you're looking at the relationship between two categorical variables, such as gender and preference for a type of shoe, or region and product sales category. There should also be a high volume of data or responses.

When to Avoid

It should be avoided if the expected frequency in any of the cells in a contingency table is too low (less than 5), as this can make the test inaccurate.

The chi-square test is appropriate for testing relationships between categorical variables without assuming a normal distribution. Avoid it when the expected frequencies in the data are too low.

Analysis of Variance (ANOVA)

Analysis of Variance, or ANOVA, is a statistical method used to compare the means of three or more samples to understand whether at least one sample mean is significantly different from the others.

How to Perform

Performing ANOVA involves calculating the between-group variability and within-group variability, and then comparing these to produce an F-statistic. A higher ratio indicates a greater probability that significant differences exist.

When to Use

ANOVA is the test of choice when comparing more than two groups, for instance, analyzing the effectiveness of more than two different marketing campaigns on customer acquisition.

When to Avoid

This test should be avoided if the assumption of equal variance between groups (homoscedasticity) is not met, or if the groups do not have independent samples.

ANOVA is useful for comparing the means across multiple groups and determining whether differences are statistically significant. It requires the assumptions of homoscedasticity and independent samples to be valid.

Correlation Coefficient

The correlation coefficient is a statistical measure that describes the size and direction of a relationship between two continuous variables.

How to Conduct

A correlation coefficient test is performed by calculating the covariance of the variables and then dividing by the product of their standard deviations. This produces a value between -1 and 1, where 1 is a perfect positive correlation, -1 is a perfect negative correlation, and 0 is no correlation.

When to Use

Use this test when you need to understand the relationship between variables, such as advertising spend and sales figures.

When to Avoid

Avoid using the correlation coefficient if your data is not continuous or the relationship is not linear. Also, correlation does not imply causation.

The correlation coefficient is ideal for measuring the strength and direction of a linear relationship between two continuous variables, but it doesn't work for non-linear relationships and does not establish causality.

Logistic Regression

Logistic regression is a statistical method for analyzing a dataset in which there are one or more independent variables that determine an outcome, which is categorical, or easy to define, such as being able to be answered with a "yes" or "no," such as whether a purchase was made or not.

How to Conduct

It is performed by using one or more independent variables to predict an outcome using a logistic function, which is an S-shaped curve that can take any real-valued number and map it between 0 and 1.

When to Use

Use logistic regression when your dependent variable is binary, such as whether a customer will buy a product (yes or no), and you want to understand the impact of one or more independent variables. Let's look at a few examples of when logistic regression might be beneficial:

- *Predicting customer conversion*: Logistic regression can help predict the likelihood that a potential customer will convert into a paying customer based on various factors, such as demographics, past buying behavior, interaction with marketing materials, and channel engagement. For example, a company can use logistic regression to analyze how factors such as age, gender, and number of email opens contribute to the probability of making a purchase.
- *Effectiveness of marketing channels*: Similar to the chi-square we discussed earlier, but with more granularity, logistic regression can assess the effectiveness of different marketing channels (email, social media, direct mail, etc.) on outcomes. By including these channels as predictors, you can estimate their impact on the likelihood of a sale, adjusting for other covariates, such as customer segment or promotion type.
- *Impact of promotional offers*: Logistic regression is useful for analyzing the impact of promotional offers on purchase behavior. Marketers can model the probability of a sale based on different types of promotions (discount percentage, BOGOF, or free shipping) to determine which offers are most likely to drive conversions.
- *Customer retention*: In customer relationship management, logistic regression can help predict customer churn based on factors such as usage patterns, customer service interactions, satisfaction levels, and payment history. This enables targeted interventions aimed at retaining high-risk customers.
- *Upselling and cross-selling opportunities*: Logistic regression can identify opportunities for upselling and cross-selling by predicting which customers are likely to be interested in additional products or services based on their purchase history and engagement.

When to Avoid

Logistic regression should be avoided when the dependent variable is not categorical or if there is non-linearity between the dependent and independent variables.

Logistic regression is used for predicting the probability of a binary outcome based on one or more predictor variables. It's best applied to binary categorical data and requires a linear relationship between the dependent and independent variables.

HOW TO SELECT THE RIGHT TEST

With a good understanding of at least a few statistical tests, you now have enough information to determine the best approach to take given the data you have and the test that would be the most beneficial to perform. Let's look at a few methods to determine whether you have selected the best type of statistical test for your marketing measurement analysis.

Criteria to Use to Select the Right Test

Selecting the right statistical test is a pivotal step in the analysis process, as it determines the validity of your conclusions. The criteria for selecting the appropriate test are based on the nature of your data and the hypothesis you aim to test:

- *Type of data*: Identify whether your data is categorical, ordinal, or continuous. Categorical data, such as gender or type of product, often requires a chi-square or logistic regression test, while continuous data, such as sales figures or time spent on a Web page, may require a t-test or ANOVA.
- *Distribution of data*: Check whether your data follows a normal distribution, which is required for parametric tests such as the t-test or ANOVA. Non-parametric tests, such as the Mann-Whitney U test or the Kruskal-Wallis test, are better suited for data that do not meet this assumption.
- *Number of variables and groups*: Consider how many variables and groups you are comparing. A t-test is suitable for comparing two groups, whereas ANOVA can compare three or more groups. Additionally, if you have more than one independent variable, you may need to consider a multivariate test such as MANOVA.
- *Scale of measurement*: Identify the scale of measurement of the data. Ratio and interval data often work with a broader range of tests than nominal or ordinal data.

How to Confirm the Test Is a Good Fit

Of course, even if a test seems like the right fit for your data, it is still important to confirm that it works well. Here are some things to check for:

- *Assumption checks*: After choosing a test, conduct assumption checks. For example, for a t-test, assess normality with a Shapiro-Wilk test or visualize with Q-Q plots, and check for equal variances with a Levene's test.
- *Preliminary results*: Run the test on a subset of data or conduct a pilot test. If the results are counterintuitive or the effect sizes are implausible, this may indicate a mismatch.
- *Consult literature and precedent*: Look at similar studies or industry-standard practices to confirm that your chosen test aligns with established research.

Ways to Tell Whether You've Chosen the Wrong Test

You may have suspicions that a test is not the right fit once you run it initially. Here are some things to look out for that point to having used the wrong test:

- *Significant violation of assumptions*: If the assumptions of the test are significantly violated (e.g., non-normality in a t-test), the test may be inappropriate.
- *Inconsistent results*: If small changes in the data result in vastly different outcomes, or if your results are markedly different from similar studies without a clear reason, you may need to reassess your test choice.
- *Lack of robustness*: If the test does not accommodate the structure of your data or ignores important facets of your data (such as the ordinal nature of a variable), it may be the wrong choice.

Choosing the correct statistical test is essential for credible analysis. This selection is guided by the type and distribution of your data, the number of variables and groups you are analyzing, and the scale of measurement. Confirming the fit involves checking assumptions, seeking consistency with preliminary results, and ensuring alignment with established research. If you encounter assumption violations, inconsistent or counterintuitive results, or a lack of robustness to your data's structure, these are signs you may need to select a different test. Ultimately, careful selection and validation of your statistical test will reinforce the accuracy and reliability of your marketing analysis.

CASE STUDY: PB SHOES' MARKETING CAMPAIGN TEST

Let's revisit our friends at PB Shoes and see how they effectively utilized statistical testing to determine the optimal launch strategy for their new line of eco-friendly running shoes. This example illustrates the entire process of applying statistical testing in a marketing context, from the formulation of hypotheses to the interpretation of results.

Background and Objective

PB Shoes aimed to introduce a new product line and wanted to identify the most effective marketing campaign to maximize initial consumer engagement and sales. The company developed two different advertising concepts:

1. An emotionally appealing campaign focusing on the environmental benefits of the shoes
2. A practical appeal campaign emphasizing the durability and cost-effectiveness of the shoes

The objective was to determine which campaign would resonate more with their target market and thus should be used for the product launch.

Hypothesis Formulation

To perform a proper test, the marketing team at PB Shoes followed best practices and formulated the following hypotheses:

- Null hypothesis (H0): There is no difference in consumer engagement between the emotionally appealing campaign and the practical appeal campaign.

- Alternative hypothesis (HA): The emotionally appealing campaign generates higher consumer engagement than the practical appeal campaign.

Experiment Design

PB Shoes decided to use an A/B testing framework to evaluate the two campaigns:

- *Sample selection*: A sample of 1,000 potential customers was randomly selected from their customer database, ensuring a representative mix of demographics and previous purchasing behavior.
- *Group assignment*: The sample was randomly divided into two groups of 500 each. Group A received the emotionally appealing campaign and group B received the practical appeal campaign.
- *Data collection*: The main metric for consumer engagement was the CTR on emailed campaign materials. Secondary metrics included time spent on the product landing page and pre-orders placed.

Statistical Testing and Results

After the two-week test period, the following results were observed:

- Group A (emotionally appealing): Average CTR of 4.5%, with a standard deviation of 0.8%
- Group B (practical appeal): Average CTR of 3.8%, with a standard deviation of 0.7%

An independent samples t-test was conducted to compare the CTRs between the two groups:

- Calculation: The t-test calculated a p-value of 0.023, which is below the significance level (α) of 0.05.

The p-value indicated that there is a statistically significant difference in CTR between the two campaigns, with the emotionally appealing campaign performing better. Thus, the null hypothesis was rejected in favor of the alternative hypothesis.

Analysis and Next Steps

With the statistical evidence supporting higher engagement for the emotionally appealing campaign, PB Shoes decided to proceed with this strategy for the nationwide launch of their new product line. The decision was further supported by the positive feedback received in follow-up customer surveys about the environmental impact message.

By rigorously testing their hypotheses and interpreting the data through the lens of statistical significance, PB Shoes was able to confidently select the marketing approach that was most likely to succeed, demonstrating the power and practicality of statistical testing in real-world marketing.

SOME COMMON TESTING AND ANALYSIS PITFALLS (AND HOW TO AVOID THEM)

Statistical testing is a powerful tool for marketers seeking to make data-driven decisions. Without careful execution and understanding, however, it's easy to fall into traps that can lead to misleading conclusions and ineffective strategies. Let's look at some common mistakes in statistical testing within the context of marketing and provide practical tips to ensure valid and reliable testing practices:

- *Ignoring sample bias*: One of the most common mistakes in statistical testing is not accounting for sample bias. This occurs when the sample used for testing does not accurately represent the target population, leading to results that cannot be generalized.
- *Overlooking the impact of external factors*: Failing to account for external factors such as seasonal variations, economic shifts, or competitive actions can skew results and attribute effects to the tested variables incorrectly.
- *Data snooping*: Often referred to as p-hacking, this involves testing numerous variables or continuously modifying hypotheses until significant results are found. This practice increases the likelihood of Type I errors, where false positives are incorrectly identified as true.
- *Underpowering your study*: Setting up a test without an adequate sample size can result in a lack of statistical power, making it difficult to detect a true effect if it exists. This can lead to Type II errors, where true positives are missed.

Preventing Common Mistakes

Now let's look at some ways to prevent some of these mistakes.

Ensure Representative Sampling

- *Tip*: Use stratified sampling to divide the total population into smaller groups, or strata, that share similar characteristics. Randomly select samples from each stratum to ensure the sample is representative of the entire population.
- *Application*: When launching a new product targeting different demographic groups, stratify your customer base by age, location, and purchase behavior to ensure all relevant consumer segments are included in your test.

Control for External Variables

- *Tip*: Incorporate control groups and use statistical techniques such as covariance analysis to separate the impact of marketing efforts from external influences.
- *Application*: If testing a holiday season campaign, compare results with a non-holiday period or use historical data to adjust for seasonal effects.

Define Hypotheses Beforehand

- *Tip*: Establish clear, testable hypotheses prior to data collection and analysis. This helps avoid data snooping and ensures that the testing process is unbiased and focused.
- *Application*: Before running an A/B test on two Web page designs, clearly define what metric (e.g., conversion rate or time on page) will determine the winning design.

Calculate Required Sample Size

- *Tip*: Use power analysis to determine the necessary sample size to achieve adequate power (typically 80% or higher) before starting your test.

• *Application*: Before testing the effectiveness of two different email marketing campaigns, perform a power analysis to determine how many recipients are needed in each group to reliably detect a difference in open rates.

More Errors to Avoid and How to Identify Them

Table 18.3 shows some more common errors, how to identify them, and how to avoid them in the future:

TABLE 18.3. Some common statistical testing errors.

Common Statistical Errors	How to Identify the Error	How to Avoid the Error in the Future
Ignoring population stratification	Uniform effects across diverse groups in data	Ensure diverse representation in samples and stratify analyses
Overlooking sample size adequacy	Statistical power is too low; results are not reliable	Use power analysis to determine the necessary sample size before data collection
Misinterpreting p-values and significance	Believing that p < 0.05 always indicates a true effect	Understand that statistical significance does not imply practical significance
Relying on convenience sampling	The sample may not represent the population well	Use random sampling methods whenever possible
Data dredging or p-hacking	Multiple tests lead to a significant result by chance	Pre-register hypotheses; correct for multiple comparisons
Confusing correlation with causation	Assuming a causal link from a correlational finding	Design experiments to test for causation, not just correlation
Using only descriptive statistics	Lack of hypothesis testing or inferential statistics	Incorporate inferential statistics to make predictions about populations
Failing to account for seasonality	Periodic fluctuations that correlate with campaign performance	Include controls for seasonal effects in the analysis
Overfitting predictive models	The model performs well on training data but poorly on new data	Validate models with new data; simplify the model if necessary
Neglecting the testing of assumptions	Violations in model residuals, such as non-normal distribution or heteroscedasticity	Check assumptions prior to analysis; use appropriate transformations or models

USING SOFTWARE TOOLS FOR STATISTICAL TESTING

While data analysis is essential in marketing, not all marketers come from a statistical background. Thankfully, a variety of user-friendly statistical software tools exist that can simplify the process of performing and interpreting statistical tests. Let's look at some of these tools and provide a brief guide on how to leverage them effectively in marketing contexts.

Statistical software tools are designed to help professionals execute complex statistical tests without needing extensive statistical knowledge. These tools often come with Graphical User

Interfaces (GUIs) and templates for common tests, making them accessible to users who may not be familiar with programming or advanced statistical methods. Here are a few popular tools that marketers can use:

- *IBM SPSS Statistics (SPSS)*: Known for its ease of use, SPSS offers advanced capabilities with a simple menu-driven interface, ideal for performing a wide range of statistical tests from basic to complex.
- *Statistical Analysis System (SAS)*: While slightly more complex than SPSS, SAS provides powerful data analysis capabilities with more customization options through SAS programming.
- *R (with RStudio)*: R is a free software environment for statistical computing and graphics, which, when paired with RStudio, becomes more accessible thanks to additional GUI features.
- *Microsoft Excel*: For simpler statistical needs, Excel offers basic tools such as t-tests, chi-square tests, and linear regression. It's widely accessible through Microsoft Office and familiar to most professionals.

By integrating these software tools into their workflow, marketers can significantly enhance their capability to conduct robust statistical analysis, ensuring that decisions are backed by solid data. These tools not only simplify the process of statistical testing but also empower marketers to derive actionable insights that can lead to more successful marketing strategies.

CONCLUSION

By understanding and applying statistical principles correctly, marketers can significantly enhance the effectiveness and efficiency of their strategies.

Also, remember that the journey of incorporating statistical testing into your marketing practices is ongoing and dynamic. This also means that you and your team don't need to be statistics experts to get started, but by committing to understanding and applying these principles, you are equipping yourself and your team with the tools to succeed in a data-driven marketing environment.

Following the more robust exploration of statistical concepts in this chapter, the next chapter will detail how to construct a single channel marketing measurement test, from identifying the test and controls, to running the test itself.

CHAPTER 19

CONSTRUCTING AND RUNNING A SINGLE-CHANNEL TEST

Running successful marketing tests is essential for the growth of businesses. As we've already discussed, every marketing test requires a clear, specific goal that aligns with your business objectives and a way to measure it.

It also requires a well-constructed hypothesis that helps you determine whether it does—or doesn't—perform as expected. Since we've already discussed these at length, let's skip to the rest of the components of a good single-channel marketing test. So, in this chapter, we will explore the essential components of a strong digital marketing test. For those more focused on offline channels, don't worry; there will still be plenty for you here as well.

CONSTRUCTING YOUR TEST

Let's start by discussing how to construct a test in terms of some key decisions you'll need to make.

Identify Your Test and Your Controls

For a test to succeed, you need to isolate the elements you are testing. This involves modifying a specific element (e.g., an email subject line, the color of a landing page button, or the image in a banner ad) while leaving the rest of the elements the same. In other words, you can only modify one element (or at least a very small number of elements) to determine what works or doesn't. Put another way, if you change *everything* about one variation versus another, it would be impossible to tell what element made it more successful.

Thus, the element that changes is your *test*, and the other elements that stay the same are your *controls*.

Back to our example

As explored previously, the falsifiable statement included two points: 1) adding more images of kids playing pickleball while wearing PB Shoes and 2) making the Call to Action (CTA) more visible.

A good test would not include making both of those changes simultaneously. Instead, a test should be performed to see the effect that changing images has, and a separate test should determine whether making the CTA more visible makes a difference. That way, a determination can be made of which, neither, or both had an impact on conversion results.

A/B or Multivariate Test?

When deciding whether to conduct an A/B test or a multivariate test—sometimes referred to as A/B/n testing—it is important to consider the questions you want to be answered (generally the hypothesis) and the goals of the test. An A/B test is a type of experiment in which two versions of something are tested against each other to determine which one performs better. This type of test is often used to test small changes to marketing collateral, such as changes to the layout or wording of a Web site.

On the other hand, a multivariate test is a type of experiment in which multiple versions are tested against each other to determine which one performs best. This type of test is often used to test larger changes to a campaign, product, or service, such as changes to multiple features or the addition of new features.

In general, an A/B test is appropriate when the goal is to test a small change, and a multivariate test is appropriate when the goal is to test a larger change. The specific choice between an A/B test and a multivariate test, however, will depend on the research question and the study's goals.

ELEMENTS TO TEST

Now that we've discussed how to construct a test, let's look at several elements you can test within your marketing channel.

Audience Segmentation

Audience segmentation is one of the most critical elements in testing. The effectiveness and accuracy of any test largely depend on the relevance of the audience you're targeting. Before running tests on marketing campaigns, it's essential to identify and understand your target audience. This involves gathering detailed information about their demographics (such as age, gender, income, and location), psychographics (such as interests, values, and lifestyles), behaviors (such as purchasing habits and Web site activity), and overall preferences. Without this level of understanding, testing outcomes may be irrelevant, as the message or offer may not resonate with the correct audience group.

Once you have this data, you can begin segmenting your audience into meaningful groups. Segmentation allows you to test how different elements of your campaign, such as messaging, creative design, or offers, perform with different audiences. For example, one segment may respond better to a discount offer, while another segment might be more motivated by an emphasis on product quality or sustainability. Testing these elements across multiple segments will give you deeper insights into your audience's preferences, enabling you to optimize future campaigns for maximum impact. Audience segmentation also helps you understand which groups are more valuable to your business, allowing you to prioritize resources accordingly.

Here are some examples of audience segments you could create for testing in a marketing campaign:

- *Age groups*: 18–24, 25–34, 35–44, 45+
- *Gender*: Male, female, non-binary, or other gender identities
- *Income levels*: Low, middle, or high-income earners
- *Location*: Urban, suburban, or rural areas; regional differences; international markets

- *Job roles*: Entry-level professionals, mid-career professionals, or executives
- *Purchase behavior*: Frequent buyers vs occasional buyers
- *Interests*: Health-conscious individuals vs fashion-focused consumers
- *Stage in the customer journey*: New visitors, returning visitors, or repeat customers
- *Technology usage*: Desktop users vs mobile users
- *Values-based segmentation*: Environmentally conscious individuals, tech enthusiasts, or budget-conscious shoppers

By segmenting your audience in such detailed ways, you can run more targeted tests and collect insights that drive better marketing decisions, ensuring that your efforts resonate with the right people at the right time.

Elements of the Creative

When testing marketing campaigns, one of the most critical components to experiment with is the creative elements. These include the layout, headline, copy, images, colors, and typography used across various channels, whether that's a landing page, email, or ad. Creative elements are the first things your audience interacts with, and even small adjustments can have a large impact on how effectively your message is communicated and received. For example, changing an image that occupies a prominent space on your Web site or email may influence how users perceive your brand or whether they engage with your CTA. By testing these elements, you can identify what resonates best with your target audience and optimize accordingly.

In email marketing, for instance, you can experiment with variations in subject lines, the imagery used in the body, and the messaging or copy. When testing creative elements, however, it's important to avoid changing too many things at once. If you alter multiple elements at the same time, such as the headline, colors, and images, it becomes challenging to isolate which variable is driving changes in performance. This is why testing one or two creative aspects at a time is best practice, as it allows you to maintain controls and pinpoint which changes yield the best results.

Here are some examples of creative elements you can test in your marketing campaigns:

- *Headline*: Test different headlines for clarity, tone, or length.
- *CTA*: Experiment with the wording, placement, or color of the CTA button.
- *Images*: Compare different images or graphics to see which engages users better.
- *Copy length*: Compare short- vs long-form copy to see what holds the audience's attention.
- *Typography*: Experiment with font styles, sizes, and boldness.
- *Colors*: Test different color schemes for backgrounds, buttons, or text.
- *Layout*: Try variations in the arrangement of content, such as where the images or CTAs are placed.
- *Email subject lines*: Experiment with different subject lines for open rates.
- *Content tone*: Test different tones of voice, from formal to conversational.
- *Video vs static content*: Compare the impact of using video content versus images or infographics.

By testing these creative elements using effective hypothesis testing, you can fine-tune your messaging, optimize engagement, and deliver more effective campaigns.

Call to Action (CTA)

Testing your CTA is one of the most impactful ways to optimize your marketing campaigns. The CTA is the point at which you ask your audience to take a specific action, whether it's clicking a button, signing up for a newsletter, downloading a resource, or making a purchase. Even small changes to the wording, design, or placement of this essential element can lead to significant shifts in conversion rates. It's crucial to test various CTA elements to determine what resonates best with your audience. Depending on the channel or medium you're using, variations can range from simple tweaks in language to significant changes in design or even timing.

For instance, if you're running a social media campaign, you might test different CTA buttons, such as "Learn More" versus "Shop Now," to see which one drives more clicks. In email campaigns, you can experiment with placement—testing whether a button performs better when it's at the top, middle, or bottom of the email. On a landing page, this type of testing might involve changing the color of the button to see whether it captures more attention or adjusting the size to make it more prominent.

Of course, each marketing channel you use offers unique opportunities to test and refine the CTA, and results can vary greatly depending on the audience and their stage in the customer journey. Here are some examples of aspects that you can test across different marketing campaigns:

- *Wording*: Test variations such as "Buy Now" vs "Get Started."
- *Placement*: Try placing the CTA at the top, middle, or bottom of the page or email.
- *Button size*: Experiment with larger vs smaller buttons to see what draws more attention.
- *Color*: Test different button colors to see which attracts more clicks.
- *Shape*: Compare rounded vs square buttons to assess user preferences.
- *Tone*: Try different tones, such as casual ("Let's Go") vs formal ("Proceed").
- *Urgency*: Test CTAs that create urgency, such as "Limited-Time Offer" or "Act Now."
- *CTA timing*: In ads or video content, test the timing of when the CTA appears.
- *Icons*: Add icons or arrows to see whether they improve clickthrough rates.
- *Hover effects*: Test whether adding a hover effect (e.g., button changes color when hovered over) improves interaction.

By systematically testing CTAs, you can better understand what drives user action in your specific campaigns and adjust your messaging accordingly. Small changes can have a big impact, and testing helps ensure that your CTA is as effective as possible, no matter the channel or medium.

Offers and Discounts

Testing offers and discounts is a powerful way to gauge what drives your audience to take action. Offers such as percentage discounts, free trials, Buy One Get One Free (BOGOF), or referral bonuses can be tested to see which generates the most engagement and conversions. By experimenting with different types of offers, you can better understand what motivates your customers. Some audiences may respond more to monetary savings (such as 10% off), while others might prefer added value (such as free shipping or a free gift). The key is to experiment with different offers to determine which provides the best results for your specific audience.

One challenge in testing offers and discounts, however, is the need for accurate tracking, especially when consumers frequently switch between channels (e.g., from email to social media to Web site). Testing a discount offer in isolation on one channel may not give you a full picture of its impact, as customers often interact with multiple channels before making a purchase decision. It's important to ensure that all offers are tracked across platforms so that you can accurately measure their effectiveness and avoid duplication of offers to the same customer across channels. This approach gives you a clearer understanding of which discount or offer is driving conversions and helps avoid "offer fatigue," where customers get desensitized to promotions.

Here are some examples of offers and discounts you can test in your marketing campaigns:

- *Percentage discount*: 10%, 20%, or 30% off specific products or services
- *Free shipping*: Offering free shipping for a limited time or over a certain purchase threshold
- *BOGOF*: Encourages more product purchases
- *Referral bonuses*: Rewarding customers for referring friends
- *Loyalty discounts*: Offering exclusive deals to repeat customers or loyalty program members
- *First-time buyer discounts*: A one-time discount for new customers
- *Seasonal offers*: Discounts tied to holidays or seasons (e.g., summer sales)
- *Time-sensitive offers*: Urgent, limited-time discounts (e.g., flash sales)
- *Bundling discounts*: Offering discounts for buying multiple products together
- *Free trials*: Offering a free trial for subscription-based services or products

Back to our example

For instance, PB Shoes could explore several scenarios to build interest in its kids' pickleball shoes. Maybe an offer of 50% off gets better results than BOGOF, or a free trial is more effective when it lasts 30 days instead of 10.

By testing various offers and tracking their effectiveness, you can fine-tune your promotional strategies. Understanding which discounts or bonuses resonate best with your audience will help you optimize your marketing efforts and drive greater engagement, loyalty, and conversions across multiple channels.

Other Personalized Elements

Of course, you can test many other elements about a marketing channel and its output, depending on which channel and what types of information you have access to. Consider testing personalized elements based on geography, time of day, past purchase behavior, or other factors you have collected about your customers.

RUNNING THE TEST

Now that we've looked at *what* we can test, let's talk about running the tests themselves, using the five steps illustrated in Figure 19.1. Of course, you should remember that if you are running multiple concurrent tests, it can be difficult to determine the effectiveness of a single aspect of a test, so be careful. That said, let's explore the steps in running a successful test.

Running a Marketing Test

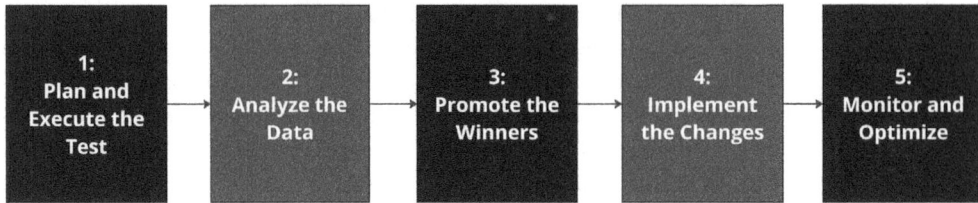

FIGURE 19.1. Running a marketing test.

Plan and Execute the Test

The first step in running a successful marketing test is to plan and execute it effectively. This involves having a clear outline of your test goals, audience segments, and the variations you will be testing. Make sure your goals are measurable, such as increasing clickthrough rates, improving conversions, or reducing bounce rates. Once your test goals are defined, carefully choose your audience segments and make sure they are relevant to the variations you're testing. It's important to consider the duration of the test—ensuring it runs long enough to collect sufficient data for meaningful analysis.

Once planning is completed, it's time to execute the test. Ensure you have the right tools and platforms in place, whether you're running A/B tests, multivariate tests, or other forms of marketing experiments. Use platforms that allow for efficient tracking and easy data collection, such as Google Optimize, Optimizely, or your marketing automation tool. During the execution phase, ensure that you're tracking the right metrics and collecting real-time data. Proper documentation of the process is also essential, as it helps with tracking progress and ensures that your testing stays on track throughout the designated timeframe.

Another critical factor in the execution of tests is maintaining proper controls. This means only testing one or two variables at a time and ensuring that you have a clear baseline for comparison. Avoid making changes in the middle of a test, as it could invalidate your results. After the test period ends, your goal is to collect enough data to draw meaningful conclusions. Always analyze whether you've reached statistical significance before moving forward with any results-based decisions.

What to Do

1. Clearly define the specific goals of your test, such as "Increase email open rates by 10% over 2 weeks."
2. Choose relevant audience segments that align with your marketing objectives and are likely to provide actionable insights.
3. Use appropriate testing platforms to ensure accurate data collection and tracking throughout the test duration.

What Not to Do

1. Avoid running a test for too short a period, which may lead to inconclusive results due to insufficient data.

2. Don't test too many variables at once (e.g., subject line, CTA, and offer) as it can become difficult to attribute changes to specific variables.

3. Never make changes during the test, such as adjusting the creative aspects midway, as this can skew your results and invalidate the test.

Analyze the Data

After running your marketing test, the next step is to analyze the data. This is where you dive deep into the results to understand which combinations of variables performed the best. Look closely at the metrics that align with your test goals, such as traffic, engagement, conversions, or any other KPIs you defined before running the test. It's important to look beyond just one metric—while conversions might be your ultimate goal, understanding other indicators, such as bounce rates or time spent on a page, can provide valuable context. For example, if you're testing different subject lines in an email campaign, you'll want to track open rates, but also look at clickthrough rates to see how well the entire email resonates with recipients.

When analyzing data, one of the most important things to check is statistical significance. Statistical significance ensures that the difference in performance between your control group and your variations is not due to random chance. Without reaching this threshold, your conclusions may be unreliable, leading to poor decisions. Use online tools or built-in analytics features in testing platforms to help determine whether your results are statistically significant. It's also essential to identify any confounding factors that might have influenced the results, such as external events (e.g., a major holiday) or even simple issues such as testing too few visitors.

Once you've identified the winning variation, compare its performance across different audience segments, if applicable. This will help you understand whether a certain variation worked better for specific segments than others. This data can inform future tests, allowing you to narrow down which offers or creative elements resonate best with different parts of your audience. It can also help you optimize campaigns to target higher-value segments more effectively.

What to Do

1. Use multiple metrics to analyze the results, such as conversion rate, engagement, and bounce rate.

2. Ensure that your results have reached statistical significance before making any conclusions or decisions.

3. Compare performance across different audience segments to get a comprehensive view of the test's success.

What Not to Do

1. Don't focus solely on one metric, such as conversions, without considering other indicators, such as engagement or bounce rates.

2. Avoid making decisions based on results that haven't reached statistical significance, as they may lead to incorrect conclusions.

3. Don't ignore possible confounding variables such as external events or seasonality that could have skewed the results.

Promote the Winners

Once you've identified the best-performing offers and discounts from your test, it's time to promote those winners to a broader audience. The goal is to capitalize on the insights gained from the test and scale your campaign for maximum impact. Whether it's a particular discount that led to higher conversions or a specific offer that drove more engagement, these winning combinations should now become the centerpiece of your marketing strategy. One way to do this is by distributing the winning content across various channels, such as email marketing, social media, paid ads, and even your Web site. Each channel should be tailored to the audience that is most likely to engage with the offer based on the test results.

To get the most out of your promotion, consider utilizing multiple channels simultaneously to increase your reach. For instance, if a certain discount performed well in an email test, expand that promotion by using paid social media ads, retargeting campaigns, and organic posts. Consistency across channels is key. Ensure that the message, creative execution (e.g. images and text), and offer are aligned and cohesive, making it easier for users to recognize the promotion, no matter what platform they are on. While promoting the winning offers, however, keep in mind that the test was likely run with a specific audience segment, so targeting should be adjusted as necessary when expanding the reach.

Additionally, consider using different marketing strategies on each platform to maximize the effectiveness of your promotion. For example, use eye-catching imagery on social media, paid ads with clear CTAs, and personalized emails for more direct engagement. Cross-channel promotion also gives you the chance to gather additional data about which platforms generate the most engagement with the winning offers. This data can be used to further refine your approach and tailor future campaigns based on the lessons learned.

What to Do

1. Distribute the winning offers across multiple channels, such as email, social media, and paid advertising, to maximize reach and visibility.

2. Ensure consistency across platforms by using similar messaging, creative elements, and offers to create a cohesive campaign.

3. Adjust targeting as needed based on the audience segment that responded best to the tested offers, ensuring relevance as you promote the winners more widely.

What Not to Do

1. Don't only promote the winning offers on one channel (e.g., just email), as this limits the reach of the successful campaign.

2. Avoid making changes to the winning offer or creative elements before launching them to a larger audience, as this may alter the effectiveness of the campaign.

3. Don't ignore performance on different platforms—continue tracking results to ensure that the offer performs well across various channels and audiences.

Implement the Changes

Once the best-performing offers and discounts have been identified, it's time to implement the changes into your broader marketing strategy. This phase involves integrating the successful elements from your test into your live campaigns across various channels. These changes can include adjusting ad copy, redesigning creative elements such as text and images, modifying landing pages, or even revamping email campaigns. It's important to ensure that the winning elements—whether they are specific CTAs, images, or messaging—are consistently applied throughout your marketing materials to maintain alignment and cohesiveness.

When implementing changes, it's critical to maintain the core elements that made the test a success. For example, if a particular headline significantly boosted conversions, that headline should be replicated across all other relevant platforms. Similarly, if a specific discount offer or creative design led to better engagement, you should apply the same elements across all marketing touchpoints, whether through digital ads, email campaigns, or Web site updates. Consistency is key, but also ensure that each platform is adapted for the specific format and audience it serves.

It's also a good idea to document the changes you are implementing and track their performance closely. Just because an element performed well in the test, doesn't guarantee that it will perform exactly the same way across all your channels or larger audiences. Monitoring the impact of these changes will help you understand whether they are scalable and which channels provide the best ROI when promoting the revised offers. This ongoing tracking and adjustment ensures that the changes have the desired impact on your marketing goals and keep your strategy optimized for success.

What to Do

1. Apply winning elements such as ad copy, images, and discounts consistently across all relevant marketing channels to maintain brand consistency.

2. Document each change you make and monitor its performance to ensure it continues to deliver positive results at scale.

3. Adjust the implementation of the winning elements to suit the specific format or audience of each marketing platform (e.g., adjusting images for mobile vs desktop).

What Not to Do

1. Don't make changes without fully replicating the elements that made the test successful; keep key variables, such as copy or design, consistent.

2. Avoid making multiple simultaneous changes beyond the tested elements, as this can skew the effectiveness of the campaign and create confusion in performance data.

3. Don't assume that just because something worked in the test it will automatically work across all channels—continue monitoring and optimizing for different audiences and formats.

Monitor and Optimize

Marketing tests should not be viewed as one-time events, but rather as ongoing processes that require continuous monitoring and optimization. After implementing the changes based on your test results, it's crucial to keep an eye on the campaign's performance over time. Regularly tracking key metrics, such as clickthrough rates, conversions, and engagement, will help you understand whether the changes continue to produce the desired outcomes. This is particularly important because consumer behavior, market conditions, and even algorithm updates can change over time, potentially impacting the effectiveness of your marketing strategies.

To monitor your campaigns effectively, use tracking codes, UTM parameters, and other analytics tools to determine the attribution of each element in your marketing mix. This allows you to see which specific test elements—whether it's the ad copy, the CTA, or the audience segment—are driving the most success. It also helps you identify underperforming aspects that may need further optimization. The more organized your tracking and attribution system, the easier it will be to make data-driven decisions and fine-tune your strategy. By continuously monitoring, you can react quickly to any shifts in performance and ensure that your campaigns remain effective over time.

Once you've gathered enough data, use these insights to scale winning strategies and eliminate the elements that aren't performing as well. This ongoing optimization process ensures that your marketing efforts are always aligned with your business goals and stay competitive. For example, if you notice that a certain discount performs better with a specific audience, you can increase the ad spend for that segment. Similarly, if a CTA is underperforming on one channel, you can test variations to improve its effectiveness. By regularly optimizing, you can ensure that your marketing campaigns evolve with the market and continue to deliver strong results.

What to Do

1. Continuously monitor the performance of your campaigns using tracking codes, URLs, and other attribution tools to understand which elements are working.
2. Use performance data to scale successful elements of your campaign, allocating more resources to strategies that generate the best results.
3. Regularly test new variations and optimize underperforming elements to keep your campaigns fresh and aligned with changing market conditions.

What Not to Do

1. Don't stop monitoring your campaigns after the initial test—failure to continuously track performance can lead to missed opportunities for optimization.
2. Avoid using vague tracking methods or failing to attribute success to specific elements of your campaign, as this can lead to poor decision-making.
3. Don't assume that strategies that worked once will continue to be effective indefinitely—ongoing monitoring and testing are essential for long-term success.

CONCLUSION

As you can see, running successful digital marketing tests involves various components that must work together. The testing process requires you to understand your audience and specific goals, create compelling variations, execute the test accurately, analyze the results, and optimize your campaigns effectively.

With effective testing and optimization, you can ensure your digital marketing campaigns get excellent ROI and your business achieves its desired objectives. Comprehending these essential components will help you conduct successful digital marketing tests.

Now that we have walked through how a single-channel marketing test is performed, the next chapter will explore what the implications of single-channel testing have in environments where customers interact with a company on more than one channel, otherwise known as a multi-channel environment.

CHAPTER 20

SINGLE-CHANNEL TESTS IN A MULTI-CHANNEL WORLD

The consumer behavior of channel switching, or using multiple devices (e.g., a mobile phone, tablet, and laptop) or channels (e.g., email, SMS, and chatbots), during the buying process continues to grow. So, marketing teams must keep up with their customers.

While many teams are focused on a single channel for their day-to-day marketing work, multi-channel marketing is the foundation of most successful marketing campaigns and initiatives these days. Through multi-channel marketing, a brand can reach its potential customers through a wide range of channels and engage with them effectively when, where, and how their customers want to engage. It's important to understand, however, that the manner and effectiveness of communication varies across different channels, making it essential to conduct channel-specific tests.

Additionally, most enterprises have teams that focus on specific channels and even specific channels at different stages of the customer journey. Thus, measuring and testing on a single channel is important to optimize its performance, and there are a few things to keep in mind to optimize your channel-specific testing. Let's explore these.

UNDERSTAND WHERE THE CHANNEL FITS WITHIN THE CUSTOMER JOURNEY

It is important to take into account the entry and exit points that a particular channel may have within the buyer's journey. For instance, a digital ad may be an important gateway to a Web site landing page or e-commerce shopping experience. Still, it may not be a factor later in the customer lifecycle. Therefore, understanding that advertisement's contribution to the whole and optimal timing and performance is based on its place in the journey.

SELECT THE APPROPRIATE METRICS FOR THE CHANNEL

While various metrics may be used to measure the effectiveness of a multi-channel campaign, selecting channel-specific metrics is important to determine effectiveness, which differs for each channel. You can see some examples in the following table.

TABLE 20.1. Some typical metrics for example marketing channels.

Channel	Typical Metrics
Email	• Open rate: The percentage of recipients who open an email • Clickthrough Rate (CTR): The percentage of recipients who clicked on one or more links within the email • Conversion rate: The percentage of recipients who completed a desired action, such as making a purchase or signing up for a service
SMS	• Delivery rate: The percentage of messages successfully received by recipients • Response rate: The percentage of recipients who reply to the SMS message • Opt-out rate: The rate at which recipients unsubscribe from SMS communications
Instagram	• Engagement rate: The total number of likes and comments per post divided by the number of followers, expressed as a percentage • Reach: The number of unique users who see your posts • Stories views: The number of views your Instagram Stories receive
YouTube video	• View count: The total number of views a video has accumulated • Watch time: The total amount of time that viewers have spent watching a video • Engagement (likes, comments, shares): Measures how viewers interact with the video
Website landing page	• Traffic: The number of visitors to the landing page • Bounce rate: The percentage of visitors who navigate away from the site after viewing only one page • Conversion rate: The percentage of visitors who complete a desired action on the landing page, such as filling out a form or making a purchase

• For instance, you can see that while Instagram and YouTube have some similarities in the measurement of engagement rate and views, there are different metrics altogether for emails and SMS.

UNDERSTAND THE CHANNEL'S CONTRIBUTION TO THE GOAL

As we explored earlier, a single channel is often only part of a customer's journey toward a sale or other type of conversion. Thus, it is important to keep this in mind and understand what anticipated behavior, both good and bad, is.

For instance, if an email is intended to drive a customer to a landing page to sign up for an event, it is important to understand its contribution to that conversion and what may happen if there is a lack of conversions on that landing page. Is the email not giving enough background information on the event, or is it potentially misleading about some details?

This is particularly important because the email itself may be performing well, with a good amount of opens and clickthroughs. Still, the true performance is less than stellar since the email fails to result in conversions on the landing page.

ATTRIBUTION MODELS

There are several types of attribution models available, each with a unique focus and methodology. The choice of model depends largely on your specific marketing objectives and the nature of the customer journey.

Let's explore a few commonly used attribution models and when they are most useful to marketers.

First-Click Attribution

First-click attribution assigns all (100%) of the credit for a conversion to the first touchpoint a customer encounters on their journey. This means that no matter how many additional interactions the customer has before converting, the first interaction is viewed as the most crucial, since it initially captured the customer's attention and started them down the path toward conversion. This model is useful when the goal is to identify which channels or campaigns are most effective at attracting new customers and generating initial interest.

First-click attribution is most often used in campaigns where the first interaction is the key moment of influence. For example, in product launches or brand awareness campaigns, it's often important to understand which channel or ad led to the first engagement, as that can be seen as the campaign's success in creating awareness. A brand running a digital ad on social media may use first-click attribution to measure the ad's effectiveness in getting users to visit their Web site for the first time. This model's strength lies in its simplicity and its focus on top-of-funnel efforts, helping marketers identify which channels are best for initiating customer journeys.

Its primary weakness, however, is that it ignores the influence of other touchpoints later in the customer's journey. Just because a customer first clicked on a Facebook ad, doesn't mean that other interactions, such as email marketing or retargeting ads, didn't play a significant role in driving the final conversion. For this reason, first-click attribution may not provide a full picture of the customer's path to conversion. This model is best used when the main goal is to track which channels are most effective at bringing new visitors to your site but should be avoided when you need a deeper understanding of the entire customer journey.

When to Use

- Brand awareness campaigns where the first interaction is the most important
- Tracking the effectiveness of top-of-funnel channels in driving new visitors to the site
- Understanding which channels are best for starting customer journeys

When to Avoid

- When you need a holistic view of the entire customer journey, not just the first interaction
- In long sales cycles with many touchpoints, where mid- or bottom-funnel interactions are also important
- For campaigns where multiple channels contribute significantly to the final conversion, and focusing only on the first touchpoint may lead to incomplete insights

Last-Click Attribution

As the name suggests, last-click attribution assigns 100% of the credit for a conversion to the final touchpoint a customer interacts with before completing the conversion. This model assumes that the last interaction was the most influential in pushing the customer to take action, whether that's making a purchase, signing up for a newsletter, or completing another conversion goal. Many businesses use this model by default because it provides a straightforward way to see which marketing effort directly led to the final action. For example, if a customer clicks on a paid search ad and makes a purchase immediately afterward, the paid search channel receives all the credit.

This type of attribution is often used when businesses want to focus on bottom-of-the-funnel activities—the touchpoints that turn potential customers into actual buyers. For example, e-commerce companies might prioritize last-click attribution to understand which ads or campaigns are most effective at driving purchases. This model's strength is that it provides a clear view of what action immediately preceded a conversion, making it valuable for performance marketing campaigns, where the final push toward conversion is crucial. It's particularly useful when the sales cycle is short, and fewer touchpoints exist.

The main weakness of last-click attribution, however, is that it disregards the contribution of any prior touchpoints that led to the conversion. Focusing only on the last interaction may overlook the impact of earlier engagements, such as an initial ad or an email campaign that nurtured the customer's interest. For instance, a customer might have first discovered a product through a social media ad, researched it via Google, and then finally purchased it through a retargeting ad. In this case, giving all the credit to the retargeting ad would ignore the contributions of the previous touchpoints. Therefore, last-click attribution can provide a narrow perspective and is best used when the final conversion step is the main priority but should be avoided when a broader view of the customer journey is required.

When to Use

- For performance marketing campaigns, where the final touchpoint (e.g., a retargeting ad or PPC ad) is critical for conversion
- In campaigns where the focus is on driving immediate conversions rather than nurturing leads through multiple interactions
- When the sales cycle is short and relatively simple, with fewer touchpoints leading to conversion

When to Avoid

- When you want to understand the complete customer journey and the contribution of earlier touchpoints
- In longer sales cycles with multiple interactions, where nurturing and mid-funnel activities play a significant role
- For brand awareness or multi-channel campaigns where earlier interactions help build interest and trust before the final conversion

Linear Attribution

This model distributes credit equally across all the touchpoints a customer interacts with on their path to conversion. In this model, every channel or interaction, from the first touchpoint to the final conversion, receives an equal share of the credit. Linear attribution is valuable for marketers who want to understand how every touchpoint contributed to the customer journey, especially in complex multi-channel campaigns where multiple interactions play a role in guiding the customer toward a conversion. This model provides a more balanced view compared to first-click or last-click attribution by acknowledging that each touchpoint, regardless of its position in the journey, adds value.

Linear attribution is commonly used when the entire marketing strategy is designed to work cohesively across channels. For instance, a customer may first encounter a product through a social media ad, then read a blog post, sign up for an email newsletter, and finally, make a purchase after receiving an email offer. In this scenario, linear attribution assigns equal credit to all touchpoints, recognizing that each interaction played a part in moving the customer through the funnel. This model is particularly useful in longer sales cycles or customer journeys that involve multiple touchpoints, as it helps marketers avoid overemphasizing the importance of one specific interaction.

A key weakness of the linear attribution model, however, is that it doesn't account for the varying degrees of influence different touchpoints may have had. Not all touchpoints are equally impactful, and by assigning equal weight to each, linear attribution can mask the true effectiveness of specific channels. For example, an early-stage awareness ad might play a smaller role in the final conversion than a targeted email offer that directly led to a sale, yet linear attribution would give them the same amount of credit. This model is best used when you want a holistic view of all touchpoints but should be avoided when some interactions clearly play a more significant role than others.

When to Use

- When you want to understand the collective contribution of all touchpoints in a multi-channel campaign
- In longer customer journeys where multiple interactions (e.g., ads, emails, social media, and content) contribute to conversion
- For campaigns where the goal is to create synergy between multiple channels and every interaction is considered equally valuable

When to Avoid

- When some touchpoints clearly have more influence over the final conversion, such as bottom-of-the-funnel activities (e.g., a sales call or retargeting ad)
- In short sales cycles where a few key touchpoints drive most of the results
- For performance marketing campaigns where specific touchpoints (e.g., last-click) are more critical in determining the ROI

Time Decay Attribution

This is a model that assigns more credit to touchpoints that occur closer in time to the final conversion, with the earlier interactions receiving progressively less credit. Its approach is based on the assumption that the touchpoints nearer to the conversion had a greater influence on the customer's decision to take action. As such, it is particularly useful in marketing campaigns where the final interactions are considered more critical than the initial engagements, such as in fast-moving or short sales cycles.

Time decay attribution is most commonly used when marketers believe that the interactions closer to the conversion carry more weight in persuading customers. For example, in a time-sensitive campaign such as a flash sale or limited-time offer, customers might engage with an initial email, see a retargeting ad, and finally, make a purchase after receiving a follow-up reminder. In this case, the reminder and retargeting ad are likely to be the most pivotal touchpoints, while the initial email, though important, may have played a smaller role in the customer's ultimate decision. Time decay attribution allows marketers to recognize this hierarchy and give more credit to the interactions that occur later in the journey.

One of the key strengths of this model is that it helps identify which late-stage touchpoints are driving conversions, which is useful for optimizing campaigns with shorter sales cycles.

One weakness, however, is that it may undervalue the early touchpoints that build awareness or nurture leads over time. For example, an initial interaction, such as a social media ad or a blog post, might have sparked the customer's interest in the first place, even though they didn't convert until much later. By downplaying the importance of these early-stage interactions, time decay attribution can give a skewed view of the customer journey. This model is best suited for short sales cycles or when the final interactions are most important, but it should be avoided for longer or more complex sales journeys where early touchpoints play a more significant role.

When to Use

- For short sales cycles where the final interactions, such as retargeting ads or reminder emails, are crucial in driving conversions.
- When running time-sensitive campaigns (e.g., flash sales or promotions) where the final touchpoints are expected to have the greatest impact on customer decisions.
- When you want to prioritize the influence of touchpoints that occur closer to the conversion and downplay earlier engagements.

When to Avoid

- In longer, more complex sales cycles where early touchpoints (e.g., brand awareness campaigns) play a significant role in nurturing leads.
- When you need to measure the overall contribution of all touchpoints equally, not just those near the conversion.
- For campaigns where the early touchpoints, such as first-click interactions, are critical to the success of the conversion path.

Position-Based Attribution

Also known as U-shaped attribution, position-based attribution is a model that allocates the majority of credit to the first and last touchpoints in the customer journey. Specifically, 40% of the credit is given to the first touchpoint, 40% to the last touchpoint, and the remaining 20% is distributed evenly among any touchpoints in between. This model recognizes that both the first interaction (which introduces the customer to the brand) and the last interaction (which leads to the final conversion) are crucial. Meanwhile, the other touchpoints are also acknowledged for their supporting roles, though they receive less credit.

Position-based attribution is valuable when both the initial engagement and the final conversion step are considered equally important in influencing the customer's decision. For example, in a multi-channel campaign, a customer might first click on a social media ad, engage with blog content or email offers, and then make a purchase after clicking on a retargeting ad. Position-based attribution ensures that both the ad that first captured the customer's attention and the final touchpoint that closed the deal are given significant credit, while intermediate touchpoints receive partial recognition for their role in nurturing the customer. This model is especially useful for marketers who want to strike a balance between understanding the channels that initiate interest and those that finalize conversions.

One of the strengths of position-based attribution is that it offers a more balanced perspective than first- or last-click models, as it gives weight to both ends of the customer journey while still acknowledging the importance of mid-funnel touchpoints. Its primary weakness, however, is that it may overemphasize the first and last interactions, potentially downplaying the influence of critical touchpoints in the middle of the journey. For instance, if an email nurtures a lead for weeks before the final conversion, this model might underrepresent its true impact. This model is best used when the initial and final touchpoints are equally critical, but it should be avoided when mid-funnel activities play a larger role in driving conversions.

When to Use

- In campaigns where both the first and last interactions are considered highly influential, such as those focused on both brand awareness and conversion
- When you want to give significant weight to both the initial touchpoint that captured attention and the final touchpoint that closed the deal
- For marketing strategies that rely on both top-of-funnel and bottom-of-funnel tactics to drive conversions

When to Avoid

- In campaigns where mid-funnel touchpoints, such as nurturing emails or product demos, are essential to the conversion process
- For very short or simple customer journeys, where the majority of influence comes from either the first or last interaction
- When equal or near-equal credit should be given to all touchpoints (e.g., linear attribution might be a better fit in such cases)

As you can see, there are unique considerations that marketers must make when choosing when to adopt one of these models. Also, as we'll soon see, in a multi-channel world, attribution on a single channel only goes so far.

CONCLUSION

Single-channel marketing tests can be valuable in a multi-channel marketing environment as they allow businesses to focus on specific channels and test different strategies to optimize their marketing efforts.

By testing different campaign elements on a single channel, businesses can gain valuable insights into what works and what doesn't, which can then be applied to other channels. Additionally, single-channel tests can help businesses to identify any channel-specific issues or opportunities that may not be apparent in a multi-channel test. Overall, single-channel marketing tests can provide valuable insights and help businesses to optimize their marketing efforts in a multi-channel environment.

Now that we have looked at single-channel measurement in the greater context of multi-channel environments, the next chapter will look at best practices and methods for measuring multi-channel marketing efforts.

CHAPTER 21

MULTI-CHANNEL MEASUREMENT

As we discussed previously, consumers increasingly engage with brands across multiple channels, completing their buying journeys through online and offline touchpoints. From social media interactions and emails to SMS messages and Web site visits, each channel offers a unique opportunity to influence consumer behavior. This complexity has made multi-channel measurement not just beneficial but essential for marketers aiming to understand the full impact of their strategies.

The importance of multi-channel measurement stems from its ability to provide a cohesive view of marketing effectiveness. Today's marketers face the challenge of allocating budgets in a way that maximizes the Return on Investment (ROI) across these diverse channels. Without a clear understanding of each channel's contribution to consumer engagement and conversions, marketing efforts can become disjointed and inefficient. Moreover, as the number of available marketing channels continues to grow, so does the need for sophisticated measurement techniques that can parse out the noise and reveal the true performance of each channel.

In this chapter, we're going to explore a few types of multi-channel measurement, focusing particularly on two pivotal techniques: Multi-Touch Attribution (MTA) and Media Mix Modeling (MMM). Both approaches offer valuable insights but through distinctly different methodologies and lenses.

MULTI-TOUCH ATTRIBUTION (MTA)

MTA is a methodology used to determine the value of each customer touchpoint leading to a conversion. It goes beyond traditional, simplistic models that attribute credit to just the first or last interaction. MTA seeks to analyze and credit each interaction in the customer journey, from initial awareness through consideration to the final purchase decision. This approach reflects the reality of modern consumer behaviors, where multiple engagements across various channels play critical roles in influencing decisions.

Why MTA Is Valuable

There are some good reasons that marketers should consider MTA:

- *Holistic view of customer journey*: MTA provides marketers with a comprehensive analysis of how each marketing touchpoint contributes to ultimate conversion goals. This is invaluable in understanding the customer journey in its entirety, allowing marketers to see which interactions are truly impactful.
- *Optimization of marketing spend*: By accurately attributing conversions to specific channels and touchpoints, MTA enables marketers to allocate their budgets more effectively. This ensures that investment is directed toward activities that are proven to drive results, enhancing the overall ROI of marketing efforts.

How to Implement MTA Successfully

Here are some things to keep in mind when implementing MTA:

- *Data collection*: Successful MTA implementation starts with robust data collection. Marketers must ensure that they have integrated systems that can track and collate data across all customer touchpoints. This often involves sophisticated tracking technologies and the integration of various data sources, including Web analytics, CRM systems, and ad platforms.
- *Choosing the right model*: There are several models of attribution within MTA, including but not limited to linear, time decay, U-shaped, and algorithmic. Choosing the right model depends on the specific business context and marketing goals:
  - The *linear model* treats all touchpoints as equally important.
  - The *time decay model* gives more credit to touchpoints closer in time to the conversion.
  - The *U-shaped model* attributes more credit to the first and last touchpoints.
  - The *algorithmic model* uses machine learning to dynamically assign credit to each touchpoint based on how likely they are to contribute to a conversion.

Caveats and Limitations

Of course, nothing is a one-size-fits-all solution, so marketers should keep the following in mind when considering whether MTA is the best fit:

- *Data silos and integration issues*: One major challenge with MTA is the integration of data across different platforms and channels. Data silos can lead to incomplete or inaccurate attribution, skewing the results and potentially leading to misinformed decisions.
- *Privacy regulations*: Increasing privacy regulations and restrictions on tracking cookies can significantly hinder the ability to collect comprehensive data. This can limit the effectiveness of MTA, as incomplete data leads to less accurate attribution.
- *Step summary*: Implementing MTA effectively requires careful planning around data collection and model selection. Marketers must ensure they choose the right attribution model that aligns with their marketing strategy and be cognizant of the data and privacy challenges that might affect the attribution accuracy. By doing so, MTA can provide deep insights into the customer journey, helping marketers optimize their strategies and budgets based on a detailed understanding of what drives conversions.

By carefully addressing these steps and considerations, MTA can significantly enhance the strategic capabilities of marketing teams, allowing for more informed and effective decision-making across multi-channel campaigns.

MEDIA MIX MODELING

After exploring MTA, let's look at a major alternative for marketers that need a multi-channel marketing measurement approach. MMM is a statistical analysis technique used to quantify the impact of various marketing tactics on sales and then forecast the impact of future sets of tactics. It uses historical data, such as sales and marketing spend across multiple channels, to determine the effectiveness of each marketing channel at scale. Unlike MTA, which is transactional and often granular, MMM provides a macro-level view of marketing effectiveness over a longer period.

Why MMM Is Valuable

There are several reasons why MMM can benefit marketers and why it might be the best approach for multi-channel measurement:

- *Strategic planning and budget allocation*: MMM allows marketers to optimize their media spending by quantifying the ROI of each channel on a larger scale. This is crucial for high-level budget planning and long-term strategy development, helping businesses allocate their marketing budgets more efficiently.
- *Holistic view across channels*: MMM takes into account external factors such as economic conditions, competitive actions, and changes in consumer behavior. This holistic approach helps marketers understand how different variables interact with each other and what drives the overall performance of their marketing efforts.
- *Causal relationship insights*: By analyzing data over an extended period, MMM can identify causal relationships between marketing spending and business outcomes, distinguishing between correlation and causation. This insight is critical for making informed decisions that drive genuine growth.

How to Implement MMM Effectively

When implementing MMM, there are several things to keep in mind:

- *Collecting comprehensive data*: Successful MMM implementation starts with the collection of comprehensive and clean data. This includes not only internal marketing data and sales figures but also external data such as economic indicators, competitive activities, and even weather patterns if they are relevant to the product being marketed.
- *Choosing the right analytical tools*: Employ robust statistical tools and software capable of handling complex econometric modeling. These tools should accommodate the integration of various data types and allow for the flexible manipulation and analysis of data to tease out nuanced insights.
- *Building the model*: Develop a model that best fits the business context and the data available. This typically involves regression analysis to determine how well each marketing channel contributes to sales while controlling for external variables. The model should be validated and continuously refined to adapt to changing market conditions and new data.

Caveats and Limitations

Here are some cautions about using MMM as your multi-channel measurement approach:

- *Data and time intensiveness*: MMM requires significant amounts of historical data to be effective, and gathering this data can be time-consuming and expensive. Smaller companies or new markets with less data may find it difficult to implement an effective MMM.
- *Adaptability issues*: MMM is less flexible in adapting to rapid changes in the market mix, or the channels utilized are likely to stay consistent throughout the duration of measurement. It is best suited for stable environments where long-term trends can be observed and analyzed.
- *Attribution challenges*: While MMM is great for overall budget allocation across media, it doesn't provide the granular insights at the customer or transaction level that MTA offers. This can make it challenging to apply in digital marketing where such granularity is often necessary.

MMM is a powerful tool for marketers seeking to understand the effectiveness of their marketing investments across various channels and optimize those investments for maximum return. While it offers great strategic insights, its effectiveness is dependent on the availability of comprehensive data and the ability to accurately model and interpret that data. When implemented correctly, MMM can significantly enhance strategic marketing planning and execution, leading to better allocation of marketing resources and improved financial outcomes.

ALTERNATIVES TO MTA AND MMM

Beyond MTA and MMM, there are several other methods used to measure and analyze the effectiveness of multi-channel marketing campaigns. Each potential approach offers unique insights and can be useful depending on the specific objectives and constraints of your marketing strategy. Additionally, there may be times when some of the attribution methods we explored in the chapter on single-channel methods may be the most beneficial as well, so it may help to revisit Chapter 20 to keep those in mind.

Here's a list of some alternative methods:

- *Customer journey analytics*: This method involves deep analysis using advanced analytics to map out the entire customer journey. It often uses big data technologies to integrate data from multiple sources and employs advanced statistical techniques to uncover patterns in the data.
- *Experimental design (A/B testing or split testing)*: This involves creating different versions of a marketing campaign and randomly assigning these versions to different audience segments to see which one performs better. It's a direct way to measure the impact of specific changes in the marketing strategy.
- *Incrementality testing*: This method involves measuring the lift that marketing efforts contribute over and above what would have occurred if the campaign hadn't been run. This is done by comparing a control group that is not exposed to the marketing activity against a test group that is.

• *Unified Marketing Impact Analytics (UMIA)*: UMIA is a more comprehensive approach that combines elements of MMM, MTA, and other analytical techniques. It provides a holistic view of marketing impact by assessing both long-term brand building and short-term sales activation.

These methods offer different lenses through which to view the impact of marketing activities, providing valuable insights that can help tailor strategies to meet business objectives more effectively. Choosing the right method or combination of methods depends on your specific marketing goals, the complexity of the customer journey, and the data available.

WHEN TO USE EACH METHOD

While it is helpful to know that there are several potential options for multi-channel measurement, there are also scenarios where one method may be more appropriate than another. Let's explore these in the following table.

TABLE 21.1. The optimal times to use multi-channel marketing methods.

Brief Description of the Scenario	Best Multi-Channel Measurement Method	Why It Is the Best Fit
Launching a new product across multiple digital platforms	Multi-touch attribution	MTA allows for granular analysis of digital touchpoints to understand the contribution of each channel in the consumer journey.
Long-term assessment of TV, radio, and print advertising impact on sales	Media mix modeling	MMM is ideal for integrating and assessing the impact of offline channels over an extended period.
Optimizing a weekly email marketing campaign	Multi-touch attribution	MTA helps in understanding the immediate impact of digital campaigns and adjusting strategies quickly.
Evaluating the impact of a nationwide billboard advertising campaign	Media mix modeling	MMM can effectively measure the broader, long-term effects of large-scale offline advertising.
Understanding the role of social media interactions in immediate sales conversions	Multi-touch attribution	MTA is best for tracking direct digital interactions and their direct impact on sales.
Assessing the effectiveness of a multi-channel brand awareness campaign	Media mix modeling	MMM provides insights into how various channels contribute collectively to brand awareness over time.
Measuring the effectiveness of a seasonal promotion across all marketing channels	Media mix modeling	MMM helps with understanding the cumulative effect of all marketing efforts across different channels during the promotion period.

(Continued)

TABLE 21.1. (*Continued*) The optimal times to use multi-channel marketing methods.

Brief Description of the Scenario	Best Multi-Channel Measurement Method	Why It Is the Best Fit
A/B testing for optimizing landing page designs on a Web site	Experimental design (A/B testing)	A/B testing is precise for testing specific digital elements such as landing pages to determine which performs better.
Incremental sales analysis for a new online advertising campaign	Incrementality testing	This method directly measures the additional business driven by the new campaign, ideal for specific digital initiatives.
Determining the immediate impact of a pay-per-click campaign on lead generation	Last-touch attribution	Last-touch attribution can clearly show the effect of the final interaction on conversion, which is useful for PPC campaigns.

CONCLUSION

In this chapter, we have explored the critical role that multi-channel measurement plays in the modern marketing landscape. As consumers increasingly engage with brands across a variety of channels, understanding the individual and collective impact of these interactions is essential. By employing sophisticated measurement methods such as MTA and MMM, marketers can gain a deeper insight into how each channel contributes to their overall marketing objectives, allowing for more informed decision-making and resource allocation.

Beyond these two predominant methods, we discussed alternative approaches such as incrementality testing and experimental design, which cater to specific needs and can be particularly effective in certain scenarios. These methods complement MTA and MMM, providing additional layers of insight and helping to refine the overall strategy.

As new channels are utilized by marketers, so too are new tools and techniques for measuring marketing effectiveness. Keeping up with these changes and continuously refining your approach to multi-channel measurement will be key to maintaining a competitive edge. By embracing these sophisticated measurement and reporting techniques, marketers can ensure that their multi-channel strategies are not only measurable but also maximally effective, driving growth and improving ROI in an environment where consumer channel-switching is the norm, not the exception.

Now that we have explored testing and measurement across single- and multiple channels, the next chapter will look at how to analyze and improve based on our measurement results.

PART 4 RECAP QUIZ

Congratulations on reaching the end of the fourth section! Let's see how well you've mastered the ideas we've covered by answering three questions on the topics covered in the chapters in this section.

To check your answers, refer to Appendix B, which lists all of the answers for the quizzes in the book.

Now, it's time to answer three questions on the content in Part 4.

Question 1
True or false: Bar charts are effective for comparing quantitative data across different categories.

Question 2
True or false: The null hypothesis (H0) is what the researcher wants to prove.

Question 3
Choose the correct answer: When testing a small change to a marketing campaign (e.g., the wording on a CTA button), it is best to use an:
a) A/B test
b) Multivariate test
c) Focus group

PART 5: REFINING AND IMPROVING YOUR RESULTS

As we've explored so far, marketing measurement, which is essential to any successful marketing strategy, requires several components working in harmony to be successful. When a strong strategy is accompanied by good data, a solid framework, and a robust testing methodology, it allows businesses to track the effectiveness of their campaigns and make data-driven decisions to optimize their efforts.

Even this, however, is not enough to be successful in the long term, as many factors that influence success and the way marketing is performed can change over time, and sometimes quite drastically—seemingly overnight. To truly understand the impact of their marketing efforts, businesses must take the time to analyze and refine their measurement results.

To do this, marketers need to understand how to perform analysis, identifying some of the common areas where mistakes can be made that lead them astray, and how to best use all of the tools at their disposal to continuously refine and improve their work.

This section will explore the process of analyzing and refining marketing measurement results, including tips for interpreting data, identifying Key Performance Indicators (KPIs), and making data-driven decisions.

We will explore the following:

- Ways to approach the analysis of marketing data
- Best practices for analyzing the results of your marketing efforts and your hypothesis testing
- Approaches to use generative Artificial Intelligence (AI) tools to analyze your data
- Exploration of how to interpret the results of your marketing measurement analysis
- Understanding continuous improvement to ensure your marketing results continue to get better

We will start with an introduction to analysis and improvement.

CHAPTER 22

INTRODUCTION TO ANALYSIS AND IMPROVEMENT

While we've discussed both single- and multi-channel data collection and measurement already in this book, this chapter will focus on optimizing a single marketing channel, and we will assume you have already begun your marketing efforts and your measurement as well.

There are three components we will focus on in this chapter, as shown in Figure 22.1: analyze the results; interpret the results; and experiment, refine, and continuously improve.

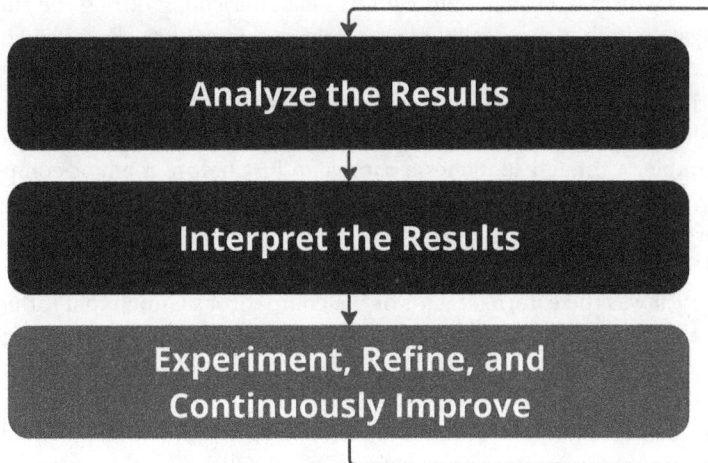

Analyze the Results

Interpret the Results

Experiment, Refine, and Continuously Improve

FIGURE 22.1. The three steps of analysis and refinement.

ANALYZE THE RESULTS

You need to analyze your data to optimize your marketing channel and the measurements you have collected. This will help you understand what's working and what's not. Use tools such as Google Analytics to track metrics such as traffic, engagement, and conversions. Analyze the data to identify patterns and trends, and use this information to make informed decisions about optimizing your marketing channel.

While many potential considerations may be specific to your business, when analyzing the results of your marketing measurement, it is important to keep in mind the following.

Context

Context is critical because it defines the environment in which the data is collected and the factors that could influence the results. This refers to external variables, such as market conditions, seasonality, competitor activities, and even larger macroeconomic trends that may affect consumer behavior. For example, the results of a marketing campaign run during the holiday season will differ greatly from those of the same campaign run during a quiet period. As such, understanding the circumstances in which the data was collected helps marketers accurately interpret results and avoid drawing faulty conclusions.

A common pitfall when considering context is neglecting the impact of external events that can skew results. For instance, a sudden spike in conversions during a campaign might not be the direct result of the marketing strategy but instead due to an industry-wide trend or a viral social media moment that temporarily increases consumer interest. Without accounting for these contextual factors, marketers may misattribute the success or failure of their efforts, which could lead to incorrect decision-making. It's essential to ask: Was there something else going on that could have affected the data? Contextualizing the data ensures that marketers consider broader influences beyond the direct impact of their campaign.

Best practices for incorporating context involve aligning data collection with specific timelines, market conditions, and cultural events relevant to the target audience. For example, if a business notices a drop in engagement with its email marketing during the summer months, it could investigate whether seasonality plays a role in this pattern. By considering the context, the business might choose to adjust its campaign timing or message to better resonate with the audience during off-peak times. This kind of analysis can prevent unnecessary adjustments to a well-performing campaign that was simply affected by temporary, external factors.

As an example, a retailer launches a campaign just before a major competitor releases a new product. The context—an impending competitive product launch—might cause potential customers to delay purchasing decisions as they wait to see the competitor's offer. If the retailer ignores this context, they may falsely conclude that their campaign was ineffective, when in reality, it was the external factor of the competitor's launch that influenced consumer behavior. In this case, adjusting the timing or messaging of the campaign could yield better results.

- *Example*: For instance, if PB Shoes launched a new product line and collected customer feedback during a major sports event such as the Olympics, the excitement around sports could positively bias the feedback. This context might not reflect the typical customer response in a non-event period.
- *Common misconceptions or mistakes*: A common misconception is that data is universally applicable, regardless of when and how it was collected. Marketers may mistakenly believe that results from one context (such as a holiday sale) will predict non-seasonal behavior.
- *How marketers can get started*: To account for context, marketers should document external factors during data collection and consider them when analyzing results. Using tools such as Google Trends can help with understanding external interest over time, while comparing data across different periods can highlight contextual influences.

Understanding context allows marketers to add nuance to their analysis. It ensures they are not making isolated assessments of campaign performance but are instead viewing results within a broader, more informed framework. By staying aware of environmental factors, companies can make better decisions and fine-tune their strategies for future success.

Sample Size

Sample size plays a pivotal role in determining the accuracy and reliability of your marketing data analysis. The sample size refers to the number of observations or data points collected to measure a particular variable or set of variables. A larger sample size generally leads to more precise and reliable data, allowing marketers to draw conclusions with greater confidence. This is because larger samples tend to provide a better representation of the entire target population, reducing the likelihood of anomalies or outliers skewing the results. For example, if you're testing two versions of an email campaign (A/B testing), a larger sample will give a clearer picture of which version performs better across a broad audience.

One of the most common mistakes marketers make when analyzing data is relying on a sample size that is too small. A small sample can lead to misleading results because it may not capture the diversity of behaviors, preferences, or responses within the target audience. For instance, if only 100 people from a target market of 10,000 are surveyed, the insights derived may not accurately reflect the attitudes or actions of the entire population. Similarly, in digital advertising, testing a campaign on a small segment of users might yield different results than a full-scale rollout, making it difficult to predict performance accurately.

That said, having a large sample size doesn't automatically guarantee success. It's essential to ensure that the sample is representative of the broader audience you're targeting. For instance, if you are marketing a product to a global audience but collect data from only one geographic region, the larger sample size will still lack representativeness and may lead to inaccurate conclusions. This highlights the need for marketers to balance both sample size and quality in data collection. Striking this balance helps marketers avoid biases and ensure their findings are applicable across different segments of their audience.

The best way to determine the most appropriate sample size depends on the goals of the analysis. For example, when running A/B tests, it's important to calculate the minimum sample size needed to detect a statistically significant difference between variations. This calculation often depends on factors such as the expected effect size and the level of confidence desired (commonly 95%). Tools such as sample size calculators can help marketers determine how many data points are needed before starting a test. This ensures that the results are not only valid but also actionable.

- *Example*: A survey on customer satisfaction with only 50 respondents may not accurately represent the entire customer base of PB Shoes, whereas a survey with 1,000 respondents would provide a more reliable picture.
- *Common misconceptions or mistakes*: Believing that sample size is the only determinant of data reliability is a common mistake. Even with a large sample, if it isn't representative or random, the results can be misleading.
- *How marketers can get started*: Marketers should determine the necessary sample size using statistical power analysis and ensure that their sampling method reaches a representative cross-section of their target population.

Sample size is a critical factor in the accuracy of marketing data analysis. By ensuring that the sample is both large enough and representative of the target population, marketers can draw more reliable insights and make better-informed decisions. A robust sample size minimizes the risks of bias and ensures that marketing strategies are backed by data that truly reflects customer behavior.

Data Quality

Data quality is fundamental to any marketing analysis because the accuracy and reliability of insights depend on the integrity of the underlying data. In marketing, high-quality data must be accurate, reliable, and representative of the target population or market segment. The goal is to ensure that the data collected genuinely reflects the behaviors, preferences, and actions of your audience, enabling more precise decision-making. Data quality involves not only collecting accurate information but also ensuring it is complete and free from errors or inconsistencies. Poor-quality data can lead to misleading conclusions, misguided marketing efforts, and wasted resources.

A critical component of data quality is the method of data collection. The techniques marketers use to gather data significantly impact its quality. For instance, using online surveys without properly vetting participants can introduce biases, as the responses may not represent the broader audience. Similarly, relying solely on automated data collection methods from digital marketing channels can introduce errors if tracking codes or tags are incorrectly implemented. Ensuring proper setup, calibration, and monitoring throughout the data collection process is essential for minimizing errors. Validating and cleaning the data post-collection—removing duplicates, correcting inconsistencies, and dealing with missing values—are also key steps in ensuring its quality.

Another factor to consider is the representativeness of the data. Even if the data collected is accurate, it must also be representative of the population you're studying. For example, if a marketing campaign targets consumers aged 18-35 but the majority of data comes from users over 40, the insights drawn from that data will likely be skewed. Marketers should always ensure that the data reflects the diversity of their target audience to avoid biases and ensure relevant, applicable conclusions. This can be particularly challenging when using third-party data or data from external vendors, as marketers may not have full control over how the data was sourced or processed.

Best practices for improving data quality include using statistical techniques to identify and correct biases, errors, or inconsistencies in the data. Statistical techniques such as regression analysis or data weighting can help adjust for imbalances in the sample, ensuring that the data better reflects the population. Additionally, marketers should employ data validation tools, run quality checks, and establish protocols for managing data collection processes. This includes ensuring that all marketing channels—whether online or offline—are consistently tracked and monitored to maintain data accuracy.

For example, a retail company collecting sales data for in-store and online purchases should ensure that both channels are tracked using uniform methods. If discrepancies arise—such as sales figures from one channel being recorded differently from another—the data may become less reliable. By instituting a rigorous process for tracking and verifying data across all channels, the company ensures that the final analysis reflects a true picture of consumer behavior.

- *Example*: Inaccurate sales tracking due to system errors could lead PB Shoes to incorrect conclusions about the success of a new marketing campaign.

- *Common misconceptions or mistakes*: Assuming that data is error-free by default is a mistake. Often, marketers overlook the potential for systemic errors or inaccuracies in data collection.
- *How marketers can get started*: Regular audits of data sources and collection processes, combined with validation techniques such as cross-referencing multiple data sources, can enhance data quality.

Data quality is a critical pillar of marketing analysis. Accurate, complete, and reliable data ensures that insights are trustworthy and actionable. By prioritizing high-quality data collection, validation, and cleaning processes, marketers can avoid the risks of faulty data and make more informed, data-driven decisions that enhance the success of their campaigns.

Confounding Variables

Additionally, there is one more element that is worth noting. Confounding variables are factors that can affect the relationship between the independent and dependent variables. It is important to control for these variables when interpreting the results of your marketing measurement. Confounding variables are external influences that can skew the results of a study by affecting the dependent variable, leading to erroneous conclusions about the relationship between studied variables.

- *Example*: If PB Shoes runs a marketing campaign simultaneously with a major discount event, the increased sales might be attributed to the campaign when, in fact, they are largely influenced by the discounts.
- *Common misconceptions or mistakes*: A common mistake is neglecting to identify or control for confounding variables, leading to incorrect attributions of cause and effect.
- *How marketers can get started*: To address confounding variables, marketers can use control groups, conduct multivariate analyses, or employ statistical controls to isolate the effects of the primary variables of interest.

Understanding and accounting for context, sample size, data quality, and confounding variables are essential components in the accurate analysis of marketing measurement results. Marketers embarking on this analysis journey can establish more robust and reliable insights by addressing each of these areas thoughtfully and systematically.

THE NEXT STAGES IN THE PROCESS

In this chapter, the next two stages will just be briefly reviewed to give context for where the analysis of results fits. We will explore each of the following two areas further in Chapters 25 and 26.

Interpreting the Results

It's not enough to just have a good understanding of your marketing channel metrics. Instead, you need to be able to turn those insights into actionable strategies, tactics, and refinements to improve the results from your marketing channel continually.

It is important to interpret the results of your marketing measurement in the context of the specific marketing strategy and objectives and to consider the limitations and potential biases of the measurement.

The goal of marketing measurement is to provide insights that can inform your marketing strategy and improve the effectiveness of your marketing efforts. Therefore, it is important to focus on the most relevant and actionable insights and to use these insights to make data-driven decisions that can improve the performance of your marketing efforts.

We will explore the interpretation of results in more depth in Chapter 25.

Experiment, Refine, and Continuously Improve

Then, once you have analyzed and interpreted your data and the results of your marketing efforts, it's time to start experimenting with different strategies to optimize your marketing channel. This may include testing different messaging, targeting, or creative. Use A/B testing to test different elements of your strategy and refine your approach. Don't be afraid to try new things and be open to learning from your mistakes. This topic will also be explored in more depth in Chapter 26.

We will also look at how to create better experiments, so there is more to come on this topic.

Finally, it's important to monitor and improve your marketing channel continuously. Regularly review your data and make adjustments as needed. Keep an eye on industry trends and changes in consumer behavior. This will help you stay ahead of the curve and ensure your marketing channel remains effective.

CONCLUSION

Optimizing a single marketing channel can be a game-changer for your business. You can ensure maximum efficiency and effectiveness by identifying your target audience, setting clear goals, measuring your data, experimenting with different strategies, and continuously monitoring your channel. Remember, there is no one-size-fits-all approach to marketing, so be open to trying new things and refining your strategy over time. With these steps in mind, you'll be well on your way to optimizing your marketing channel and achieving success for your business.

In the next chapter, we're going to explore analysis in greater depth, including questions to ask to gain deeper insights and understandings about how your marketing efforts are performing.

CHAPTER 23

ANALYZING YOUR RESULTS

As is the case with any marketing team, you'll have your marketing measurements, whether from a single channel or across multiple channels. At first glance, they may look good across the board, but it's not time to celebrate just yet. Instead, it is time for a deeper analysis to figure out what went well and what didn't go as well. Even if your numbers are positive—or negative—there might be some conflicting messages in the results.

So, when analyzing the results of your efforts, it is important not to get distracted by very good—or very bad—anecdotal results or results that may be extreme but not directly related to success or failure.

In this chapter, we will explore some questions to ask about your results, as well as some common misconceptions that may be masking the truth. All of this will help you gain a more robust understanding of how your marketing is performing. So, let's go.

QUESTIONS TO ASK TO GAIN A DEEPER UNDERSTANDING OF YOUR MARKETING RESULTS

I'm going to assume you've done at least a top-level analysis and have concluded that things are either on the right track or not. That said, gaining a deeper understanding will help you understand what is working and what needs improvement, as it is rare that you've done *everything* right or wrong. To do this, you can start by asking a series of questions.

What Are Our Goals and Did We Achieve Them?

It sounds pretty obvious to state, but before analyzing any of your marketing results, it's vital to remember and acknowledge what you were trying to accomplish in the first place.

This requires revisiting the business KPIs that drove your marketing KPIs and ensuring that the goals of your efforts were aligned with those. Refer to Chapter 2 if you need to refresh your memory on that part of the process.

Again, a number of results have occurred from your marketing efforts that may or may not be directly related to your goals, but whether or not you achieved your primary goal(s) is of utmost importance. Did you achieve what you set out to do? Even if something else really good happened, ensure you stay focused on your goals and are not distracted by other information that may cloud your judgment.

Back to our example

If PB Shoes beat their sales target for *basketball* shoes last quarter, that's a really good thing. If, however, their primary goal was to grow their *pickleball* shoe sales, then as good as increased sales in another product category may be, it's not directly aligned with their goals.

What Are the Primary Reasons We Succeeded (or Failed)?

As important as the last point is, it's not enough to know whether you have achieved your goals or not. You also need to be able to explain *why* you got the results you did. After all, if you did well, you will likely want to try to do more of the same, and if you didn't do well, you want to know what to avoid.

Understanding the primary reasons why a marketing effort succeeded or failed is crucial for continuing to improve your efforts. By analyzing the results of your marketing campaigns, you can identify what strategies worked and what didn't and make data-driven decisions to optimize your efforts. For example, if a campaign was successful, you can determine the specific tactics that contributed to its success and replicate them in future campaigns. On the other hand, if a campaign fails, you can identify why it failed and make changes to address those issues in future campaigns. By understanding the primary reasons for the success or failure of your marketing efforts, you can continuously improve your strategies and achieve better results over time.

Are There Particular Areas We Succeeded in More Than Others?

Average or mediocre results of your marketing efforts may not always mean that you didn't succeed in some respects. It may simply mean that you were very successful in certain areas, but in others, your efforts failed to perform. For instance, this could apply to:

- Audience segments
- Content variations
- Times of day

If your marketing efforts overperformed with professionals aged 35–44 in metropolitan areas but failed to gain traction in the suburbs, unless you look granularly by audience segment, you may miss the positive impact on that first audience segment.

What Are the Industry Benchmarks and Did We Exceed Them?

It is great to exceed your organization's numbers from the last week, month, quarter, or year, but it is also extremely helpful to understand the norms in your industry or on a particular channel. For instance, understanding industry-average email open and clickthrough rates can help you set the right goals for your own.

Considering industry benchmarks when analyzing your marketing campaign results is important because it provides a point of comparison and helps you understand how your results stack up against industry standards. Industry benchmarks can help you identify areas where you are performing well or poorly compared to your peers and provide insights into best practices and strategies working for other companies in your industry. Additionally, industry benchmarks can help you set realistic goals and track your progress over time. By using industry benchmarks, you can identify areas for improvement and make data-driven decisions to optimize your marketing efforts. Overall, having industry benchmarks is important for measuring and improving your marketing performance.

If you are well below the industry average, I recommend setting incremental goals to ultimately reach and exceed that standard instead of trying to change things overnight.

Are the Numbers Too Good (or Bad) and Why?

Having a wildly successful-looking number is always a great thing, right? Not always, especially if a spike (or dip) is too extreme to be possible. This might be an indication that there is an error in your data collection or something abnormal is happening, as in Figure 23.1, where we see that Web site traffic increased several-fold in Q2 versus the other quarters. It is likely that there was some miscounting, double counting, or other errors that caused this anomaly.

Website Traffic Q1-4

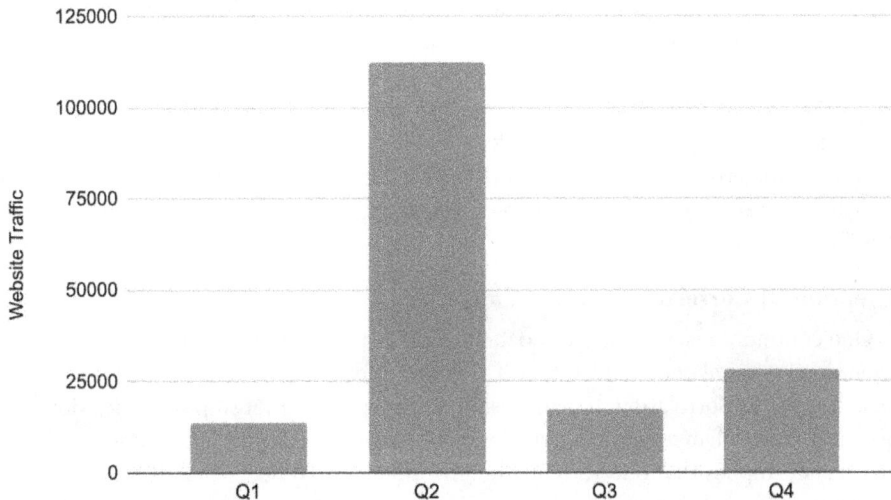

FIGURE 23.1. A chart that shows a possible error or miscounting in the data.

While runaway success is certainly possible, too-extreme numbers often point to something that needs further review. Ensure to look closely at these types of results and teach your team members to do the same. Quite often, this might even point to an error in the data collection methods, meaning your entire set of results needs to be recaptured.

What Could We Have Done Better?

Finally, when analyzing your marketing results, it's essential to identify any areas of improvement. No marketing campaign is perfect, and there's always room for improvement. Once you've analyzed your results, ask yourself, "What could I have done better? What did I do wrong? What changes can I make to improve my future campaigns?" The answers to these questions will help you identify areas of weakness and guide you in making necessary improvements.

There's no doubt that analyzing your marketing results is essential to the success of any business. Asking the right questions will help you gain valuable insights into your campaigns and ultimately guide you in making key decisions to improve your marketing strategy. Before analyzing any marketing results, be clear on your goals, define your target audience, track your campaign's performance across multiple channels, analyze your content, and identify areas of improvement. Doing this allows you to continuously improve your marketing strategies while maximizing resources for better ROI.

COMMON MISCONCEPTIONS

Analyzing data is a crucial part of your job. While data analysis is essential to determine the success of your marketing efforts, it can, however, also be daunting. It's common to fall into the trap of misconceptions that may negatively impact your marketing campaigns. Let's discuss this to understand better how to interpret data accurately and make smarter marketing decisions.

Misconception 1: More Data Equals Better Insights

It's a common misconception that having more data means you'll have more insights. That is rarely the case. It is important to define the data that will be helpful to you and your team to measure the effectiveness of your efforts according to your marketing measurement framework, but if you have too many data points to work with—and worse still, if you are reporting on too many data points—it can distract everyone from their primary objectives. Data overload can also lead to decision fatigue, making it challenging to identify critical insights.

Instead, focus on collecting specific data that aligns with your business goals. Also, remember to analyze the data regularly and extract insights that can help you make informed marketing decisions.

Misconception 2: Correlation Equals Causation

One common misconception in data analysis is the confusion between correlation and causation. Many mistakenly believe that if two variables show a correlation, one must necessarily cause the other. Correlation, however, simply implies a relationship or association between two variables, where changes in one variable are mirrored by changes in the other. Causation, on the other hand, implies that one variable directly affects the other, which is a much stronger assertion requiring more rigorous validation.

To differentiate between correlation and causation, it is crucial to conduct thorough statistical analysis and experiments. This involves looking beyond the data to consider external factors and using statistical tools to test the strength and significance of the correlation. For instance, regression analysis can be used to control for other variables that might influence the relationship, and randomized controlled trials can help to establish causality by isolating variables and directly observing the effects of changing one variable on another.

Case Study: PB Shoes

For example, PB Shoes observed that higher sales volumes were correlated with increased social media engagement. The initial assumption might be that increased engagement on social media platforms causes higher sales. Before drawing this conclusion, however, PB Shoes conducted a deeper analysis to explore this relationship.

Using statistical tools, PB Shoes first confirmed that the correlation was statistically significant and not due to chance. They then designed an experiment where they deliberately increased social media engagement through targeted campaigns to see whether there was a corresponding increase in sales independent of other variables, such as seasonal effects or promotions.

Furthermore, they analyzed other potential confounding factors, such as an increase in overall marketing spend or the introduction of new products that coincided with the rise in social media activity. By controlling for these variables, PB Shoes aimed to isolate the effect of social media engagement alone on sales.

The analysis revealed that while social media engagement was indeed correlated with higher sales, the effect was significantly amplified by simultaneous promotional campaigns. Thus, the causal relationship was not as straightforward as initially assumed. Social media engagement did contribute to higher sales, but it was most effective when combined with other marketing efforts.

Misconception 3: Anecdotal vs Statistical Significance

Humans are inherently prone to cognitive biases, one of which includes the tendency to overemphasize certain pieces of information that appear more salient or memorable for various reasons. This can be due to the recency or primacy effect, where the first or last pieces of information encountered are given undue weight. Alternatively, it might be because the information aligns well with our existing understanding, or it stands out due to its uniqueness or emotional impact.

Such biases can lead to overreliance on anecdotal evidence—individual stories or examples that may seem compelling but are not necessarily representative of the larger reality. Anecdotal evidence can skew perception and decision-making processes in significant ways, especially when contrasted with data-driven insights derived from statistically significant information.

When making critical decisions, especially in marketing and strategic planning, relying on anecdotes rather than rigorously collected data can lead to strategies that are not only ineffective but potentially detrimental. Anecdotes often fail to capture the full complexity of a situation and can be exceptions rather than the rule. Decisions based on such evidence might cater to outliers rather than the typical experiences or behaviors of the majority.

Case Study: PB Shoes

Let's revisit PB Shoes, where the company is deciding whether to launch a new product line. Suppose a handful of high-profile, enthusiastic customers provide glowing feedback about a prototype. While these anecdotes are positive and potentially persuasive, they do not necessarily represent the broader customer base's perspective.

To avoid the trap of anecdotal bias, PB Shoes conducts a comprehensive market analysis, gathering data from a diverse and statistically significant sample of their target market. They utilize surveys, focus groups, and a pilot sales program to collect and analyze data on customer preferences and behaviors. This approach ensures that the decision to go ahead with the product launch is informed by reliable data that accurately reflects the sentiments of a broader customer base, not just a few vocal individuals.

By prioritizing statistical significance and representative data, companies such as PB Shoes can make more informed, effective, and strategic decisions. This shift not only mitigates the risk of bias but also aligns business strategies with the genuine needs and preferences of the market, leading to better outcomes and higher customer satisfaction.

Misconception 4: Data Analysis Is Always Objective

While data provides a quantitative measure of your marketing campaign's success, it's important to consider the qualitative context surrounding the data. For instance, analyzing social media metrics without considering customers' sentiments can lead to incorrect conclusions. It's vital to consider qualitative factors that may impact your marketing campaigns, such as consumer feedback or competitor analysis.

Misconception 5: Data Speaks for Itself

The saying goes, "Numbers don't lie," yet as we've seen, marketing results and other statistics can be interpreted in a number of ways.

Data is complex, and it doesn't always speak for itself. It requires interpretation and analysis to identify trends and insights. Even the most visually appealing data visualization can be misinterpreted if not properly analyzed. Therefore, it's vital to ask the right questions when analyzing data to ensure you extract accurate insights.

Misconception 6: Predictive Analytics Is Always Precise

Predictive analytics is an essential tool for identifying future trends. It's important, however, to understand that predictive analytics can't always be 100% precise. There's always a chance of unexpected external events impacting the predicted outcome. Therefore, it's essential to view predictive analytics as a guide and make adjustments based on new data or unforeseen circumstances.

Additionally, we explored the concept of bias getting introduced into datasets that are then fed into machine learning algorithms. When those algorithms lack transparency into how they are making decisions, it can be hard for humans to understand when and where inaccuracies may exist.

CONCLUSION

It's essential to recognize that data analysis is complex and requires a thorough understanding of the subject matter. It's crucial to avoid common misconceptions in data analysis to make accurate decisions that align with your marketing goals.

You can effectively analyze marketing data by focusing on gathering specific data, digging deeper, considering the qualitative context, interpreting data accurately, and recognizing that predictive analytics aren't always precise. As a result, the insights and trends you identify will help you make informed decisions that drive growth for your business.

Building on the methods discussed in this chapter, the next chapter will explore how to use generative artificial intelligence (AI) tools to assist in your marketing data analysis.

CHAPTER 24

USING GENERATIVE AI FOR ANALYSIS

W e've explored usages of AI in earlier parts of the marketing measurement process, and it may come as no surprise that generative AI can play a role in the analysis stages as well.

For most companies, the ability to both anticipate change and quickly react and adapt to it can be a significant competitive advantage. Generative AI facilitates this by processing and analyzing data at a scale and speed unattainable by human analysts. This enables marketers to identify trends, predict market movements, and optimize campaigns with a level of precision and foresight previously deemed impossible.

In this chapter, we will explore how generative AI can be specifically applied to marketing measurement analysis, enhancing traditional methods and introducing new capabilities that allow businesses to measure, understand, and influence consumer behavior more effectively than ever before.

GENERATIVE AI AND MARKETING DATA ANALYSIS

Because Generative AI systems are trained on large datasets to recognize patterns and predict outcomes, it enables them to generate insights that would be nearly impossible for human analysts to derive due to the volume and complexity of the data.

Generative AI models go beyond simple analysis; they can simulate potential future scenarios by generating data that mimics real-world behaviors. This predictive capability allows marketers to see not only what has happened or what is happening but also what could happen under different strategies. For instance, AI can simulate the impact of a new marketing campaign on customer purchasing behaviors before it is launched, providing a valuable "test" of potential outcomes.

Comparing Generative AI Analysis with Traditional Data Analysis Methods

Let's look at some ways that the utilization of generative AI for marketing data analysis differs from more traditional methods, and benefits the marketers using them:

- *Speed and scale*: One of the most significant advantages of generative AI over traditional data analysis methods is its ability to process information at an unparalleled speed and scale. Traditional methods, often manual or semi-automated, involve linear and time-consuming processes that struggle to handle today's big data demands. Generative AI, however, can analyze petabytes of data in real time, delivering insights almost instantaneously.

- *Predictive power*: Traditional data analysis typically focuses on descriptive analytics, which explains what happened, and diagnostic analytics, which explains why it happened. Generative AI extends these capabilities to predictive and prescriptive analytics, not only forecasting future trends but also recommending actions to achieve desired outcomes. This is achieved through sophisticated models such as neural networks, which can extrapolate future outcomes based on historical data.
- *Accuracy and learning ability*: While traditional methods rely on static models that need human intervention for updates, generative AI continuously learns and improves its algorithms based on new data. This self-learning capability reduces the likelihood of bias and error over time, leading to more accurate analyses. Traditional methods, however, can become outdated quickly and may retain biases from initial model assumptions.
- *Novel insight generation*: Generative AI can identify patterns and correlations that are not immediately obvious to human analysts. This not only improves understanding but can also lead to the discovery of new marketing strategies or target previously unconsidered demographics. In contrast, traditional methods might only confirm known patterns or trends already visible to analysts.

Generative AI's ability to process vast datasets rapidly, predict future trends, and continuously learn and adapt offers a significant advantage over traditional data analysis methods, making it an invaluable tool in the marketer's toolkit.

EVALUATING THE EFFECTIVENESS OF MARKETING CAMPAIGNS WITH AI

With generative AI, marketers can leverage deeper insights and predictive analytics to truly understand and enhance the effectiveness of their marketing efforts. Let's look at a few ways that generative AI can enhance marketers' ability to understand this.

Measuring Campaign Success Against KPIs

- *Data integration and analysis*: Generative AI can ingest data from multiple sources—social media, CRM systems, sales data, and even third-party data—to create a unified view of campaign performance. By applying machine learning algorithms, AI systems analyze this data to assess how well the campaign is meeting its KPIs. This might include complex calculations such as attribution modeling, where AI determines the contribution of each campaign element to the overall goal.
- *Real-time reporting and adjustments*: One of the strengths of using AI in campaign evaluation is its ability to provide real-time insights. This is particularly useful for long-running campaigns where ongoing adjustments may be necessary. AI systems can continuously analyze incoming data and suggest modifications to optimize the campaign's performance, such as reallocating budget to more successful channels or tweaking the messaging based on audience response.

Uncovering Patterns and Predicting Future Campaign Performance

- *Pattern recognition*: Generative AI excels at identifying patterns and anomalies in large datasets that might elude human analysts. For instance, AI can detect emerging trends in consumer behavior or shifts in sentiment that are subtly developing across platforms. These patterns can indicate underlying factors driving campaign success or failure, allowing marketers to better understand the dynamics at play.

- *Predictive analytics*: Beyond analyzing current campaigns, AI can forecast future performance based on historical data and ongoing trends. Using techniques such as regression analysis, clustering, and even sophisticated neural networks, AI models simulate different scenarios and predict their outcomes. This predictive capability enables marketers to anticipate market reactions and adjust their strategies proactively.
- *Look-alike simulations*: AI can also create simulations based on past campaigns to predict how a similar future campaign might perform under various conditions. This is especially useful when venturing into new markets or testing new marketing channels. Additionally, case studies of AI-driven campaigns often reveal insights about which strategies yield the best ROI, helping to refine future campaigns.

By utilizing generative AI to analyze campaign success against detailed KPIs and utilizing AI's capability to uncover patterns and predict outcomes, marketers can not only see what strategies worked but also why they worked and how they can be improved in the future. This approach enhances the efficiency and effectiveness of current campaigns and informs the development of future marketing strategies, ensuring that they are data-driven and dynamically tuned to meet evolving market demands.

CASE STUDY: OPTIMIZING PB SHOES' MARKETING MIX

Let's explore how PB Shoes leveraged generative AI to optimize its marketing strategy, including the mix of channels used to reach customers, leading to significantly improved campaign performance and customer engagement.

Analyzing Marketing Channel Effectiveness with Generative AI

- *Initial assessment*: PB Shoes initially conducted a broad marketing strategy that included online ads, social media, email marketing, and traditional print advertising. The ROI from these channels was unclear, however, and the marketing team needed a way to identify which channels were most effective.
- *Implementation of generative AI*: PB Shoes implemented a generative AI system designed to analyze marketing data across all channels. The AI was tasked with processing sales data, marketing spend, customer interactions, and engagement metrics to evaluate the performance of each channel.
- *Data analysis and pattern recognition*: The AI system used advanced machine learning algorithms to identify patterns and correlations between marketing activities and sales outcomes. It considered various factors, including the timing of campaigns, customer demographics, and the customer journey across touchpoints.

Insights Gained

- *Social media efficiency*: The AI analysis revealed that social media campaigns were particularly effective in driving engagement among younger demographics, especially on platforms such as Instagram and Snapchat.

- *Email marketing personalization*: Email campaigns had a high engagement rate when messages were personalized based on previous purchase behavior and browsing history.
- *Underperforming traditional ads*: Traditional print advertising showed a lower-than-expected impact on sales and was more costly compared to digital channels.

Actions Taken

- *Resource reallocation*: Based on these insights, PB Shoes reallocated its marketing budget, significantly reducing spend on traditional print ads and increasing investment in social media and personalized email marketing.
- *Campaign optimization*: The marketing team used AI-generated insights to tweak the content and scheduling of social media posts and emails, aligning them more closely with customer preferences and behaviors identified by AI.
- *Enhanced customer segmentation*: The AI tools helped refine customer segmentation, which allowed for more targeted and effective marketing campaigns. Segments were adjusted in real time based on continuous AI analysis, keeping the marketing efforts aligned with dynamic customer behaviors.

Outcomes

Following the adjustments made using AI-driven insights, PB Shoes observed a 25% increase in overall campaign effectiveness and a 40% increase in engagement rates on personalized marketing channels. The shift in strategy also led to a 15% reduction in marketing costs due to the decreased use of underperforming channels.

Furthermore, the enhanced customer segmentation and targeted marketing efforts improved customer satisfaction scores and increased repeat customer rates, showcasing the extended benefits of a well-optimized marketing mix.

By embracing AI-driven analytics, PB Shoes was able to make informed decisions that maximized the impact of their marketing spend, improved customer engagement, and ultimately drove greater sales performance.

ENHANCING MARKETING ROI WITH GENERATIVE AI

While the marketing channels that customers prefer may evolve over time, as do the methods that marketers use to reach them, the need to achieve ROI is a constant. AI-based tools, and generative AI in particular, can help marketers understand where they are spending money wisely and where they need to make adjustments. Let's look at a few ways to do this.

Leveraging AI Analysis to Optimize Budget Allocation and Resource Investment

- *Data-driven investment decisions*: Generative AI can analyze past marketing performance data alongside current market trends to determine the most cost-effective allocation of marketing budgets. By predicting the future performance of different channels based on historical data, AI helps marketers invest more in channels that offer higher returns and cut back or optimize those that underperform.
- *Scenario simulation*: AI tools can simulate various budget allocation scenarios to forecast potential outcomes. These simulations can include adjustments to spending in specific channels, shifts in timing, or strategic changes in targeting. By visualizing the potential

returns of different scenarios, marketers can make more informed decisions about where to allocate their budgets for maximum impact.

- *Dynamic budget reallocation*: AI systems can monitor ongoing campaigns in real time and suggest budget reallocation when certain channels perform above or below expectations. This dynamic approach allows marketers to adapt quickly to market changes, optimizing spend throughout the campaign lifecycle for the best possible ROI.

Incorporating AI Insights into Financial Decisions in Marketing

- *Integration of cross-functional data*: To enhance ROI, it's crucial that AI systems have access to wide-ranging data beyond just marketing metrics. Incorporating data from sales, customer service, and even inventory management can provide a more holistic view of how marketing efforts affect the broader business. This comprehensive data integration helps AI generate more accurate and impactful insights.
- *Continuous learning and adaptation*: AI models should be continually trained and updated with new data to improve their accuracy and relevance. As market conditions change, the AI system needs to learn from these changes to refine its predictions and recommendations. Regularly updating AI models ensures that the insights remain applicable and that the marketing strategies align with current market dynamics.
- *Stakeholder education and buy-in*: For AI-driven financial decisions to be effective, it's important that all stakeholders understand and trust the AI's insights. Educating stakeholders about how AI works, the benefits it offers, and how it derives its recommendations can foster trust and encourage wider adoption. Additionally, involving stakeholders in the AI implementation process can help align the AI's outputs with business goals and ensure that its insights are actionable.
- *Transparent metrics and reporting*: Maintain transparency in how AI-driven recommendations are calculated. Clear reporting on AI findings and the rationale behind its recommendations can help stakeholders understand and act on AI insights more confidently. Transparent metrics and methodologies also make it easier to evaluate the AI system's effectiveness and make adjustments as needed.

Incorporating generative AI into marketing financial decision-making processes can significantly enhance ROI by ensuring that marketing budgets are allocated to the most effective channels and strategies. By following best practices for AI integration, businesses see improved financial returns while gaining deeper insights into the complex dynamics of their market environments.

LIMITATIONS AND CHALLENGES IN AI-POWERED ANALYSIS

As good as all of this sounds, there are still some limitations within AI-based tools and methods, and there can be challenges for any organization adopting these approaches. Let's explore a few of these:

- *Data quality and availability*: The accuracy of AI-powered analysis is highly dependent on the quality and quantity of the data available. Incomplete or biased datasets can lead AI systems to generate misleading insights. Additionally, smaller companies or newer brands might not have access to the extensive historical data that AI models require for optimal performance.

- *Over-reliance on technology*: There is a risk that marketers may become overly reliant on AI for decision-making, overlooking the importance of human intuition and experience. AI should support, not replace, human judgment, especially in complex and nuanced marketing environments where emotional and cultural factors play a significant role.

- *Interpretability of AI decisions*: Often referred to as the "black-box" issue, many AI models, especially those involving deep learning, do not easily reveal how decisions are made. This can make it challenging for marketers to trust and understand AI-generated recommendations and insights fully.

- *Compliance and privacy issues*: With increasing regulations around data privacy, such as GDPR and CCPA, using AI to analyze customer data can pose legal challenges. Ensuring compliance while leveraging AI for marketing analysis requires careful navigation of these regulations.

Some Ways to Mitigate These Challenges

There are several ways to address these challenges and overcome them so that AI tools can play a stronger role in your marketing analysis. Let's look at a few, keeping in mind that we may have discussed some in previous contexts as well.

- *Ensuring data integrity*: Invest in robust data management practices to ensure the data feeding into AI systems is accurate, comprehensive, and clean. Regular audits and updates of data sources can help maintain the quality of data.

- *Balanced approach to decision-making*: While AI can provide powerful insights, integrate human judgment into the decision-making process. Use AI as a tool for generating hypotheses and insights, which should then be reviewed and contextualized by experienced marketers.

- *Transparency and explainability*: Choose AI tools and platforms that offer greater transparency about how their algorithms work. Some AI systems are designed to provide explanations for their predictions and decisions, which can help build trust and understanding among marketers.

- *Stay informed and compliant*: Keep abreast of the latest developments in data privacy laws and regulations to ensure that your use of AI in marketing analysis remains compliant. Consider working with legal experts to navigate complex privacy issues.

- *Continuous learning and adaptation*: AI technologies and marketing landscapes are continuously evolving. Engage in ongoing learning and training programs to keep up with the latest AI advancements and their applications in marketing. This ensures that your marketing team can adapt and make the most of AI technologies effectively.

While generative AI brings significant advancements to marketing analysis, understanding and addressing its limitations and challenges are crucial for maximizing its benefits. A balanced approach ensures that AI acts as a powerful assistant in the complex, dynamic world of marketing.

CONCLUSION

From optimizing marketing mixes based on precise, data-driven insights to enhancing ROI through strategic budget allocation and advanced customer segmentation, generative AI has proven to be an invaluable asset in decoding complex marketing data.

Generative AI can automate the analysis process while bringing a level of depth and precision that was previously unattainable. By leveraging predictive analytics and machine learning, this technology can forecast trends, anticipate market changes, and provide recommendations that are both actionable and forward-thinking. It enables marketers to move beyond traditional descriptive analytics to embrace a more dynamic approach to understanding consumer behavior and campaign performance.

Now that analysis has been discussed using both manual and AI-assisted methods, the next chapter will explore how to interpret the analysis.

CHAPTER 25

INTERPRETING RESULTS

S tringent analysis of your marketing performance metrics is important for several reasons. Firstly, it allows you to track your progress over time and identify areas where you are improving or experiencing challenges.

This information can help you make data-driven decisions about your marketing strategy and adjust your tactics to meet your goals better. Additionally, analyzing your performance metrics can help you identify areas where you are underperforming compared to industry benchmarks, allowing you to optimize your efforts and improve your results. Furthermore, a stringent analysis of your marketing performance metrics can help you measure the ROI of your marketing campaigns and demonstrate the value of your marketing efforts to stakeholders. Overall, a stringent analysis of your marketing performance metrics is important for understanding your marketing performance and making informed decisions to improve your results.

Thus, the effectiveness of your marketing efforts relies not only on the activities you do but also on the results you get. Also, how do you prove that your efforts are working? Let's explore a few ways to make sure your analysis can be used to have a direct impact on marketing and the business.

TELL A STORY WITH THE RESULTS

One of the most effective ways to interpret and utilize your marketing results is by crafting a compelling narrative around the data. The ability to tell a story with your analysis not only tests your understanding of the results but also enhances your ability to communicate their significance to others, particularly a non-technical audience. This approach involves translating complex data insights into relatable and engaging narratives that highlight the successes and shortcomings of your marketing efforts without relying heavily on technical jargon or complex marketing terminology.

The Art of Simplification and Connection

The first step in storytelling is simplification. This means distilling complex data into key takeaways that capture the essence of what the data reveals about consumer behavior, market trends, or campaign performance. It's about focusing on what matters most to the audience, be it the ROI, the growth in customer engagement, or the impact of a specific marketing strategy.

The next step is to connect these key points in a logical sequence that builds toward a conclusion or a call to action. For instance, if your analysis shows that a particular campaign led to a significant increase in customer retention, the story might start with the campaign's goals, describe the tactics used, detail the outcomes, and conclude with what this means for future strategies.

Case Study: PB Shoes' New Ad Campaign

Consider PB Shoes, which recently launched a targeted ad campaign aimed at increasing sales among first-time buyers. After the campaign, the marketing team analyzed the results and prepared to present their findings. They noticed that while the campaign did generate an increase in first-time purchases, the cost per acquisition was higher than expected.

To communicate these results effectively, the team crafted a story that began with the campaign's ambitious goals and innovative tactics. They highlighted how these tactics resonated well with the target demographic, as shown by the increased purchase rates. They also addressed the high costs involved, framing them as a learning opportunity for optimizing future campaigns. This narrative was structured to affirm the campaign's successes while transparently addressing its challenges, making it accessible and actionable for stakeholders, including those without a deep understanding of marketing analytics.

Engaging and Persuasive Communication

The ultimate test of your interpretation is your ability to engage your audience. A good story does not just inform; it persuades. It should explain the "why" and "how"—why the results are important and how they can inform future decisions. This means not only recounting what happened and what worked but also offering insights into why certain outcomes occurred and how these learnings can be applied moving forward.

By telling a story with marketing results, you transform raw data into a powerful narrative that can inform strategy, persuade stakeholders, and guide future actions. This method makes your findings not only more understandable and relatable but also more impactful, driving home the relevance of marketing efforts in a way that charts and numbers alone cannot achieve.

WHEN IN DOUBT, TEST AND VALIDATE YOUR ASSUMPTIONS

As we navigate through the complexities of interpreting marketing data, it is vital to ensure the validity of the numbers underpinning your analysis. Doubts about data validity can undermine the credibility of your insights and potentially lead to flawed strategic decisions. To mitigate this risk, it's advisable to adopt a rigorous approach to reviewing and validating your data before presenting it to stakeholders.

Re-Evaluating Data with a Critical Eye

The first step in ensuring the reliability of your data is to double-check the sources and methods used in your initial analysis. If there are any concerns about the accuracy or relevance of the data, consider running additional reports or using alternative metrics that might provide a different perspective on the same issue. This can help confirm findings or reveal new insights that were not apparent in the original analysis.

Using Statistical Tools for Deeper Insights

Leveraging statistical tools can provide another layer of validation. Statistical analysis can help identify outliers, trends, and patterns that support or challenge your initial conclusions. Techniques that we've discussed earlier in the book, such as regression analysis, hypothesis testing, and confidence intervals, can strengthen your understanding of the data and help substantiate your findings.

Collaboration and Critical Review

Engaging with peers and soliciting feedback is another effective way to validate your analysis. Working collaboratively allows you to explore different viewpoints and question assumptions through a process akin to playing "devil's advocate." By challenging each other's findings and interpretations, you can uncover potential weaknesses in the analysis and refine your approach. Encouraging a culture of critical review and open dialogue ensures that the analysis is robust and comprehensive.

Case Study: PB Shoes' Quarterly Performance Report

Our friends at PB Shoes routinely employ these validation strategies in their marketing analysis. Before finalizing their quarterly performance report, the analytics team conducts a series of validation checks. They re-run the sales and customer engagement reports using different segmentation criteria to confirm the consistency of the trends they observe. Additionally, they employ statistical tests to verify the significance of the changes noted in customer behavior patterns over the quarter.

Once the team feels confident in the data's accuracy, they organize a review session with representatives from sales, marketing, and product development. This cross-functional meeting serves as a platform to critique the findings, challenge the underlying assumptions, and discuss the implications of the analysis. This rigorous review process helps PB Shoes ensure that their insights are not only based on solid data but are also aligned with the broader business context and strategic goals.

Validating your marketing analysis is crucial to building confidence in your insights and recommendations. By taking the time to review data critically, utilize statistical tools, and engage in collaborative scrutiny, you can enhance the integrity and impact of your marketing analysis. This rigorous approach not only fortifies your findings against potential criticism but also ensures that strategic decisions are made on a foundation of reliable and thoroughly vetted information.

USE ATTRIBUTION MODELING TO MEASURE THE IMPACT OF DIFFERENT TOUCHPOINTS

As we explored in Chapters 20 and 21, attribution modeling is an essential analytical technique used to assess the influence of various touchpoints throughout the customer journey on the final conversion. This approach helps marketers understand which channels, messages, and activities have the greatest impact on achieving their marketing goals, enabling more informed strategic decisions.

Each model has its advantages and disadvantages, and the choice of model can significantly influence how credit is allocated across channels. Therefore, it is crucial to align the selected attribution model with your strategic objectives and the specifics of your marketing funnel.

Case Study: PB Shoes' Multi-Channel Marketing Campaign Analysis

The PB Shoes marketing team uses attribution modeling to optimize their multi-channel marketing campaigns. Recognizing the complexity of their customer journey, which includes interactions across social media, email, paid search, and direct Web site visits, PB Shoes employs a position-based attribution model. This model helps them understand the significance of initial awareness created through social media and the effectiveness of final touchpoints such as email campaigns that close the sales.

By applying this model, PB Shoes can accurately measure the impact of each channel and adjust their budget allocation accordingly. For instance, if data shows that social media campaigns are crucial in driving awareness but do not directly result in conversions, the team might decide to increase spending on social media for awareness while refining their closing strategies in email campaigns.

By choosing the appropriate attribution model, marketers at companies such as PB Shoes can ensure they are not only crediting the right channels but also optimizing their marketing spend based on solid data-driven insights. This approach allows for a balanced evaluation of each channel's contribution to conversions, ensuring that all efforts are recognized and appropriately valued in the broader marketing strategy.

CONNECT MARKETING METRICS TO REVENUE AND ESTABLISHED BUSINESS KPIs

The ultimate goal of marketing is to generate revenue for your business. Therefore, tying your marketing metrics to revenue is perhaps the most crucial step in providing results from your marketing efforts.

You can use different methods to achieve this, such as tracking the ROI of each campaign, calculating the cost per lead or acquisition, or measuring customer lifetime value. By connecting marketing metrics to revenue, you can demonstrate the actual impact of your marketing activities on your business's bottom line.

WATCH OUT FOR BIAS

Interpreting the results of your marketing measurement efforts requires a thorough understanding of the data and the context in which it was collected.

One key aspect of effective interpretation is understanding the limitations and potential biases of the metrics used. For example, tracking Web site traffic and social media engagement may not accurately reflect the success of a marketing campaign if the metrics are not properly aligned with business goals.

COMMUNICATE RESULTS EFFECTIVELY

Finally, once you have proven results from your marketing efforts, it is essential to communicate them effectively to the stakeholders in your business. This can include executives, investors, sales teams, or other departments that may benefit from your insights.

Use visual aids, such as graphs, charts, or dashboards, to illustrate your points clearly. Also, tailor your communication to your audience's preferences and priorities to ensure you make an impact.

CONCLUSION

Interpreting the results of your marketing measurement efforts requires a thorough understanding of the data and the context in which it was collected. This can mean considering the broader marketing landscape, which includes understanding industry benchmarks and comparing your performance to those benchmarks to identify areas where you are underperforming. Additionally, it is important to consider changes in the marketing landscape, such as shifts in consumer behavior or new technologies, that may impact your results.

Finally, as mentioned in the previous chapter, it is always important to consider the specific goals of your marketing campaigns when interpreting results. Different goals may require different metrics, and choosing metrics aligned with your objectives is important. For example, tracking Web site traffic or social media engagement may not be the most relevant metric if your goal is to increase sales. Instead, you may want to focus on metrics such as conversion rates or ROI.

Overall, effective interpretation of marketing measurement results requires a nuanced understanding of the data, the marketing landscape, and the specific goals of your campaigns. By considering these factors, you can make informed decisions to improve your marketing performance and achieve your business objectives.

Now that we have an understanding of how to analyze and interpret our results, the next chapter will explore methods to refine your results and take your analysis further through continuous improvements.

CHAPTER 26

EXPERIMENTING, REFINING, AND CONTINUOUS IMPROVEMENT

O f course, your initial results and analysis are only the beginning of your marketing measurement journey. Continuously testing and refining your marketing channel can help you reach the right audience, engage with them effectively, and ultimately keep them as loyal customers. Let's explore some ways to implement continuous experimentation in marketing to help you achieve better results in the long run.

BENEFITS OF EXPERIMENTATION

Experimentation is a cornerstone of effective marketing measurement and analysis, providing marketers with a systematic way to test hypotheses, explore new ideas, and refine strategies based on real data. One of the primary benefits of experimentation is the ability to minimize risk by testing concepts on a small scale before rolling them out to a broader audience. By running controlled tests—such as A/B or multivariate experiments—marketers can see how different variables, such as creative elements, messaging, or offers, impact customer behavior. This evidence-based approach helps organizations avoid costly mistakes by focusing resources on strategies that have been proven to work.

Moreover, experimentation drives innovation by allowing marketing teams to move beyond assumptions and gut instincts. Instead of relying on what has worked in the past, marketers can explore new approaches, test bold ideas, and discover unexpected insights that lead to better outcomes. Experimentation encourages a culture of curiosity and learning, empowering teams to question the status quo and continuously optimize their efforts. For example, testing different audience segments or channels can reveal previously untapped opportunities that would otherwise go unnoticed. Through experimentation, marketers not only improve the effectiveness of individual campaigns but also gain a deeper understanding of their customers.

Continuous experimentation also fosters agility. In today's fast-paced marketing environment, consumer preferences, technologies, and market conditions are constantly evolving. Experimentation allows marketers to stay ahead by continuously testing, refining, and adapting their strategies based on real-time data. This ongoing process ensures that marketing efforts remain relevant and impactful, even as external conditions shift. By integrating experimentation into their overall strategy, organizations can remain flexible, improve decision-making, and maximize ROI in an ever-changing marketplace.

Let's look in more depth and explore some benefits of experimentation in your marketing measurement and testing.

Understand Your Customers' Behavior and Preferences

Understanding customer behavior is one of the most valuable outcomes of running marketing experiments. Through testing different marketing elements—whether it's channels, messaging, creative design, or Calls to Action (CTAs)—you can observe how your audience interacts with your content and offerings in real time. These insights are crucial because they move beyond assumptions and allow marketers to see how actual customers behave when presented with different choices. For instance, an experiment testing two different email subject lines may not only reveal which one performs better but also offer insight into how your audience prefers to engage with your brand (e.g., a preference for humor over straightforward messaging). This data-driven understanding of customer preferences enables more informed decision-making, reducing the guesswork in marketing.

Experimentation also highlights the diversity of preferences within your audience. Not all customers react the same way to a single message or channel. For example, younger consumers might respond well to social media ads with concise, direct CTAs, while older demographics may prefer detailed, informative content through email marketing. Running segmentation-based experiments across different audience groups can help identify these nuances and allow for more tailored approaches. Over time, consistently testing and refining your campaigns can paint a comprehensive picture of what drives engagement, what motivates conversion, and what turns off your audience. This ensures that every marketing decision is aligned with customer behavior, improving the likelihood of campaign success.

Another key benefit of understanding customer preferences through experimentation is the ability to future-proof your marketing strategy. Consumer preferences change, sometimes rapidly, and what works today may not be effective tomorrow. Through continuous testing, marketers can stay ahead of these changes and be more responsive to shifts in behavior. For instance, as consumers shift from desktop to mobile devices, experimenting with mobile-first strategies can provide early insights into how to optimize for this growing segment. This proactive approach ensures that your marketing stays relevant, avoiding the trap of relying on outdated methods that may no longer resonate with your audience.

Ways You Can Apply This Idea

- *Test landing page designs* to see which version keeps customers engaged longer and leads to more conversions.
- *Experiment with email subject lines* to understand whether your audience prefers curiosity-driven or straightforward messaging.
- *Run A/B tests on social media ads* to determine whether customers respond better to short-form video content versus static images.
- *Segment audiences for personalized offers*, testing different discount strategies to see which results in higher clickthrough rates and purchases.
- *Experiment with CTA placements* on your Web site or email campaigns to see which location drives the most action from users.

Understanding your customers through experimentation ensures you're not just following marketing trends but are developing strategies rooted in real, actionable insights. This helps create more personalized and effective campaigns, leading to better engagement, higher conversions, and, ultimately, stronger customer relationships.

Stay ahead of Your Competitors

In today's rapidly changing digital landscape, staying ahead of competitors requires constant innovation and adaptability. Marketing channels, platforms, and consumer preferences are evolving faster than ever, and companies that fail to keep up risk falling behind. By continuously experimenting with new marketing tactics, strategies, and platforms, you can maintain a competitive edge. This ongoing experimentation allows you to discover what works best for your brand while your competitors may be sticking with traditional or outdated methods. For instance, being an early adopter of emerging social media platforms or leveraging new ad formats before they become widely popular can give your brand a distinct advantage.

One of the key benefits of continuous experimentation is the ability to identify growth opportunities that your competitors may have overlooked. For example, while competitors may focus solely on established platforms such as Facebook or Instagram, experimenting with emerging platforms such as TikTok or newer content formats such as interactive ads may open up untapped markets. By testing new channels and formats, you can reach different segments of your audience, attract new customers, and expand your reach. Staying ahead of your competitors means not waiting for others to adopt successful strategies—you are the one setting trends and blazing new trails in your industry.

Furthermore, experimentation allows you to refine your marketing efforts continuously and pivot faster than competitors. For example, if a new advertising feature is introduced on a platform, early testing can provide insights into how well it works for your brand, giving you the flexibility to optimize your campaigns while others are still figuring out the basics. Competitors that rely on static, "tried-and-true" methods may find themselves left behind as your brand evolves and innovates. Staying agile through constant testing positions your company to be more responsive to market changes, customer preferences, and new technologies.

Ways You Can Apply This Idea

- *Test emerging social media platforms* (e.g., TikTok or Threads) to see whether they are viable for engaging your target audience before competitors.
- *Experiment with new ad formats* such as shoppable ads, interactive ads, or augmented reality ads, giving your brand a unique edge in digital advertising.
- *Try different content types*, such as podcasts or live streaming, to see whether these formats resonate with your audience better than traditional content.
- *Run pilot campaigns* on new marketing automation tools or AI-based analytics platforms to improve efficiency and stay ahead of competitors stuck with older technologies.
- *Test niche or micro-influencer partnerships* to see whether they drive better engagement than high-profile influencer campaigns, which may be oversaturated in your industry.

Staying ahead of competitors through experimentation not only allows you to differentiate your brand but also ensures that you are constantly refining your strategy to keep up with or even outpace market changes. This proactive approach to marketing gives you an edge in capturing new audiences, expanding your reach, and maintaining relevance in a fast-moving landscape.

Optimize Your Budget Allocation

Optimizing budget allocation is one of the most critical benefits of marketing experimentation. With budgets often stretched across multiple channels—such as paid social media ads, search ads, display ads, and email marketing—it's essential to understand where your marketing dollars are delivering the most value. By running controlled experiments, marketers can identify which channels generate the highest Return on Ad Spend (ROAS) and focus resources where they deliver the best results. Experimentation provides clear data on which platforms, campaigns, or creative elements such as image selections, videos, headlines, and other copy are performing well, allowing you to make more informed decisions about budget allocation, leading to more effective marketing spend and improved financial outcomes.

ROAS is a key metric in evaluating how effectively your marketing dollars are working. It measures how much revenue is generated for every dollar spent on advertising. For example, if you spend $1,000 on a Facebook ad campaign and generate $5,000 in revenue, your ROAS would be 5:1, meaning you earned five times what you spent. Running experiments can reveal which campaigns or channels yield the highest ROAS, allowing marketers to funnel more budget into those high-performing areas. Conversely, channels or strategies that underperform can be scaled back or abandoned, optimizing overall budget allocation. Without experimentation, marketers run the risk of inefficient spending, investing heavily in channels that may not provide the best returns.

Another benefit of experimentation is the ability to test new budget strategies in a controlled environment. For example, testing how increasing or decreasing spend in a particular channel affects ROAS can provide insights into the optimal budget allocation for maximum return. You may discover that investing more in retargeting ads generates a significantly higher ROAS compared to other digital ads, or that scaling down underperforming search ads and reallocating that budget to social media leads to better outcomes. These insights help marketers refine their budget allocation strategy over time, ensuring that every dollar is spent as efficiently as possible to generate the greatest impact on revenue.

Here Is How You Can Apply This Idea

- *Test different budget allocations across channels* (e.g., allocate 60% to search ads and 40% to display ads versus 70% to social media and 30% to email) to see which mix generates the highest ROAS.
- *Run experiments on different bidding strategies* for paid media, such as manual bidding versus automated bidding, to determine which delivers better ROI.
- *Test different daily ad spend caps* on various campaigns to see where additional investment drives diminishing returns and adjust accordingly.
- *Experiment with seasonal budget adjustments* (e.g., increasing ad spend during peak sales periods such as Black Friday) to find the most efficient times to allocate larger portions of the budget.
- *Compare performance across platforms*, such as Facebook versus Google Ads, to see which delivers a higher ROAS and reallocate budgets based on findings.

Experimentation is a powerful tool for optimizing budget allocation by providing clear data on which channels and strategies generate the highest ROAS. By continuously testing and refining your ad spend across different platforms, audiences, and creative approaches, you can ensure that every marketing dollar is used effectively, leading to improved financial outcomes and a better overall marketing strategy. This approach allows marketers to maximize the impact of their advertising efforts while minimizing waste and inefficiency.

How to Calculate ROAS

The formula for calculating ROAS is:

ROAS = Revenue Generated from Ad Campaign / Cost of Ad Campaign

Where

- *Revenue Generated from Ad Campaign* refers to the total revenue driven directly by the advertising effort. This should be the revenue attributable to the ads, which can typically be tracked through conversions that result directly from the ads.
- *Cost of Ad Campaign* is the total expenditure on the advertising campaign. This includes all costs associated with the campaign, such as media buys, ad placement costs, and any other relevant expenses.

Example Calculation

Suppose you spent $1,000 on a digital advertising campaign and tracked that the campaign directly generated $5,000 in sales. The ROAS would be calculated as follows:

ROAS = $5,000 / 1,000 = 5

This means that for every dollar spent on the advertising campaign, five dollars in revenue were generated.

By testing and analyzing the performance of different channels and campaigns, you can identify the ones that deliver the best results for your business. This helps you allocate your budget more effectively and generate more leads at a lower cost.

Measure the Impact of Your Marketing Efforts Toward Business Goals

Measuring the impact of marketing efforts in relation to overarching business goals is a critical component of any marketing strategy. Marketers need to ensure that their campaigns are not just driving clicks, likes, or shares, but are directly contributing to tangible business outcomes, such as revenue growth, customer acquisition, or brand awareness. Establishing clear Key Performance Indicators (KPIs) tied to business goals provides a roadmap for evaluating campaign success. By continuously measuring the right metrics, marketers can assess whether their efforts are aligned with the broader objectives of the organization. For example, a campaign focused on lead generation may have KPIs such as Cost per Lead (CPL) and conversion rates that align with the business goal of increasing sales.

It is not enough to simply run campaigns without understanding their impact on business goals. Tracking the right metrics allows marketers to evaluate whether their strategies are effectively moving the needle. For instance, a marketing campaign that boosts Web site traffic but doesn't translate into conversions or sales is not delivering on key business objectives. By measuring both marketing-specific outcomes (e.g., engagement and traffic) and business-level outcomes (e.g., revenue and customer lifetime value), marketers gain a holistic view of their campaign's effectiveness. This comprehensive approach to measurement ensures that marketing activities are making a meaningful contribution to the bottom line, rather than just meeting vanity metrics.

Experimentation plays a crucial role in refining this measurement process. By running tests, marketers can evaluate which tactics, messaging, and channels deliver the greatest impact on business goals. If campaigns are falling short, the insights gathered from experimentation allow marketers to make informed adjustments to improve performance. For example, if a campaign is not meeting its goal of increasing customer acquisitions, experimentation may reveal that a different CTA, channel, or audience targeting strategy could drive better results. This iterative process of testing, measuring, and optimizing ensures that marketing efforts are always aligned with business objectives, maximizing ROI.

Ways You Can Apply This Idea

- *Align KPIs with business goals* by setting measurable objectives such as revenue growth, customer acquisition, or brand awareness, and track these metrics across all campaigns.
- *Experiment with different campaign strategies* (e.g., product launches versus promotional campaigns) to determine which type best aligns with key business outcomes such as market penetration or customer retention.
- *Test different attribution models* to ensure that credit is being given to the marketing channels most responsible for driving conversions and sales, ensuring alignment with business revenue targets.
- *Use data from CRM systems* to link marketing activities directly to business outcomes such as sales pipeline growth or customer lifetime value.
- *Run A/B tests on different sales funnels*, analyzing which approach converts the most leads into paying customers, and continuously refine the process to better achieve business objectives.

Measuring the impact of marketing efforts toward business goals ensures that marketing campaigns are not just successful in isolation but are directly contributing to the overall success of the organization. By tracking the right KPIs and metrics, marketers can make data-driven decisions that optimize campaign performance and maximize ROI. Through continuous experimentation and refinement, businesses can ensure that their marketing strategies are always working in service of their larger goals.

Improve Your Customer Experience

The customer experience is one of the most important factors in the success of any marketing campaign. In today's highly competitive environment, consumers have endless choices, and providing a seamless, enjoyable experience can make all the difference in securing conversions and building long-term loyalty. Continuously experimenting allows marketers to fine-tune the customer journey at every touchpoint. Whether it's the ease of navigating a Web site, the clarity of messaging, or the personalization of offers, every interaction contributes to the overall customer experience. Through A/B testing and multivariate experiments, marketers can identify the elements that resonate best with their audience and optimize them for maximum impact.

For example, a company might run an A/B test on two different versions of a product landing page—one with a video introduction and one without. By analyzing metrics such as time spent on the page, bounce rates, and conversions, they can determine which version provides a better user experience and drives more engagement. The same principles apply to multivariate testing, where multiple variables (such as layout, CTAs, and imagery) are tested simultaneously. This allows marketers to see how different combinations affect customer interactions and discover the optimal setup for improving the user experience. Over time, these experiments can lead to more intuitive customer journeys, from first contact to conversion, ultimately improving satisfaction and retention rates.

Improving the customer experience through experimentation also enhances customer engagement and loyalty. Customers are more likely to return to and engage with a brand that consistently provides a frictionless and enjoyable experience. As businesses gain more insights into what customers prefer, they can personalize the experience even further, tailoring content, offers, and interactions based on individual behaviors and preferences. The result is not only better performance from marketing campaigns but also a stronger connection between the brand and its customers. This leads to long-term value, as customers who enjoy their experience are more likely to become repeat buyers and brand advocates.

Ways You Can Apply This Idea

- *A/B test Web site navigation changes* to identify the user flow that results in more conversions and fewer drop-offs during the checkout process.
- *Experiment with personalized email campaigns*, testing different levels of personalization (e.g., first name inclusion and personalized recommendations) to see how they affect open and clickthrough rates.
- *Test the impact of customer support features*, such as live chat versus an FAQ section, to determine which method provides a better experience for customers needing assistance.
- *Run experiments on mobile versus desktop experiences*, optimizing for the growing number of customers interacting through mobile devices and ensuring a seamless experience across platforms.
- *Conduct tests on social media ad formats* (carousel ads versus single-image ads) to find out which formats deliver the most engagement and create a more interactive user experience.

By continuously refining the customer journey through experimentation, marketers can enhance every touchpoint, resulting in a more satisfying and seamless experience. This not only leads to immediate improvements in engagement and conversion rates but also builds long-term customer loyalty and retention. Ultimately, focusing on improving the customer experience is a win-win strategy: customers enjoy interacting with the brand, and businesses see stronger marketing results and a more dedicated customer base.

The Critical Role of Experimentation

Experimentation is the key to a successful marketing strategy. By continuously testing and refining your campaigns, you can gain valuable insights into your customers' behavior, optimize your budget allocation, stay ahead of your competitors, measure the impact of your marketing efforts, and improve your customer experience. Whether optimizing your existing channels or testing new ones, experimentation should be an ongoing process that provides insights to guide your marketing decisions. So, keep experimenting and refining your marketing channels to achieve better results in the long run.

Of course, you also need methods to ensure that your experiments are improving your results over time, as well as ways to improve your experiments themselves. This is where continuous improvement comes into play.

CONTINUOUS IMPROVEMENT

Continuous improvement is a process of constantly enhancing and refining marketing strategies to achieve maximum efficiency and effectiveness. This approach allows marketers to stay competitive in the industry's ever-changing landscape and ensure that they consistently deliver value to their customers. Let's explore what continuous improvement means for marketers and how to apply it to your strategy for better results.

Continuous Improvement

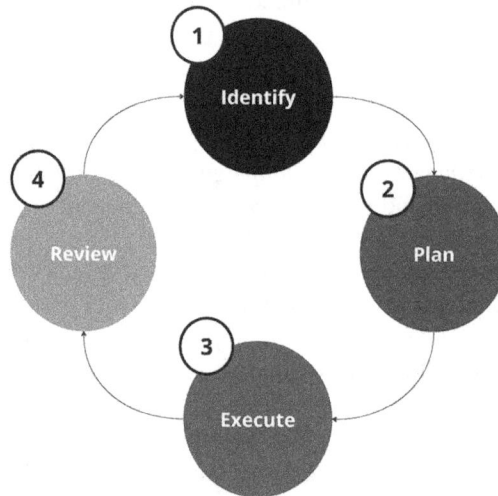

FIGURE 26.1. Continuous improvement cycle.

Continuous improvement is a philosophy that involves seeking out opportunities to make incremental improvements in various aspects of a marketing strategy. This can be achieved through data analysis, experimentation, and collaboration with other departments. The goal is to identify areas for improvement and implement changes that lead to better outcomes. By embracing a continuous improvement mindset, marketers can remain agile and adaptable to changing customer needs and market trends.

As you can see in the preceding diagram, continuous improvement involves a four-step process of:

1. Identifying areas of improvement
2. Creating a plan to improve
3. Executing the plan
4. Reviewing the results of the plan and determining further refinements

The Benefits of Continuous Improvement

Continuous improvement offers many benefits for marketers, including increased productivity, higher customer satisfaction, and better ROI. By consistently analyzing and refining your marketing strategy, you can identify opportunities to streamline processes, reduce waste, and deliver more value to your customers. This leads to better results and can improve overall team morale and satisfaction as progress is continually being made.

Applying Continuous Improvement to Your Strategy

Implementing continuous improvement in your marketing strategy requires a commitment to ongoing analysis and experimentation. Start by defining your KPIs and regularly tracking data to identify areas for improvement. Then, brainstorm solutions and implement changes to test their effectiveness. It's critical to involve all relevant team members in this process, gather their feedback, and collaborate to implement the best changes.

Common Continuous Improvement Tools and Techniques

Marketers can use various tools and techniques to implement continuous improvement more effectively. For instance, Lean Six Sigma can help identify inefficiencies and waste in processes, while design thinking can be used to solve customer problems and generate new ideas. Additionally, A/B testing and multivariate testing can help assess the effectiveness of various strategies and identify areas to refine and optimize.

Measuring the Success of Continuous Improvement

Continuous improvement requires ongoing measurement and analysis of your strategy's effectiveness. By evaluating KPIs regularly, you can track the success of your improvements and make further changes where necessary. Using metrics such as customer feedback, conversion rates, and ROI will enable you to evaluate the effectiveness of your marketing initiatives continually.

CONCLUSION

Continuous improvement is essential for marketers looking to stay ahead in a rapidly evolving industry. By constantly refining your marketing strategy, you can make incremental improvements that lead to better results and higher customer satisfaction. Apply a continuous improvement mindset to your marketing strategy, focusing on data analysis, experimentation, and collaboration.

Use tools and techniques such as Lean Six Sigma, design thinking, and A/B testing to refine your marketing strategy effectively. You can accurately measure the success of your continuous improvement efforts by tracking metrics, including customer feedback, ROI, and conversion rates. Embrace the philosophy of continuous improvement and you'll stay competitive and positioned for success.

PART 5 RECAP QUIZ

You've now reached the end of the final section of the book. Take one last quiz to make sure you have a good understanding of the concepts we've discussed in this part.

To check your answers, refer to Appendix B, which lists all of the answers for the quizzes in the book.

Question 1
Choose the correct answer: The three steps of analysis and refinement are: 1) Analyze the results, 2) Interpret the results, and:
a) Define the hypothesis
b) Experiment, refine, and continuously improve
c) Adjust the P-level

Question 2
Choose the correct answer: Which of the following are reasons that generative AI can be beneficial when analyzing marketing results?
a) Speed and scale
b) Predictive power
c) Accuracy and learning ability
d) Novel insight generation
e) All of the above

Question 3
True or false: Return on Ad Spend (ROAS) is a marketing metric that measures the effectiveness of a digital advertising campaign.

Epilogue

taying ahead of the competition and customer expectations has become paramount for marketers. Not all marketing investments, however, yield the same results, so focusing your future investments on the areas with the highest impact is increasingly important. As we conclude this book, let's explore how you can use your past marketing results to improve your future investment plans. We will also check in with the team at PB Shoes one last time to see how they are utilizing best practices in their marketing measurement and analysis.

START WITH THE AREAS THAT WILL HAVE THE HIGHEST IMPACT WITH THE LOWEST INVESTMENT OF TIME AND RESOURCES

When developing a marketing strategy, it's essential to prioritize efforts that deliver the highest Return on Investment (ROI) while requiring minimal time and resources. By focusing on these areas, marketers can achieve significant results without stretching their budgets or overburdening their teams. A prime example is email marketing, which consistently ranks as one of the most cost-effective channels. With the ability to personalize content and directly target customers, email marketing can deliver high conversion rates with relatively low investment. The key is to identify marketing activities that have the potential for high impact with minimal input, maximizing ROI.

Example from PB Shoes

PB Shoes discovered through data analysis that email marketing offered the best opportunity for customer engagement. By segmenting their email lists into new customers, returning customers, and high-value repeat buyers, PB Shoes was able to tailor personalized offers and recommendations to each group. They invested minimal time and budget into creating these campaigns using an email automation tool, yet the returns were substantial. Open rates and clickthrough rates were significantly higher for emails that offered targeted product recommendations, leading to an increase in online sales without the need for heavy ad spending.

Another high-impact, low-cost strategy PB Shoes adopted was content marketing through a series of blog posts and how-to guides on their Web site. By focusing on trending topics in the pickleball community—such as tips for improving performance or selecting the best shoes for different playstyles—they drove organic traffic to their Web site. This content was optimized for search engines, allowing it to rank well for relevant keywords over time, which brought in a steady stream of new visitors. The initial investment in content creation was minimal, but the long-term benefit of organic traffic resulted in ongoing brand visibility and customer acquisition.

To identify areas with the highest potential, PB Shoes also evaluated which marketing channels showed the most promise for engaging their customers. They discovered that while paid social media ads brought in some traffic, organic Instagram content performed better in terms of engagement with their target audience of pickleball enthusiasts. As a result, they reduced their ad spend and focused more on creating high-quality, shareable content for social media, such as behind-the-scenes videos, customer testimonials, and pickleball tips. This strategy allowed PB Shoes to maintain a strong presence without excessive spending on paid advertising.

By using email marketing and content creation, PB Shoes was able to increase customer engagement and online sales with minimal investment. Rather than spending heavily on acquiring new customers through costly digital ads, they nurtured relationships with existing customers, resulting in more repeat purchases and a stronger brand presence in the pickleball community.

Focusing on areas that yield the highest impact with the lowest investment is key to smart marketing. By leveraging cost-effective channels such as email marketing, organic social media, and content marketing, PB Shoes maximized their marketing returns without overspending. This approach allowed them to build a sustainable marketing strategy that could scale over time while staying aligned with their broader business goals. Prioritizing marketing efforts this way is essential for any business looking to achieve growth without draining resources.

FOCUS BY PICKING ONLY A FEW KEY METRICS TO TRACK

With the vast array of data available to marketers, it can be tempting to track as many metrics as possible. This, however, often leads to data overload and an inability to derive meaningful insights from the clutter. The most effective marketing strategies are those that focus on a few key metrics that align directly with business objectives. This focused approach allows marketers to allocate resources more efficiently and make data-driven decisions that improve campaign performance.

Example from PB Shoes

PB Shoes initially tracked a wide range of metrics across their campaigns, from email open rates to page views and everything in between. After refining their strategy, however, they decided to concentrate on a few high-impact metrics that were most aligned with their core business goals, such as Customer Lifetime Value (CLV) and customer retention rate. By narrowing their focus, PB Shoes was able to better understand how their efforts directly impacted long-term customer relationships and business growth. Tracking these key metrics allowed them to refine their campaigns to improve customer loyalty and ultimately increase sales.

Focusing on specific metrics also enables clearer reporting to stakeholders and helps streamline decision-making processes. When marketing teams present data to executives, a cluttered dashboard with dozens of metrics can be overwhelming and lead to decision paralysis. By selecting the most relevant metrics—whether they are related to engagement, conversion rates, or customer retention—marketers can provide concise, actionable insights that help drive business decisions. In the case of PB Shoes, focusing on engagement metrics such as customer retention allowed the team to highlight the success of their loyalty programs and justify further investment in retention strategies.

PB Shoes decided to emphasize CLV, customer retention, and purchase frequency as their primary metrics. By doing so, they aligned their marketing strategies with their business goal of increasing repeat purchases. Rather than getting bogged down by secondary metrics such as clickthrough rates or vanity metrics such as follower counts, they concentrated on understanding and optimizing customer behaviors that had the greatest financial impact on their bottom line.

The key to effective marketing measurement lies in simplicity and alignment with business goals. By focusing on a few carefully chosen metrics, marketers can avoid unnecessary complexity, improve clarity in reporting, and make more informed decisions. Whether it's customer engagement, retention, or lifetime value, identifying the right metrics ensures that marketing efforts remain efficient, effective, and always aligned with the broader objectives of the business. This focused approach is essential for marketers who want to drive meaningful, data-driven results.

COMMUNICATE EFFECTIVELY TO GET FURTHER INVESTMENTS

Once you've gathered valuable insights from your marketing efforts, the next crucial step is to effectively communicate those insights to executives and stakeholders. These individuals often hold the decision-making power for future investments and strategic direction. The key to gaining buy-in and further investment is presenting your data in a way that is both compelling and clear. By leveraging hard data and highlighting the direct impact on business goals, you can build a strong case for why additional resources or funding should be allocated to specific marketing initiatives.

To start, use hard data to support your claims and ensure that your insights are tied to relevant Key Performance Indicators (KPIs) that align with business goals. For example, PB Shoes measured the impact of their marketing campaigns on customer retention and lifetime value. When presenting these findings to their executives, they showcased how an increase in retention directly correlated to increased revenue and customer loyalty. This hard data demonstrated the tangible benefits of their marketing efforts and made a clear case for investing more in customer retention strategies, such as loyalty programs or targeted email campaigns.

It's also important to develop a clear narrative around your insights. Avoid bombarding executives with too much data. Instead, focus on telling a story that connects the marketing results to business outcomes. Explain how each campaign or initiative supported key business goals and what the next steps are to scale success. For example, PB Shoes presented the case for increasing investment in their email marketing efforts by showing how segmented and personalized email campaigns led to higher customer retention rates. By making a direct connection between marketing actions and business growth, they were able to secure further investment in their email marketing platform.

Example from PB Shoes

When PB Shoes discovered that customers who received personalized recommendations via email had a 25% higher likelihood of making repeat purchases, they presented this data to their executive team. By clearly communicating the value of personalized marketing, they were able to secure additional resources to expand this initiative, including hiring more marketing staff and investing in advanced email marketing tools.

Effective communication with executives and stakeholders is essential for gaining buy-in and driving further investment in your marketing efforts. Presenting clear, data-backed insights that align with business goals will make your case stronger. Whether it's illustrating success with customer retention, ROI on ad spend, or engagement metrics, the ability to articulate your results and create a compelling case will help ensure that your marketing efforts continue to receive the resources needed to thrive.

LEARN WHEN AI-BASED METHODS CAN BENEFIT YOUR EFFORTS

As we have already explored in this book, Artificial Intelligence (AI) is increasingly transforming how marketing measurement is conducted, offering powerful tools to enhance decision-making. The key to using AI effectively, however, is understanding when and how it can truly benefit your efforts. While AI can automate and optimize many aspects of marketing analysis, it's not a one-size-fits-all solution. Certain situations lend themselves well to AI-driven tools, such as analyzing large datasets, identifying patterns, and personalizing customer experiences. On the other hand, relying on AI for areas that require human intuition or creative direction, or where data quality is inconsistent, can introduce unnecessary complexity.

For example, a marketing team working on a campaign for a niche product might want to utilize AI to analyze customer behavior and predict purchase trends. This data can be used to identify target audiences and personalize offers that resonate more deeply with specific segments. If the data inputs are sparse or not well structured, however, the AI model may return unreliable predictions, potentially leading the team down the wrong path. In such cases, relying on traditional marketing intuition or manual data analysis may be more effective than introducing AI-driven methods that could add complexity without clear benefits.

Example from PB Shoes

One of the growing advantages of AI-based methods is how accessible they are becoming for marketers. Many modern AI tools require minimal data science or coding knowledge, allowing marketers to integrate them into their strategies easily. AI platforms designed for marketing can now handle tasks such as A/B testing, predictive analytics, and dynamic content generation. For instance, PB Shoes utilized an AI-driven email marketing tool to automatically recommend personalized products to customers based on their past purchases and browsing behavior. This allowed the team to scale their marketing efforts without requiring a deep understanding of how the underlying algorithms worked.

If PB Shoes had decided to overcomplicate their marketing strategy by using AI for tasks that could easily be handled manually—such as making slight adjustments to ad copy—they might have risked introducing inefficiencies and delays. By identifying the right moments to use AI, such as optimizing their email recommendations or predicting customer churn, they were able to enhance their efforts without added risk.

While AI can offer significant advantages in marketing measurement and analysis, knowing when and where to apply these tools is crucial. AI methods can accelerate tasks and improve the accuracy of predictions, but they should complement human-driven strategies rather than replace them. As AI-based methods continue to advance, marketers should keep them in mind for future planning and consider where they can bring the most value to their current efforts without introducing unnecessary risks.

HOW TO PRIORITIZE FOR THE FUTURE

Finally, it is essential to prioritize your marketing investments for the future. You can focus on three key areas: driving innovation, improving the customer experience, and driving better business results.

Firstly, identify areas where innovation can help to create more captivating campaigns, appeal to new target audiences, and improve the customer experience. Secondly, focus on improving the customer experience to increase engagement and customer loyalty. Finally, prioritize marketing investments likely to drive better business results based on the insights gained from your performance metrics.

Optimizing your marketing investments requires data-driven insights from past performance, understanding where to focus, and prioritizing the areas of highest impact. By implementing these strategies, you can optimize your marketing investments and maximize your ROI.

We now find ourselves at the end of this book. I hope you've enjoyed it and gained some insights into how you can improve your marketing measurement and performance. Remember that continuous improvement will lead to better performance, happier customers, and better returns for you and your marketing team.

GLOSSARY OF SELECT MARKETING MEASUREMENTS AND FORMULAS

M arketers should be familiar with some of the common metrics as well as how to calculate them. This glossary provides several key marketing measurement terms for review.

AUDIENCE GROWTH RATE (AGR)

Audience Growth Rate (AGR) is the percentage increase in your total audience size over a specific period of time. Essentially, it measures your brand's ability to attract new followers and retain existing ones. A robust AGR not only reflects engaging content but also a magnetizing brand presence that compels viewers to tune in.

The formula for AGR is surprisingly simple:

```
AGR = ({New audience} - {Lost audience}) / ({Total audience at the
start}) × 100
```

AVERAGE ORDER VALUE (AOV)

Average Order Value (AOV) is a metric that calculates the average amount of money spent per order by a customer. AOV is calculated in the following way:

```
AOV = {Total revenue} / {Number of orders in a given period}
```

For example, if a business has $10,000 in monthly revenue with 100 orders, their AOV would be $100. This means that on average, each customer spends $100 when they make a purchase. This can be calculated on a per-channel basis (e.g., on the Web site or a mobile app), or omnichannel, encompassing the average amount a customer spends regardless of where the order originates.

AVERAGE REVENUE PER USER (ARPU)

Average Revenue per User (ARPU) is a metric that measures the average revenue generated by a single user of a particular service or product over a certain period of time. Essentially,

ARPU calculates the amount of money each individual customer contributes to a company's overall revenue. When you calculate ARPU, you get a precise estimation of how much a brand is earning per customer.

ARPU is calculated by the following:

```
ARPU = {Total revenue generated} / {Number of users who purchased a
product or service over a given period}
```

Suppose a company generated $10,000 in revenue and 1,000 users in a month. In that case, the ARPU would be $10,000/1,000, giving us an ARPU of $10 per customer.

BOUNCE RATE

Bounce rate measures the percentage of visitors who land on your Web site and then leave after viewing just one page. In other words, they "bounce" off your site without exploring further. Generally, a high bounce rate is considered to be a bad thing since it indicates that visitors aren't finding what they're looking for or aren't interested in your Web site's content.

Google Analytics is a popular tool used by many marketers to track their Web site's performance, including bounce rate. By logging in to your Google Analytics account, you can access data on your Web site's bounce rate and see how it compares to industry benchmarks. You can also use Google Analytics to drill down into specific pages on your Web site to see where visitors are bouncing the most.

CHURN RATE (CR)

Churn Rate (CR) measures how many customers stop doing business with a company in a particular period. CR is an essential metric for businesses to track, especially those with a subscription-based model. CR is calculated by dividing the number of customers lost during a specific period by the total number of customers.

```
CR = {Customers lost (in a specific period)} / {Total number of
customers}
```

For instance, if a business had 100 customers at the beginning of the month and lost 10 by the end, their CR would be 10%. As a business, understanding what causes high CR is vital to prevent customer losses.

CLICKTHROUGH RATE (CTR)

Clickthrough Rate (CTR) calculates the percentage of users who click on a specific link out of the total users who view a Web page, email, or advertisement. The CTR is pivotal for marketers to gauge how well their ads, keywords, and free search engine listings are performing, offering insights into the engagement and interest levels of their audience.

While it isn't always vital to know how the CTR is calculated as it is a built-in measurement in the reporting function of many platforms, understanding its basic formula is straightforward:

```
CTR = ({Number of clicks} / {Number of impressions}) x 100
```

Where:

- *Number of clicks* refers to how many clicks were carried out on the advertisement or link.
- *Number of impressions* is how many times the advertisement or link was displayed to users.

The formula calculates CTR as a percentage, indicating the proportion of views that resulted in clicks.

CONVERSION RATE (CR)

The Conversion Rate (CR) quantifies the percentage of users who have completed a desired action out of the total number of visitors. This metric is crucial for evaluating the success of various online activities, including e-commerce transactions, sign-ups, and other conversion goals on a Web site or within a digital marketing campaign.

The formula for calculating the CR is straightforward:

```
CR = ({Number of conversions} / {Total visitors}) x 100
```

Where:

- *Number of conversions* is the total count of the specific desired actions completed by visitors.
- *Total visitors* refers to the total number of unique visitors during the same period.

COST PER ACQUISITION (CPA)

Cost per Acquisition (CPA) is a marketing metric that measures the cost of generating a new lead or customer. It represents the total amount of money spent on advertising campaigns divided by the total number of customers acquired through those campaigns. CPA allows you to understand the effectiveness of your advertising campaigns and how much each lead or customer is costing your business. This data can then be used to optimize your campaigns for better ROI.

Calculating CPA is relatively simple:

```
CPA = {Total cost of your advertising campaigns} / {Total number of
customers acquired through those campaigns}
```

For example, if you spent $500 on Facebook advertising and acquired 25 new customers, your CPA would be $20. By tracking your CPA regularly, you can identify trends, optimize your campaigns, and improve your overall marketing ROI.

CUSTOMER ACQUISITION COST (CAC)

Customer Acquisition Cost (CAC) is defined as the cost of converting a lead into a customer and is typically used to calculate the cost of resources that it takes to acquire potential customers. It is a critical metric that is used by businesses to determine the effectiveness of their marketing strategies.

You can calculate CAC by dividing the total amount spent on sales and marketing in a specific time period by the number of customers acquired during that same period.

CAC can be calculated in the following way:

```
CAC = {Sales and marketing costs} / {Number of new customers}
```

For instance, if sales and marketing costs equal $1 million, and 25,000 new customers are gained, the CAC equals $40, or $1 million divided by 25,000.

CUSTOMER LIFETIME VALUE (CLV)

Customer Lifetime Value (CLV) is a calculation of the total value of a customer over their entire journey with a brand. This can be calculated by looking at the total amount a customer has paid, subtracting the gross margin, and dividing by the CR (or cancellation rate) for that customer.

CLV is calculated in the following way:

```
CLV = ({Purchase Frequency [PF]} × {Average Order Value [AOV]} × {Gross
Margin [GM]} × {Customer Lifespan [CL]})/{Number of new customers}
```

Where:

- *Purchase Frequency (PF)*: This is how often the average customer makes a purchase from you. Choose a measurement for frequency that makes sense for your business. For instance, a car manufacturer and a quick service restaurant are going to have different time frequencies that make sense. The former might be in years and the latter in weeks.
- *Average Order Value (AOV)*: This is the average amount a customer spends with your brand.
- *Gross Margin (GM)*: This helps you calculate the amount of profit you make on each order, and gets to a much more accurate number than simply using the AOV as your measurement of how much you make from the average customer.
- *Customer Lifespan (CL)*: Again, make sure to make this take the same unit of measurement as your purchase frequency (weeks, months, or years).
- *Number of new customers*: This is the number of new customers you gain within the same unit of frequency chosen for purchase frequency and customer lifespan.

LEAD VELOCITY RATE (LVR)

Lead Velocity Rate (LVR) is a metric that measures a brand's lead generation rate over a specific period. In simple words, LVR focuses on tracking the growth in your sales leads month over month. The calculation of LVR is pretty straightforward—it's the percentage increase or decrease in the number of leads generated each month. A positive LVR indicates growth, while a negative LVR suggests a decline in lead generation.

To calculate LVR, you can use the following formula:

```
LVR = ({Number of leads generated} - {Number of leads lost}) / ({Number
of leads generated} - {Number of leads won})
```

Where:

- *Number of leads generated* is the total number of leads generated during a given period, such as a month or a quarter.
- *Number of leads lost* is the total number of leads that were not qualified or did not meet the desired criteria and were therefore disqualified or rejected.
- *Number of leads won* is the total number of leads that qualified and met the desired criteria, and were therefore accepted as sales-ready leads.

For example, let's say you have the following data for a given month:

- Number of leads generated: 100
- Number of leads lost: 20
- Number of leads won: 80

Using the preceding formula, we can calculate LVR as follows:

```
LVR = (100 - 20) / (1000 - 80) = 0.9 or 9%
```

This means that for every 100 leads generated, 900 were successfully converted into sales-ready leads, while 100 were lost.

RETURN ON AD SPEND (ROAS)

Return on Ad Spend (ROAS) helps marketers measure the effectiveness of an advertising campaign.

ROAS can be calculated in the following way:

```
ROAS = R divided by C (or R / C)
```

Where:

- C = Cost of the advertising campaign, or the amount spent on advertising
- R = Revenue that was generated as a direct result of that same campaign.

RECAP QUIZ ANSWERS

PART 1 QUESTIONS

Question 1

Which of the following are true about Key Performance Indicators (KPIs)? Choose all that apply:
a) KPIs help you set achievable goals
b) KPIs increase transparency and accountability
c) KPIs help you measure the effectiveness of campaigns
d) KPIs improve the customer experience
e) All of the above

Answer: a, b, c
Regarding d, KPIs themselves don't change anything for better or worse. Only making changes based on KPIs and the information they present can improve things.

Question 2

Which of the following are part of gaining stakeholder support? Choose all that apply:
a) Think outside marketing: what is best for the business at large?
b) Make sure stakeholders understand the marketing jargon you use
c) Choose metrics that tell a story
d) Keep it straightforward
e) All of the above

Answer: a, c, d
Regarding b, you should strive to use as little jargon as possible when presenting information such as marketing measurements.

Question 3

Which kind of data does this describe?
It is descriptive and conceptual. It is data that can be observed but not measured.
a) Quantitative data
b) Qualitative data
c) Categorical data
d) Continuous data

Answer: b

PART 2 QUESTIONS

Question 1

True or false: Alignment of metrics and KPIs to the strategy and goals of the business is a key reason to invest in a marketing measurement framework.

Answer: True.
This is one of the core reasons for the investment in a marketing measurement framework.

Question 2

Which of the following are reasons an AI tool may not be a good fit for your marketing measurement framework? Choose all that apply:
a) It does not integrate well with your existing marketing stack, leading to fragmented data and insights
b) Its capabilities are too specific to your needs, and it doesn't provide generic functionality you may need at some point in the future
c) The learning curve and operational overhead outweigh the potential benefits, making it a resource-intensive option without offering proportional advantages
d) a and c
e) All of the above

Answer: d
You really can't be *too* specific in this instance. It could be argued that an AI tool that is too narrowly focused and also expensive may not be as good an investment, but that factor still doesn't make it a bad fit.

Question 3

True or false: The fourth step in our Marketing Measurement Framework (MMF)—results and analysis—is where we set our business goals and KPIs.

Answer: False.
If you haven't set your goals by this point in the process, you are going to have issues. Goals and KPIs should be set well before measurement as well as the results and analysis stage.

PART 3 QUESTIONS

Question 1

True or false: Alignment of metrics and KPIs to the strategy and goals of the business is a key reason to invest in a marketing measurement framework.

Answer: True.
This is one of the key reasons we want to create a marketing measurement framework in the first place.

Question 2

Select the correct answer: The four Vs of big data are volume, variety, veracity, and:
a) Value
b) Velocity
c) Vivid

Answer: b
Velocity. This is the speed at which data is generated, collected, and processed.

Question 3

Pick the correct answer: The following is a benefit of single-channel measurement:
a) It can often be easier to measure a single channel rather than reconcile or aggregate numbers from multiple channels
b) Analytics and reporting are often (for digital channels) built natively into the platforms themselves, which can simplify getting a quick view
c) A single channel can often be integrated into a more robust reporting tool more easily than multiple channels
d) All of the above

Answer: d

PART 4 QUESTIONS

Question 1

True or false: Bar charts are effective for comparing quantitative data across different categories.

Answer: True

Question 2

True or false: The null hypothesis (H0) is what the researcher wants to prove.

Answer: False

Question 3

Choose the correct answer: When testing a small change to a marketing campaign (e.g., the wording on a CTA button), it is best to use an:

a) A/B test

b) Multivariate test

c) Focus group

Answer: a

An A/B test can be easy to implement and understand the results from. You might use a multivariate test if you have several different ideas, but that gets more complex, and a focus group can be pretty cost and time-intensive for testing such a small feature.

PART 5 QUESTIONS

Question 1

Choose the correct answer: The three steps of analysis and refinement are: 1) Analyze the results, 2) Interpret the results, and:

a) Define the hypothesis

b) Experiment, refine, and continuously improve

c) Adjust the P-level

Answer: b

Question 2

Choose the correct answer: Which of the following are reasons that generative AI can be beneficial when analyzing marketing results?

a) Speed and scale

b) Predictive power

c) Accuracy and learning ability

d) Novel insight generation

e) All of the above

Answer: e

Question 3

True or false: Return on Ad Spend (ROAS) is a marketing metric that measures the effectiveness of a digital advertising campaign.

Answer: True

www.ingramcontent.com/pod-product-compliance
Lightning Source LLC
Chambersburg PA
CBHW080522220326
41599CB00032B/6172